ORDEAL BY WATER

DURING WORLD WAR II, much of the success of British naval operations in the Mediterranean hinged on the courage and resourcefulness of one man. That man was Peter Keeble—a skillful, fearless diver involved in the perilous job of naval salvage and harbor clearance.

Lieutenant Commander Keeble and his men worked under grueling pressures. At no time could they forget that a troop landing could be delayed or an entire campaign lost if their diving operations were not successful.

There were always personal dangers: from too many hours in oily, mine-infested waters, from booby traps, from the dreaded "bends," from failing mental alertness while working at depths of over two hundred feet. And on the surface was the ever-present danger of enemy attack.

Here is one of Britain's top war heroes telling his own "war story"—a story hard to equal for excitement and personal courage.

L. A. J. "Peter" Keeble

ORDEAL
BY WATER

Peter Keeble

With drawings by the author

Doubleday & Company, Inc.

Garden City, New York

1958

Dedicated to those members of the
United States Navy who inspired
and assisted me.

FOREWORD

THIS is a war book that was badly wanted. It is the story of a side that is little known, although from first to last, hundreds of men took part in the scenes described and on the many stages on which the Company was billed to perform. Not infrequently the curtain had to go up for an opening night which gave them insufficient time to get ready, and irrespective of whether there were pulleys and ropes to raise it or props with which to set the stage. The principal actors are the divers, and these pages tell how a chance remark and a few ideas scribbled on a signal pad removed Commander Keeble from his mine-sweeper and in due course enrolled him 'in a brotherhood which in the seafarer's world is unique and select'; a brotherhood of danger and great loneliness where the unexpected can always happen and death very suddenly overtakes even the most experienced. It is a story of the extraordinary things that must be done when armies and air forces need the sea-roads to sustain their operations, and a story, too, of one of the most important of the Navy's roles.

Seeing that so many of the happenings took place in the Mediterranean after the Germans had fastened on to Greece and Crete, no one will be surprised to find in the earlier chapters a tale of makeshift and empty shelves when almost the only things not in short supply were guts, determination and the habit of tackling the impossible. True, as the months went by more men and better gear arrived, but as these benefits multiplied so, it seems, did the jobs to be done. The reader will, therefore, not be surprised when he finds the Author and a body of South African Sappers led by an old friend, pulling up sewer pipes from the Benghazi streets to make pumps and equipment to salve a French destroyer. But this was a side-line, for by then most of North

Africa was in our hands and Tripoli had been opened in the meagre ten days they were given, in spite of the immense trouble the enemy had taken to seal the entrance. Perhaps it was then that Commander Rippon, the Fleet Salvage officer, and Commander Keeble began to realise, with justification, 'how much difference our small efforts here could make to the Desert war'. They may even—though the Author does not mention it—have found themselves wondering what strange optimism had once induced the Authorities at home to believe we could effectively block Tripoli with a battleship, in a hurry and at night. Not that they could have found much time to ruminate over theories, for the present and future were both marked urgent, and, as the days went by, there seemed to be no limits to what the word Salvage could mean.

I doubt if, when Commander Keeble flew to South Africa to see what help General Smuts could give to the sorely tried Fleet in Alexandria, he ever imagined that the course of events would dump him into a Grecian pig-sty for twenty-four hours where, with his Coxswain, Petty Officer Holloway, they were to listen with interest to the German bicycle patrols passing on their rounds. Or that some weeks later they would again have to lie doggo, this time in Athens and in the flue of a baking oven. Those who know something of the Greek capacity for mental gymnastics when it comes to politics will readily understand that, whilst their first hosts would willingly have given their own lives for them, in the second picture their 'murderous-minded Allies' wanted to cut their throats. It was, I suppose, all in the day's work for a Senior Salvage Officer; but whilst I knew something of what he was up to—at times—and some of the lights and shades of his job, I now realise how much I missed. He never told me, for example, what it is like doing 'a bit of dissection—and not very scientifically', with a saw-backed knife in a sunken enemy submarine; nor, for that matter, that a dead man can tap on one's helmet as if trying to attract attention. That Commander Keeble then got cross and found he had 'no time to be sociable' is, I feel, allowable. Moreover, since such odd things can happen under water, most of us would have been ready to pardon him and his companions for being 'in low spirits' when, after some quayside explanations and a few rough sketches on the ubiquitous signal pad, they dropped down into a sunken enemy minelayer to start removing the primers. Seeing that it was all dark down there, and that there was a whole shipload to tackle they had, too, the right to feel it was not a job to do in a hurry. It is perhaps interesting today to wonder how long they would have taken to deal with the ships said to be carrying explosives in the recent Suez operations. Certainly no one will doubt that the date the Admiralty originally gave would have seen the Canal open.

Reading of the Liberty ship which he refloated, I rather fancy (though I have forgotten her name) that it was she whose Captain came out tops in a short radio contest with Alexandria. The Red Sea though narrow, is many hundreds of miles long, and so I hope it was not a very stupid thing to do when, on getting the signal that he was ashore and needed immediate help, we asked him to say where he was. I still wonder whether it was just a man dealing factually with the situation or a slight desire to put one over on the Limey Admiral that brought the unambiguous reply, 'If I knew it I wouldn't be here.' That, if in fact it was the same ship, is where Commander Keeble entered the competition and got on with the job. It was indeed this habit of getting on with the job, whatever it might be, which was the mark of those with whom he worked, irrespective of what Service uniform they wore or to what nation they belonged. So, whilst above them strong arguments on strategy flew to and fro across the Atlantic and great men met and debated the next move, the people on the spot got on with things until the days came near when the Master Race, which he had seen come in 'red eyed and merciless with benzedrine and the fumes of destructive power', began to yield and 'we, the ordinary people, were ready to move in again'.

Perhaps, after all, this is largely a tale of ordinary people sidetracked by war into jobs few had ever envisaged and which demanded and got devotion, pertinacity and not infrequently heroism. In the end, however, it was on those working below the surface that nearly everything finally depended, and for all his other adventures it is mainly as a diver that Commander Keeble writes; manifestly that is where his heart lies. It may be that the same curious magnet which first drew him is responsible today for the growing numbers who, in their shallow water outfits, set out in their quests along the shore; they are perhaps a counterpart of those who like 'messing about in small boats', and both, again, are phases of man and his dealings with the sea. But big ships or small, shallow water or deep, most will instinctively recall such feelings as were the Author's when he writes 'taking the great waste of the sea bed and the fallibility of men and their instruments the odds seemed collossal, and as the hours passed they lengthened'. Those who have served the sea in any guise know well what that fallibility can bring, even when one is on the surface and in God's open air. But translating it, in time of war, into what can happen when, to the constraint of darkness there is added the unknown and the unforeseeable, and when life depends on a rubber hose, I find myself strongly subscribing to the idea that theirs is a unique and select brotherhood. It occurs to me, too, that it is a very courageous company.

BERNARD RAWLINGS

CONTENTS

CONTENTS

PLATES

ORDEAL BY WATER

I. ALTERING COURSE

THE wind had dropped, as it often did towards sunset in the eastern Mediterranean. From the bridge of the Fleet Sweeper *Harrow* I watched the convoy of grimy merchant-men ease into line ahead, losing way as they swung to pass the boom of Alexandria Harbour. We had swept right up to the entrance of the Great Pass for them and were now lying astern, graciously giving our charges the benefit of the failing light to find their moorings. Outside the harbour entrance a light chop ruffled the surface of the water, grey now with an occasional russet tinge as it picked up the thin rays of the sun setting behind a thickening curtain of mist. I cursed as I saw the slowness with which the convoy was making its way through the boom gate. It would be dark long before the last of them was safely inside and we had, as usual, a filthy berth to find for ourselves, stern on to the Arsenal Mole.

It had been, by local standards, a quiet run from Tobruk. A couple of Jerry reconnaissance aircraft had come out to take a look at us and we had had enough Asdic contacts reported to keep us closed up to Action Stations most of the time, but no attack had developed. It was just as well. *Harrow* was low on ammunition and the ship's company was tired and edgy, like every other ship's company that had survived six months in Bomb Alley. All we asked of life at the moment was for these limping merchantmen to get a move on and let us tie up alongside and have a night's sleep.

The last ship churned slowly through the gate. As the phosphoresence of her wake died on the night sea I rang down for more revolutions, gave the helmsman his course and jockeyed up to the entrance. The thin whistle of the bos'un's pipe was followed by the hoarse bellow of the Duty P.O.: 'Special sea duty men close up to harbour stations!' Above the throb of our engines I could hear the clank and whir of the winches as behind us the steel curtain of the boom was dragged shut. We were in, but we did not know what we had brought in with us. It was the 18th of December 1941.

I conned *Harrow* through the craft scattered at their moorings in the harbour, keeping a wary eye out for the irresponsible feluccas and the picket boats and duty launches scurrying single-mindedly about their business in the crowded anchorage. The base at Ras-el-Tin flashed us. We identified ourselves and picked our way onwards to where the other ships of my flotilla were already tied up. Below, unseen in the wheelhouse, the Cox'n repeated the helm orders I gave him down the voice-pipe. The dim outlines of the Mole emerged from the drizzle-thickened darkness.

I bent over the voice-pipe again. 'Stop both! Port thirty, Cox'n!' We lost way and the bows started to slew. Behind me I heard Number One clump on to the bridge and take over from the Officer of the Watch who departed for'ard to his station on the fo'c'sle with the cable party.

'Half astern port, slow ahead starboard!' Even as I heard the Cox'n repeating my orders, the ship's head came easily to port, beginning that slow swing that would bring us parallel to my next in line and stern to the Mole. I waited. Then, 'Stop starboard . . . 'midships . . . slow astern starboard'. I stuck my head over the dodger on the forepart of the bridge and hailed the cable officer: 'Let go!' On the fo'c'sle a rating threw his weight on the windlass brake and the anchor, released, splashed into the dark waters and arrowed its way to the bottom in a deafening roar as the heavy chain danced after it through the hawse-pipe. We dropped slowly astern into our berth. Aft, a heaving line snaked ashore, our stern wires followed it over the side and were made fast. I leant over and said thankfully into the voice-pipe—'Stop both!—finished with engines!' We were home. I took a last long look round the blacked-out harbour, left the ship to Number One, and went below.

Accommodation in a mine-sweeper is not notably luxurious, but my cabin contained an armchair, filched many months ago, which swallowed me as completely and comfortably as any I had slept in after lunch at my club. It swallowed me now as I waited for the post-berthing bustle to begin. First came a Signalman with a file of signals from C-in-C's Office. I leafed through them lazily and Number One joined me to claim his gin and talk about the innumerable routine problems of running a ship. His voice made a soothing refrain to my thoughts, which were turned entirely towards a long and peaceful night in my bunk. We were both perfectly happy, acting out the simple domestic scene that would be repeated in hundreds of H.M. ships all over the world.

The Yeoman knocked, entered briskly and with a flourish handed me another signal: 'It's an Urgent Important, Sir,' he said. I looked at it, groaned aloud and signed the receipt angrily. 'Read that, Number One!' I tossed the signal over to him and watched his face lengthen as his eyes took in the faded pink text of the mimeographed message:

General 37   *To all concerned*   *From C-in-C*

ATTACK ON ALEX BY AIR, BOAT OR HUMAN TORPEDO MAY BE EXPECTED WHILE PRESENT WEATHER CONDITIONS PREVAIL STOP LOOKOUTS AND PATROLS SHOULD BE WARNED ACCORDINGLY

T.O.O. 1025 B 18

'It's the middle watch,' Number One muttered savagely.

'They want to turn us out in the middle watch. I can feel it in my bones. Are they serious, do you suppose? Human torpedoes in Alex!'

'Anyway . . .' I roused myself with an effort: 'We'd better do something about it. See that sentries posted are warned to be on their toes, will you, Number One? Duty Officers to do rounds of the upper deck frequently. Have a copy of this stuck on the notice board for'ard. And—wait a minute . . .' I broke off as a Signalman arrived with another flimsy.

'Oh God!—it's a "further to their 1025 B". They want us to draw bottom lines immediately!' The First Lieutenant got wearily to his feet, drained the tail-end of his gin at a gulp and reached for his cap. 'They couldn't even wait for the middle watch,' he said sadly. At the door, he added over his shoulder: 'The lads will be pleased about this!'

It was bad luck. We had earned a quiet night, but there was another hour's work in making up the bottom lines, getting them over the bows and sawing them aft along the ship's keel plates in the hope that any limpet mines that had attached themselves to our bottom would quietly drop off. Even if there was anything in the scare, which to me seemed highly unlikely, no enemy who'd succeeded in penetrating Alexandria's boom defence was going to waste his time on an insignificant little tub like ours. There were two capital ships in the harbour.

I gave Number One ten minutes and then slipped on a raincoat and went on deck. The Duty Watch were cursing as they struggled with the heavy, obstinate bottom lines on the slippery, rain-wet decks. As I watched them I heard at intervals from across the harbour a series of dull thuds and guessed that the Guard boats were lobbing small charges into the water as a sharp warning to underwater attackers. There was a flap on all right.

I stayed on deck until Number One and his men had finished their fruitless task and were stowing away the gear; then I went into the lobby to write a couple of routine signals. 'For tonight,' I thought, 'that's that!' I climbed heavily over the washplate into my cabin and was soon snugly in my bunk.

It seemed only a few minutes before I was awake again, roused by the sound or sensation of an explosion, a deep and distant *thump*. The sound seemed too heavy to have come from one of the charges the Guard boats were playing with: perhaps I had imagined it, my dreams conditioned by that signal. Then, as my wits gathered themselves and I shook off the vestiges of sleep, I registered another impression. The glasses in the rack over the pantry hatch had rattled. No question about it; what I had heard had been an explosion, and a big one.

I swung my legs out of the bunk and was fumbling around for a pair of trousers when the R.N.R. Midshipman who was Duty Officer pulled aside my door curtain and stuck his head into the cabin. Water was still running down his oilskin coat and I did not have to ask him how the weather was.

'What's up, Mid?'

'An explosion somewhere over Gabbari way, Sir. Can't see a thing.'

'All right. I'll be up in a minute.' I grabbed the nearest clothes, stepped into my seaboots and pulled on an oilskin.

Up on deck it was pitch black. Even when my eyes had settled to the dark my visibility was limited to about twenty yards. Now and then I could hear a power boat's engine some way off, and on the far side of the coaling jetty somebody was using an Aldis as a searchlight. The pencil beam looked pale and watered and I wondered what on earth was going on over there, over where the big ships lay.

The big ships . . . We had only two left in the Mediterranean; *Queen Elizabeth* and *Valiant*. If anything happened to put them out of action, even for a few weeks, there would be nothing powerful enough to face the Italian battle fleet if it came out. The entire naval situation in the Mediterranean would be changed. Standing there on the bridge of my small sweeper I shuddered at the possible consequences; but there was nothing I could do about it.

I told the Midshipman to keep his eyes skinned and to call me at once if anything happened. Then I slid back down the ladder to my warm cabin and its comfortable armchair, and lit a cigarette. For more than half an hour I sprawled there, smoking and turning over in my mind the possible grounds for alarm in the combination of C-in-C's signal and the following explosion. I had almost decided to turn in for the second time when the glasses clattered again. Looking up quickly I saw the needle on the barometer above my desk quivering as if it had been given the fright of its life. At the same time I heard the distant *whumph* of another explosion, another big one.

I was halfway up the ladder before I had begun to think about it. At the top, moving fast, I met Number One and almost bowled him over. He straightened his cap and told me breathlessly: 'It came from *Q.E.*, Sir. I was looking over that way and I saw the flash out of the top of her funnel before I heard it.' I stared at him, feeling very cold, wondering: if the *Q.E.*'s had it, what do we do now?

Number One asked, 'Shall I send the hands to Action Stations, Sir? Do you want the boat away?'

'No. Call the Duty Watch to stand by. Double up sentries and shake the officers.'

'Aye, aye, Sir.' The First Lieutenant hurried for'ard, shouting for the Quartermaster who had gone for'ard himself to call the Watch.

For the rest of the night I prowled around the greasy decks, smoked cigarettes in my cabin, drank raw tea with Number One. I hadn't a doubt now that something disastrous had happened, and I longed for a signal that would tell us exactly what. I was leaning on the rail when the Guard boat passed, thundering by at full throttle, no doubt driven that way by some snottie anxious to get back to his hammock. I watched the bow wave and spreading wake as my Quartermaster challenged with his strident, shattering yell: 'Boat aho-oy!' Across the dark water the picket boat's answer floated back: 'Gua-ard!' The night wore on.

By the time the sky turned grey and changed to pink and the ships took shape with the dawn, I was sick of the taste of tea and cigarettes. I climbed up to the bridge and focused my binoculars on the upperworks of the battleships. Over the coaling arm nothing else was visible, but at least it was reassuring that what could be seen looked normal. There was no smoke or obvious activity. And behind us, at the Ras-el-Tin base, all seemed as it had been before, a few early boats moving around the jetty's end, but nothing that could be regarded as significant. Then as I swept round with my glasses I took it all back with one swift presentiment of disaster. The two fleet tugs, *Roysterer* and *Respond*, were not in their berths. . . .

At that moment the duty despatch boat from Ras-el-Tin swept around our bow, just clearing the cable which led out from the starboard hawse and slanted down into the water. The skimmer slid up to the gangway and the Marine orderly in her sternsheets pushed the morning's signals into my Quartermaster's outstretched hands. The little boat spun on its heel and sped away to the next ship, farther along the mole. I hurried down and grabbed the wad of messages from the Q.E. Number One was there too, as eager for news as I. He followed me down to my cabin and hovered impatiently while I read quickly through the routine signals. There was nothing of interest in them. I dropped the lot on the table and stared disgustedly at the barometer. Number One shrugged his shoulders.

'What's the answer, Sir?'

'I don't know a damn' thing more than you do. Until they tell us we might as well forget it.'

All the same I had to have another look at Gabbari, and Number One climbed up to the bridge after me. The sun was just rising over the low land to the east of us, brightening the roofs of the dockyard sheds across the harbour. I mastered my impatience and curiosity, stifled my fears and went below for a hot bath. Just as I was getting into it I remembered that I had left Number One without instructions, so I called the steward and sent up a message that the ship was to revert to normal harbour routine.

Soaking in the bath I felt some of the weariness fade out of

my bones, and I was beginning to recover from the effects o
the night when Number One banged on my bathroom doo
and yelled: 'Commander Wheeler to see you, Sir!'

'Wheeler?' I thought. 'Wheeler?' And then I remembered
'Sit him down,' I shouted back. 'I'll be out in a jiffy.'

Wheeler was Fleet Salvage Officer. As I reached for a towe
I remembered that I had taken him to Malta once, on passage
when he was going to inspect the latest damage to shipping i
the harbour inflicted by the Luftwaffe. We had talked a lot o
that trip, Wheeler complaining savagely about the impossibility of carrying out an effective salvage campaign with the
incredibly limited resources of men and material at his disposal
I had suggested to him then that he could get, if not all the
help he wanted, at least a sizeable contribution from South
Africa. I felt I was in a position to comment, for I knew the
problem and I knew South Africa. I had been a professional
sailor, a deck officer in the Merchant Navy for ten years, and
during that time I had also qualified as an engineer. When I
swallowed the anchor—temporarily, as it turned out—I had gone
to work with a large engineering concern in the Union. Even
before the war South Africa's industrial potential had been increasing at a tremendous rate and I had told Wheeler I was sure
that if he tried he could get trained men and the right sort of
equipment out of the South African Government for the asking. Wheeler had not been impressed, but before he had gone
over the brow in Malta he had asked me to put my ideas into
a memorandum and I had scribbled one for him on a few sheets
of a signal pad. All very well, but what did Wheeler want with
me now? And if our suspicions about last night's events were
reasonably founded, why was he wasting good time calling on
me like this?

But I was forgetting my manners. I called out: 'Number One!
Ask the steward to bring Commander Wheeler some coffee!'

Wheeler's voice came back crisply. 'Skip the coffee, Keeble.
C-in-C wants to see you in his office. Right away!'

That brought me rocketing out of the bathroom, a damp

wel round my middle. I greeted the tall thin Commander
acing nervously up and down my cabin and scrambled for
ie clothes I had thrown over a chair. Wheeler glanced at his
vatch. 'Ready?' he asked, as I wrenched my monkey jacket on.
hadn't even found my socks, but I nodded and Wheeler made
or the door. A minute later I joined him on deck, wrapping
n old muffler about my neck to disguise the fact that I had not
ad time to don a tie. It was only when we had dropped into
is launch that Wheeler started to talk.

'It's been a hell of a night. Four Eyetie two-man torpedoes
ot through the boom last night—I fancy you brought them in
vith your convoy. We've got the crews of two of them so far.
he bastards have blown holes in *Valiant* and in *Queen Eliza-*
eth.' He paused, then added as if it did not matter: 'That tanker
ying near *Q.E.* had her stern blown off, too.'

It was at least as bad as I had imagined it could be. 'How
erious is the damage?' I asked.

Wheeler stared over the launch's bow at the distant, dusty
utline of Gabarri. It was a moment before he answered. 'The
Valiant's got a sixty-foot hole in her bows: luckily the charges
were a bit too far for'ard for maximum effect, and I think we'll
oe able to dock her. But *Q.E.*'s holed worse—her boilers bloody
aearly went through her funnel and she's sitting on the mud aft.
Seven stokers killed. She's an unholy mess.'

As the launch cleared the end of the jetty we could see the
oows of *Queen Elizabeth* surrounded by small craft, mostly
ighters. (She was berthed with her stern to the Gabarri pier,
her long bow pointing out towards us.) We passed down her
port side, and as the launch swung out for the turn that would
oeing us alongside the quarterdeck gangway I saw with amazement that the huge battleship had a freeboard aft of only a couple
of feet. It was a staggering sight.

We chugged up alongside and jumped aboard. Wheeler
grabbed my arm and we followed the Officer of the Watch in
through the screen door and past a Marine sentry into the Captain's day cabin. As I stepped into this spacious apartment, which

was crowded with senior officers and Naval Constructors, I was
acutely conscious of my miserable two stripes, their twisted braid
peeling off my old reefer, and of the scruffy scarf around my
neck. It was not a company in which a Lieutenant, R.N.R.,
could be expected to feel entirely at ease at the best of
times.

With his elbow on the fireplace mantel, and looking remark-
ably cheerful, was Admiral Sir Andrew Cunningham, in conversation with some official from the dockyard. Near-by were
Captain Edelsten, the Chief of Staff, and the Captain of the
Fleet, Richard Shelley. Presiding over the coffee service—no
stewards were admitted to this highly confidential gathering—
was Q.E.'s commanding officer, Captain Claud Barry. He greeted
Wheeler and, when I was introduced, handed me a cup of coffee.
Nobody seemed much to mind my disreputable attire, and I was
beginning to stand easy. Except for the Constructors, who look
pretty miserable at the best of times, every man in the cabin
seemed brisk, cheerful and apparently quite undaunted by the
disaster which had come so suddenly.

While we waited Wheeler told me in an undertone that the
Constructors were for giving up Q.E., stripping her of her fighting gear and using her as a depot ship. C-in-C had other ideas,
however, and had been giving them hell. He was still going for
them hot and strong at intervals after we arrived.

Suddenly the C-in-C looked up and spotted Wheeler. He
beckoned him over and asked: 'Wheeler! Did you find this
fellow?' I put down my coffee cup and in answer to Wheeler's
wave stepped forward to be introduced. The Admiral shook my
hand and came straight to the point.

'You've ideas about salvage, Keeble, eh?'

'Yes, Sir,' I said. It was what one is supposed to say to Admirals. 'I have.'

'I read your minute to Commander Wheeler. All very well
on paper, Keeble, but do you *really* think South Africa can give
us what we need?'

'I'm sure we can get the men, Sir, trained harbour divers;

nd I believe we could get a ship. If you were to send a signal——'

'I'm sending no signals. As far as the enemy's concerned the
ttack on Alex was a failure—until he finds out for himself
what's happened, and I'm not going to help him about that.
You a South African?'

I nodded.

'Then get you off to South Africa and see what you can do
or us. Don't come back without results. My secretary will
arrange an appointment for you in my office this afternoon:
get packed meanwhile and we'll have a final talk then. . . .
Edelsten—get the R.A.F. to play. I want this officer flown out
in a hurry. And Shelley—dig out a relief C.O. for Keeble, will
you?' The great man turned brusquely back on his Constructors
and I retired, dazed, from the presence.

Within a week I was back in South Africa. The absurdity of
the situation had hardly dawned on me before I was rolling up
in an official car to Groot Schuur, the gracious, Dutch-gabled
house given to the nation by Cecil Rhodes as a residence for
its Prime Ministers. I stepped out of the car, smoothing the
creases in my white drill uniform, and was greeted by Mrs.
Coaton, General Smuts's daughter. She settled me in the General's
small, book-lined study, and there I had tea and waited, half-
apprehensively, for the Prime Minister's return from the House,
which was then in session. It would be a little awkward if the
great man were prepared to accept none of my proposals. Beyond a signal to announce my arrival, he knew nothing of the
nature of my mission: Admiral Cunningham's insistence on
secrecy had been absolute.

At about six-thirty the General arrived. It had been a hot day
and he looked drawn and tired, but the weight of affairs in
wartime South Africa had done nothing to bow the straight,
spare figure, and in the flesh he looked even more like a Spanish
grandee than in his pictures. If he was disturbed at my invasion
of his domestic privacy, he did not show it. I indicated briefly
what I wanted to talk about; he suggested I keep it for the morning, and we sat down together to dinner.

The next day we talked. In General Smuts's long, panelled office in Parliament Street, I drew a chair up to his desk and sitting beside him, described in detail the events in Alexandria which had led up to my visit. The Prime Minister appreciated at once the situation that had emerged in the Mediterranean from the crippling of our only two capital ships and his thoughts turned quickly to Table Bay where more than a hundred ships lay open to similar attack. He questioned me closely in his sharp high-pitched voice, and I illustrated my answers with rough sketches on his blotting pad. Then I came to the point.

'The Mediterranean Fleet is desperately short of divers with experience of salvage, Sir. It was possible to dry-dock *Valiant*; this was done before I left, but there is a tremendous amount of underwater work to be done on *Queen Elizabeth* if she's ever to be brought back into commission. The Navy simply can't cope. I've come to appeal to you, Sir, to provide us with the trained men who can do the job. They exist, there are several of them in Cape Town Harbour. I know they can ill be spared: but it would be a temporary expedient—the divers could be flown back when they'd finished their job—and they would have a magnificent opportunity to do really significant work in Alexandria. . . .'

The Prime Minister needed no urging. 'This is Sturrock's Department,' he said, referring to the Minister of Transport. 'I'll see him about it at once. You had better see him too, and his colleagues: you will be able to tell them precisely what is wanted. And I think you should also speak to some of our senior Defence Officers. There is a lesson for us to learn from what has happened at Alexandria. You have my full support. Now, is there anything else?'

There was. My excitement built up as I launched into an account of the sorry state of salvage in the Mediterranean. I pointed out the value there would be in a ship equipped with workshops and all the tackle required for salvage work and manned with skilled personnel. I said that the Union's potential was hardly realised in the Middle East, and if the South African

Government would provide a ship and the men to go with it
that it would be a gesture of far-reaching consequences. The
words came tumbling out as I elaborated on my theme, hardly
daring to glance at the Prime Minister to see how he was taking
it; but he listened sympathetically, interposing an occasional
question. Again he offered his support.

The interview came to an end. As I rose to go, I remembered
the sketches on the blotting pad and suggested that they ought
to be destroyed. The General agreed, and I felt in my pockets
for matches, but I had none, and he did not smoke. He pressed
a button on his desk and a burly, plain-clothes officer burst into
the room with alarming suddenness. General Smuts asked him
mildly, in Afrikaans, for a box of matches, and the detective
watched in amazement as the Prime Minister and an R.N.R.
Lieutenant knelt side by side on the floor and kindled a fire in
the office grate in the middle of a hot Cape summer.

With the General's co-operation, my visit reached a successful
conclusion. Forty-eight hours after my talk with him I had collected four volunteer divers from Cape Town Harbour, and a
fifth, T. F. Devonshire, a Petty Officer Diver in the South
African Naval Forces, was flown down from Walvis Bay to join
the group. I packed them all off to Alexandria by air, in civvies
and under an oath of secrecy, and there they were promptly
arrested by an ambitious Provost Marshal as suspected spies.
Fortunately Commander Wheeler was expecting them, and he
had the five men released before anyone called a firing squad.
Then, still wondering what had hit them, they were set straight
to work in the thick, clinging mud under *Queen Elizabeth*.

Meanwhile, I continued to scrounge. In Cape Town I hurried
from official to official, discussing what equipment might be
borrowed or purloined. Three months passed, mainly on these
negotiations, and it was March 1942 before I found myself back
in Alexandria and was ushered once more into the office of the
Commander-in-Chief, to make my report.

The Admiral was at his desk, eyes red-rimmed from a night
in the operations office, but brisk and jaunty as ever. He rose to

greet me; then, before we had seated ourselves, a roar of cheer ing rolled across the harbour. The Commander-in-Chief rushe to his verandah and, following him, I could see at intervals be tween the trees that partially screened the garden the ships c Admiral Vian's battle fleet steaming slowly back to their buoy.

It was one of the greater moments in the history of the Roya Navy. All ships in harbour had their men on deck, cheering lik thunder as Vian's three cruisers and eight destroyers steamed inti their berths. Back from escorting a convoy to Malta, three c the four merchantmen they had started out with were at thi moment discharging their cargoes in Valetta. With his puny bu now glorious force, Vian had held off one Italian battleship o the *Littorio* class, one eight-inch cruiser and five six-incl cruisers. He had held them off, and turned them, and as dark ness had fallen, shepherded his precious charges into Malta.

The C-in-C was greatly moved at the sight of his ships in the full pride of their victory. As the trees blotted them moment arily from his sight he stood on tip-toe or bobbed up and down unashamed of his excitement and open emotion, anxious to lose nothing of the great occasion. The ships churned past, severa clearly showing their scars of battle. Then, as the cheering faded away, Sir Andrew turned abruptly on his heel and led the way back into his office.

'Well, Keeble, you found the men. They've done good work Now what about the salvage ship?'

'We can have that too, Sir,' I said, savouring the pleasure of the moment. 'The Union Government is willing to commandeer the *Gamtoos*—she's been on coastal work—fit her out in the Union with workshops and what equipment we need, man her with South African personnel and put her at our disposal. She's about 900 tons, coal-burning. She won't be able to tow, I'm afraid, Sir; but she's ours for the asking.'

'Good!' The Admiral spun a signal pad across his desk at me. 'I know your General Smuts. Draft me a signal to him and we'll have that ship.'

I scrawled laboriously on the pad and handed it back to the

C-in-C for approval. In a few minutes, heavily amended, the signal was on its way to South Africa. It read:

Personal for Field-Marshal Smuts from Admiral Cunningham

It would be much appreciated if it were possible for a salvage vessel to be fitted out in the Union for employment in the M.E. There is unfortunately only too much work for this class of vessel. I would be very happy if she could be manned by your Seaward Defence Force whose men are doing excellent work here. It is understood that KEEBLE discussed ways and means during his recent visit.

I am bidding farewell to the Seaward Defence Force with great regret. As you are aware, they have done magnificent work here, and I have always been able to place complete reliance in them. I am sorry that I shall not have the opportunity of seeing you before I leave. Please accept all my good wishes for the future.

A few kind words from the Admiral ended the interview, and I went back to my hotel to ponder the events of the day and wait, not without anxiety, for another signal of strictly personal moment. Admiral Cunningham had hinted that there might be a salvage job for me, but it was quite on the cards that the Captain of the Fleet would discover a drearier alternative, and for two days I waited in trepidation.

When the signal came it seemed to confirm my worst fears:

LIEUTENANT KEEBLE RNR IS APPOINTED TO HMS *BULL*, MASSAWA, AS FIRST LIEUTENANT, WITH EFFECT FROM APRIL 15TH.

I stared stupidly at the signal. First Lieutenant of a shore base! I knew just about enough of Massawa to give myself heat stroke thinking about it, but it was not the climate of the place that made my heart sink like a stone. After what I had hoped for it was the thought of a shore appointment that sent me reeling. I thought with suddenly renewed love and longing of my old fleet sweeper and plodded heavily off to seek further details of my draft.

The Secretary to Captain of the Fleet, who ran officers' appoint ments, was used to men with a grievance. I told him what I had wanted and reminded him of what I had got. I had not expected him to be moved, and he was not; but to my surprise he gave me a ray of hope. 'If you're looking for extra duties, old boy, you'll get 'em,' he said breezily. 'Especially at *Bull*. There's plenty of salvage work going there, don't you fret. You'll be up to your neck in it before you know where you are!'

And that, as events proved, was an understatement.

II. INITIATION

As the Dutch troopship which carried me to Massawa neared the mainland I got my first sight of the country which was to be my home for almost a year. It was not enticing. A long, low, dirt-coloured coastline sprawled monotonously to the horizon. Here and there an untidy scatter of boulders, a clump of faded, wilting vegetation accentuated the drabness of the scene. A bald, hard sun hurled its strength on the baked ground and forced out of the earth a film of moisture which rose up as a tremulous curtain. Beneath this curtain the shore danced and shimmered like a picture projected without much focus on to an unsteady and rather dirty screen. The waters of the Red Sea lapped listlessly at the margin of the land, and like a clammy and unwelcome handshake the damp heat reached out to greet me.

From this uninviting coast a stubby spit of coral poked out and swelled into a small island, rather like the neck and head of a dumb-bell in shape. On this promontory the Italian empire builders had chosen to erect the fair-sized township of Massawa, at one time the commercial capital and port of Eritrea, and, just before the Royal Navy entered its history, an important Italian naval base. Most of the township and the naval base had been built by the Italian army and from the deck of the trooper I could see clusters of single-storey, wide-eaved bungalows in colonial style, once white, now a dirty cream enlivened only by bursts of colour from bougainvillaea and other creepers gasping for existence on the trellis-work attached to most of the houses.

The main basin of the harbour which we were now entering was wide and modern, with well designed jetties and sheds. It had been built by the Italians to shelter and serve a large operational fleet. To the north we had already passed another almost naturally enclosed reach of deep water; to the south lay a third safe anchorage with some sixty feet of clear water. It was easy to imagine, even in this killing, sun-blasted spot, the busy purposefulness of an active port: the swaying cranes, the fussy, hooting tugs, the scurrying, ant-like stevedores watched as they went about their labours by bored, suspicious deck-officers. But now, early in 1942, the small forest of masts, funnels and upperworks was conspicuously absent. A dead silence brooded over the harbour. Massawa was a ghost port.

My gaze ranged across the still waters and picked out here the superstructure of a sunken merchantman just breaking the surface, there the slick turn of a bilge, black as a whale's back except for a growing streak of rust, denoting a vessel capsized at her moorings. Square in the entrance to the port lay a large liner on her beam-ends, almost denying access to all but the smallest craft. This was a graveyard of ships that had died before their time.

The Italians had made a good job of building their port. With the assistance of their German partners they had made an equally good job of wrecking it. Alongside the fine wharves lines of scuttled ships—freighters, barges, coasters, minor war vessels—lay silently on the bottom silt. Even with the main basin blocked and the shore installations wrecked, the Italians had realised that Allied ships could anchor in the south harbour and discharge their war cargoes into lighters; so before they had evacuated the port to British forces, they had scuttled sixteen ships in a wide circle. In the north harbour, completing the havoc, two big floating docks squatted heavily on the mud. Looking at the desolation all around us as we docked I could see what the

Captain of the Fleet's secretary had meant when he talked about the scope for salvage at Massawa.

* * *

Captain Colin Lucas, R.N., was Naval Officer in Charge of the base, and I couldn't have asked for a better officer to work under. The morning I reported for duty he took me out on the verandah of his bungalow and waved an expressive hand at the litter of wrecks visible in the port.

'You must remember, Keeble,' he said genially, 'we may not be able to hold the Afrika Korps in the desert. If the worst happens and we have to pull out of the Canal Zone, which God forbid, this malodorous hole will become our main naval and air base. Look at it! The entrance to the main harbour is almost completely blocked and the north and south harbours are little better; every quay is fouled with wrecks. The port is virtually unworkable. We've got to get it cleared if it's to be of any use at all.'

'I'd like to have a smack at it, Sir.'

'You're welcome to, Keeble, but most of your effort will have to be made outside of routine working hours. Actually, your duties as Number One shouldn't be too onerous, but you'll have the devil's own job raising the equipment you need. We're due some from America, but God knows when it'll pitch up—I'm afraid you'll have to scrounge what you can.'

'And trained men, Sir?' I asked.

'We've got a couple of divers on the strength, although I don't know how experienced they are; and you may be able to dig a few artisans out of the Eyetie P.O.W. camps. Then there's McCance. He represents the Admiralty contractors: a good chap, I think, but as badly stuck for equipment and skilled labour as everybody else. You'll not find things easy, but see what you can do and let me know if I can help in any way.'

* * *

Tropical routine meant making a start at 5 a.m. In the afternoon everything shut down under the fierce heat, and work, generally speaking, was resumed after tea. Between morning and afternoon sessions I toured the base getting to know people, sizing up the problems and noting what equipment might be useful.

On one of these tours I met McCance. He was a remarkable character who might have stepped out of a Captain Kettle novel: a cultured man, always immaculate in a spotless white suit that seemed uncreasable; a dandy with impeccable manners, an immense capacity for hard work, and a monocle. He delighted us and amazed the Americans who were to join us later. But if his appearance seemed eccentric in the squalid conditions at Massawa, it could not conceal the fact that Captain McCance, a Younger Brother of Trinity House, was a fine seaman and an exceptional Salvage Officer, although during the time I knew him he laboured long for small reward. As a civilian contractor he had to recruit his labour locally and when he wanted equipment he had to rely, in the old-fashioned way, on being able to buy it. In spite of this, in the course of a nine-month struggle, he raised the German steamer *Gera*—a triumph of single-mindedness which would have cost a less stable man his sanity.

At the same time I ran down a good supply of Italian Naval diving sets in the Regia Marina stores, along with tools and a quantity of valuable timber. I made the acquaintance of the naval divers, Collins, a rating whom the heat had driven to his last gasp and who had to be shipped north shortly afterwards, and P.O. Sinfield, a prime product of naval training with something like fifteen years of diving experience to his credit. In the P.O.W. camp Sinfield had found Angelo Sodini, a veteran diver who had been with the famous Sorima Company when they recovered the bullion from the wreck of the *Egypt* off Ushant, and he was at once roped into the small team. He proved to be an asset of almost incalculable value to the salvage effort at Massawa and, with the boundless energy and single-minded devotion to detail which is the hall-mark of the good diver, he was my adviser-in-chief throughout the arduous operations that were to follow. I started with hopes of being able to use Sodini for underwater work, but it was firmly pointed out to me that if he showed a tendency towards heroics the possibilities of sabotage by a man working below the surface were almost unlimited. So instead of diving he became a helper on the surface and in time established himself as my personal aide.

Within a week or two of my arrival in Massawa I had got a fair picture of our resources in terms of salvage, and a good picture of the work that had to be done, to which there was no end. I was still plugging away at my routine duties as First Lieutenant of the base, but my real energies, and certainly my enthusiasm, were reserved for the salvage jobs that I lay awake at nights to plan.

The first job to be tackled, I decided, was to raise one of several Italian tugs sunk in the main harbour. One of my duties was to act as pilot to visiting ships calling at the port and to guide them through the wrecks and alongside the quays. Lacking a tug I had to snub the heavy-laden single-screw merchant ships round on their anchors and then nose them in between the wreck-blocked berths and alongside. This was often a harrowing experience and one which could be greatly eased with a tug suitable for ship-handling.

The tug I picked on was not chosen exclusively for suitability for the job, but lying at the westerly end of the main harbour she had the signal merit of being in shallow water. The top of her bridge and funnel showed above water, and although with her low freeboard she had little reserve buoyancy and was therefore an awkward proposition to raise, she was reasonably accessible and seemed a good prospect for a first venture. I sent Sinfield down several times to investigate, and from his reports it appeared that little damage had been done to the tug in scuttling her. Restoring her for active service promised to present few difficulties. But there was a limit to what I could learn from Sinfield's reports and to what the man himself could do, however willing. In the conditions that prevailed at Massawa nobody could work under water for more than half an hour at a time and expect to survive for long. It behoved me, I felt clearly, to lend a hand.

Once, in the years before the war, the company for which I worked had installed a piece of machinery some twenty feet below the surface in a quay wall of Port Elizabeth harbour. I decided to go down and have a look at it, less from an excess of dutiful zeal than to satisfy my curiosity about what it was like to make a dive. It was terrible. I had been inducted into a diving suit a size too small for me, dunked briefly in the murky harbour waters, and hauled in to express my opinion of the job. I had not even found the harbour wall. My few minutes on the bottom had been spent fighting off a fearful panic which swept over me the moment my suit was sealed and which had not left me till a helper unscrewed my front glass and admitted a few lungsful of air to my craving, quaking body.

The thought of diving again after my total failure at Port Elizabeth was exciting and disturbing. I felt strongly the urge to discover whether I could master not merely the mechanics of the operation—I was confident enough about that—but the physical and psychological circumstances which were, in a straightforward dive at least, the principal obstacles to success. So at two o'clock on a steaming afternoon, the worst possible time for the venture, I boarded a launch we had equipped for diving with Sinfield, Collins, Sodini and a jabber of Eritreans who represented our hard labour force. We pushed off from the jetty, nosed out to the tug and made fast to her bridge. I settled myself on the hard, solid diving bench, feeling like an offering about to be burnt, while Sodini lovingly laid out the gear at my feet. The shot-rope which I was shortly to follow to the bottom went over the side with a whang and a splash.

I proposed to remove only my shoes for the dive, and to retain the khaki shirt and shorts I was wearing. They were soaked already with perspiration, and in the clammy heat I felt the less I wore below my diving dress the less I would suffer. But Sodini chattered shrilly at Sinfield, who turned to me with an apologetic grin. 'Sorry, Sir, but I think you'd better cover up a bit more. If you try going down in a suit dressed like that the wet twill'll rub every square inch of skin off you before you've got time to shout for mother. First class abrasive, a diving suit, Sir.'

Reluctantly I allowed myself to be talked into a smelly pair of heavy, woollen, thigh-length stockings and a thick, roll-neck submariner's jersey. I suppose the temperature on the deck of that launch was 120 degrees: in the jersey reaching down to my knees and the stockings reaching up to my crutch, it was astronomical. I flopped down on the stool again and panted.

Helpers dragged over to me the heavy rubberised twill diving dress made in one piece from the gaping neck to the absurd-looking flipperish feet. I inserted my legs into the mouth of the thing and wriggled and struggled my way down into it, sweating and cursing, until my toes found the extremities. Sinfield stretched the dress to its full length to let me duck my head and shoulders into the body in order to thrust my arms through the sleeves. The stench inside the suit was indescribable, but I got my arms through, and the rubber cuffs in which the sleeves terminated, designed to make the suit water-tight but equally effective as tourniquets, clamped dank and hard on my wrists. The olive oil with which my wrists had been smeared prevented chafing, but it didn't help my circulation and gradually my hands tightened and my fingertips hardened as the flow of blood was restricted. But at least I could get my head out of the infernal suit again and when I emerged, blinking in the bright sunshine, the sweat pouring as in a Turkish bath, even the foetid air of Massawa seemed sweet.

I felt as if I had run the course, but the fun was only beginning. Sodini's Eritrean attendant carted over the fantastic boots which went with the suit and dropped them at my feet, almost amputating my toes in the process. They weighed fourteen pounds each. Their uppers of heavy leather were triple-strapped for buckling on, and they had brass protective toe-caps and lead soles an inch to an inch and a half thick. I thrust my twill-clad feet into them and jumped up and down until I was satisfied that I'd got myself firmly lodged. Then the attendant stepped on to the brass toe-cap and further secured the boots by heaving on a heavy point-line lanyard. The suction of clinging mud in which the diver commonly works would just about pull a limpet off a rock and there has to be no danger of the diver's boots coming adrift under water, for he relies on their ballast to keep him right way up as he works. The buckles on the boots were savagely tightened and the security lanyard wound like the toe tapes of a ballet dancer's pumps round my ankles before being made fast in a reef knot.

I stood almost literally rooted to the spot while Sinfield buckled a heavy leather belt round my middle, pulling the spare of the suit up round my chest and back as he fastened it. Arms dangling, shoulders bulging, with a dummy chest like a barrel, I felt —and probably looked—like an over-dressed gorilla. On the left-hand side of the belt a canvas pouch contained spanners, wrenches and a pair of pliers, for use below. The pouch was pierced all over by brass-eyeletted holes like a colander, to deprive it of buoyancy under water. The rest of my main armament consisted of a diver's knife carried in a brass scabbard on the right-hand side of the belt.

For the next operation I was allowed to return to my stool. Sinfield bore down on me carrying my corselet, a kind of out-size fore-and-aft bib made of copper, similar in general shape to the cuirass of a Life Guard. The corselet, topped by a bronze dog-collar designed to fit a rubber cuff on the top opening of the dress, had somehow to be rammed over my head inside my suit. Sodini preserved my features from damage from the collar by wrapping his hands round my face while Sinfield heaved and pushed on the breast-plate. We all oozed sweat and imprecations. Once inside the suit the corselet was joined to it in a water-tight union by the front and back brasses—flanges used to force the neck-cuff of the suit against the rim of the corselet. These were forced into place and locked with shaped brass nuts bolted on with a special two-handled box spanner. As the nuts were made fast by Sinfield, Sodini, with his usual motherly care,

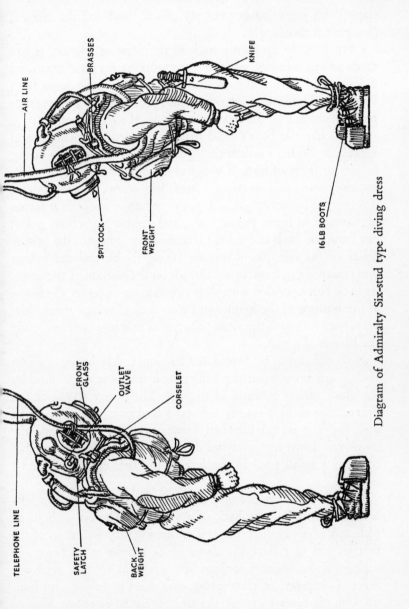

Diagram of Admiralty Six-stud type diving dress

clapped his bony hands over my ears to ward off the blow if the spanner should slip.

I was literally up to my neck in the dressing routine. It had taken us ten minutes, where a team working on an experienced diver would have had him ready to go over the side in four. Dressing, like most diving operations, proceeded in almost complete silence except for a constant refrain of muffled oaths.

Then, like the boar's head making a ceremonial entrance at a banquet, Sodini's assistant stepped forward bearing my diving helmet in front of him. It weighed about twenty pounds without telephones and its copper dome had a port on each side of it protected by heavy grids. A round window, about four inches in diameter in front, swung open, and stubby projections poked out from the back and sides. I retracted my chin into the bronze collar of the suit, like a tortoise taking fright, and the helmet was clamped on. Interrupted threads on the outside of the corselet neck corresponded with their opposite numbers on the flange at the bottom of the helmet and were locked with a quick sideways turn on much the same principle as that involved in closing the breech of a gun.

Now the ordeal by fire neared its climax. My heavy woollen undergarments generated a stifling heat that was augmented by the close, airless confines of the suit. The brassy Massawa sun beat almost audibly on my helmet. Ventilation was virtually nil and, sopping wet, I hunched forward on the stool while the sweat ran down my jaws and dripped off the point of my chin to form a small pool in the face of the helmet. I stank and I steamed.

The air hose was brought forward and fastened to the left-hand connection at the back of my helmet. The hose, about an inch and a half in diameter, is buoyant for fifty feet or so of the first section to relieve the diver of its weight as he begins to submerge. Subsequent sections are weighted to sink after the diver. Composed of wire spring embedded in rubber and built up with reinforcing canvas, the air hose has to be tough. It must not kink or pinch under pressure, and at the same time it must be flexible enough to allow of reasonably free movement. With a breaking strain in the region of 1,300 pounds, the diver can be hauled up by it in an emergency. From the connection on my helmet the hose was led down the back of my left shoulder, under my armpit and up again past my helmet, to which it was lashed, and thence on to a neat coil on the deck and so to the pump. Lashing the hose to my helmet meant that I could find it easily with my hand, and the fact that under water it would run straight up above my head and not trail over my shoulder behind me, eased the drag on my movements. In the spigot of the air-hose connection a spring-loaded, non-return valve was situated. Once under water, this was my link with life. Air pumped through the hose forces the spring valve open, enters the suit and provides a cushion against pressure as well as the essential oxygen the diver breathes. If the valve sticks, get a new diver.

On the right side of my helmet I felt for the outlet valve, also spring-loaded. Through this valve excess air and nitrogen escape in a stream of bubbles to the surface. The flow can be varied by flicking a milled wheel on this exhaust valve with the thumb in much the same action as is used to operate a cigarette lighter. I knew that as I went down, the pump hand on deck, if he wasn't lying on his back having a smoke, would be watching two gauges, one showing my depth in feet and fathoms, the other showing air pressure, which should be kept a few pounds per square inch above the water pressure at the diver's level. One of the few conveniences of diving is that maximum comfort in the suit indicates correct air pressure: too much air, and the diver will find himself involuntarily taking off for the surface; too little air, and his suit presses in on him and it seems as if the world is resting on his shoulders. When the pressure is right his movements are comparatively free, his breathing almost easy. He suffers no more discomfort than, say, a straight-jacketed contortionist buried in a box at Brighton.

Beside the air hose connection on the back of my helmet protruded a second connection which would normally have been used for a combined telephone and life-line, but at Massawa we had no telephones, and communication was by significant pulls either on the air hose or on the breast-line which was lashed round my waist, led up my right armpit behind me and secured in passing to my helmet.

To complete my burden only the front and back weights had to be added. These are 35 to 45 lb. each, depending on the depth to which the diver is descending. For my jaunt I got away with the 35 lb. ones. The shaped weights were shackled by a faintly grinning Sinfield to the clips on the front and back of my corselet. Sodini then ran a lanyard through the front weight, over a lug on one side of my helmet, through the back weight, over a second lug on the other side of the helmet and back to the front weight again. Looping the lanyard over my helmet was a precaution against the helmet's becoming unscrewed under water, which, should the safety catch fail, can only happen to any diver once. The lanyard was tied in front with a slip knot for easy release in an emergency.

Sodini darted for'ard to start the pump. The air hissed into my helmet, rubbery-smelling but sweet in comparison with what I had been breathing for the last five minutes. I would not have exchanged the soothing jet playing about my head and filtering down to my sticky body for a bath in asses' milk as the impure atmosphere of my helmet was swilled out.

I could have sat there all day, but Sodini signalled to me to rise and helped me shuffle across to the bulwarks. I was carrying, between helmet, suit and ballast, just about my own weight—cunningly distributed for maximum discomfort. With a prodigious effort I swung a leg over the side, gripping the bulwark firmly, and got a foot on the ladder leading some six feet down below the surface. I lowered myself carefully down until the water reached my waist. Sinfield and Sodini hung on to my lanyards for all they were worth: if I toppled off the ladder with my front glass missing, as it was, my salvage career was over before it had started. I nodded inside my helmet to Sinfield, signalling insincerely that I was O.K., and he reached down and screwed in the heavy half-inch-section brass-rimmed front glass.

From the time I was introduced to my thigh-length stockings until that moment I had been utterly preoccupied with personal discomfort, which was of a high order. But with the screwing into place of the front glass my mind jumped the points and careered off on a new course. While there was a four-inch hole in front of my helmet, I still belonged to the world. Now I was cut off. All sounds stopped except the hiss of air through my diffusors, the flop-flop of the pump and the slightly magnified sighing of my own breath. I felt frighteningly alone and for an instant quite helpless.

Much later in the war when I was training divers I discovered that the sealing of the suit gets everybody in the same way. Burly A.Bs. who had never admitted fright in their lives suddenly discovered claustrophobic tendencies and screamed like trapped animals to be released. As soon as the front glass came off they relaxed, shamefaced at their lack of control; but they were not to be blamed. The fear of confined spaces, in one degree or another, is common to most of the human race and it cannot be mastered by guts alone.

From my brief experience at Port Elizabeth I had known what to expect, and although I flinched involuntarily as the glass went in, I braced myself to suppress the flicker of panic. My concern was with the next move. This time I had to achieve something. I knew that if I came back up after staggering blindly about for a few minutes on the bottom with nothing done, I couldn't continue to send men down on diving inspections, briefing them before they went, cross-examining them on their return, behaving as if but for an accident of circumstances I should be making the inspection myself. I had in fact already realised that, to get the best out of my own experience, in many salvage jobs it would be necessary for me to gain first-hand knowledge of the problem. That could not be acquired on the topside end of a diver's telephone. This dive *had* to come off.

As far as the descent itself was concerned, although my inexperience exaggerated the difficulties it presented, I was surprisingly unperturbed. I knew I could get down and, unless I did something pretty stupid, I knew I could get up again. I descended to the bottom rung of the ladder so that my helmet was just below the surface of the water and pressed the spindle to close my exhaust valve. With no air escaping, the pressure in the suit built up and the stiff twill filled out. Any leaky joints or tears in the fabric would at once be demonstrated to my helpers on top by a flow of bubbles. I leaned back, stiff as a board, for under water a diving suit is inflexible and with one's vision restricted and canalised by the narrow front glass it is usually necessary to move the whole body to look in any direction other than straight ahead. Above me I saw a reassuring flash of white teeth as Sodini grinned his approval of the test. I acknowledged him with an upraised thumb and stretched out my right hand, already puffy from the constriction of the cuffs, to grope for the shot-line, found it, and swung across.

At once I felt my suit urging me upwards. Too buoyant. I flicked at the spitcock to reduce pressure, but even so I had virtually to drag myself down the shot-line foot by foot. For the novice, getting under is one of the most difficult parts of a routine dive. But I was gaining confidence by the second, forgetting in my pleasure at making progress about the nerve-searing pain that assails all divers once the first fathom is passed. I was sharply reminded. The pressure in my helmet built up until suddenly a streak of blinding agony shot through both ears and halted me in a minor and frightening convulsion. I swallowed, grimaced, waggled my jaw, blinked at the tears smarting in my eyes and then, in a moment of blessed relief, my ears 'clicked' and the ferocious pain passed, leaving only an aftermath of tenderness.

I pressed on, much happier. In front of me my hands, magnified to twice their natural size by the water, brushed a delicate stream of minute bubbles from the shot-line. It was all rather fascinating and much, much more comfortable than the Port Elizabeth plunge. For one thing, the water was crystal clear, light and bright. For another, it was as warm as milk: although my

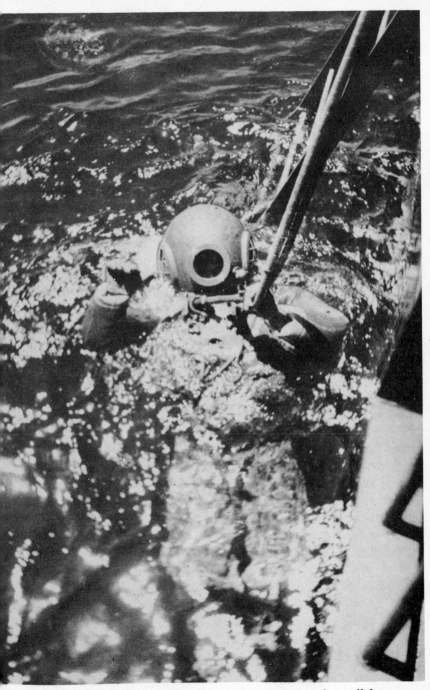

The beginning of a dive. The hand is raised, not in jaunty farewell, but to adjust the exhaust valve in the helmet preparatory to submerging.

hands were numb they still retained some feeling. In Port Elizabeth the chill water of the harbour had desensitised them at once.

Halfway down the line I leant out from it and peered down
at the bottom. I found I had to concentrate hard to get anything
to focus, but after a moment I could see the bottom quite clearly
—sparkling white coral sand with here and there a burst of
marine growth, an outcrop of delicately shaped coral rock. It
looked attractive and I rejoiced to find myself so much at ease.
There were going to be no difficulties after all.

I slid gently down the line until my feet touched bottom, stir-
ring up a little fog of sand. I let my weight go on my feet and
immediately lurched about like a drunken sailor, which for the
moment to all intents and purposes I was. Too much buoyancy
again. I fiddled with the exhaust valve, waving one arm about
in an effort to retain my balance, while I tried to adjust the
pressure in my suit so that the weight just lifted off my shoulders and the lead on my boots gave me a hold on the bottom.

Movement under water is ponderous. As I lumbered and
almost fought my way around the bottom of the shot-line I felt
like a fly struggling out of treacle. I discovered that leaning forward at an angle of sixty degrees made progress easier, and in
fact an experienced diver in my position would probably have
flopped flat on his face and wriggled on his tour of inspection
in order to decrease resistance. I spent a couple of minutes trying
to get full command of my movements and then paused to take
stock. In the conditions at Massawa underwater visibility was
excellent. Although by a freak of optics it is difficult for a diver
to see anything through his front glass without conscious effort,
I reckoned my visibility on the bottom there at twenty to thirty
feet. It was a pleasant, drowsy sort of world to which a gentle
translucence—the kind of soft diffusion of light one associates
with the interior of a cathedral—dimmed to a grey-green twilight and dwindled into the velvety darkness of an African night.
Nothing was harsh. At my feet I could see scattered about the
sea bed scores of *bêches de mer*, brown, furry, sausage-shaped sea
slugs which are found all over the Red Sea. Then with a slight

start I realised that I had attracted what seemed like shoals of garfish, brilliantly incandescent blue creatures about six inches long with spiny swords projecting from their snouts. They had crept up on me impelled by a curiosity that seems to be their main characteristic. They were not in the least diffident, nosing at my suit, nuzzling in a tentative sort of way at my fingers and darting off only when I shooed them away. They followed me about like a cloud of flies, persistent, irritating, yet ethereally attractive.

But I had to be getting on. By a brilliant feat of memory for which I duly congratulated myself, I remembered to pick up the distance line, a rope attached a few feet above the shot which the diver uncoils as he goes and which directs him back to his starting point. I moved off heavily to a dark shape discernible a few yards away as the hull of my tug. At close quarters I could see it was deeply coated with marine growth which in these parts is luxuriant and quick growing—weed, grass, oysters, mussels, knobs of coral. I put my hand out to steady myself to examine the six-inch growth more closely and collected in my palm a quiverful of the sharp spines of a sea egg. These poisonous things break off flush with the skin, and although my dose did not worry me much when I got it, I had a painful session later when the spines had to be dug out one by one.

Paying out my distance rope carefully, I edged along the keel of the ship, thrusting my front glass at intervals against the hull, looking for trouble. I worked my way aft, and saw the propeller blades and rudder in black silhouette against the bright sand. A single pull travelled down my breastline, an enquiry from the watchers on top after my welfare and, with another tug, I telegraphed back cheerfully that I was O.K. These checks were made periodically, and this one served to remind me that if I went round the ship on the bottom I would almost certainly foul my air-line on the superstructure. So coiling my precious distance rope in my hand I retraced my steps, working up to the bow without discovering damage, and then returning to midships. Sinfield's earlier reports were so far confirmed.

I decided I had better try to get myself on to the deck of the tug, cross it and go down the other side to complete my circuit of inspection. The shot-line was a bit too far from the wreck for use in the ascent, so I shut the exhaust valve on my helmet, pumped up the suit, flexed my knees inside it and sprang upwards. The impetus took me gently and pleasantly up from the bottom in a kind of slow-motion Martian leap. I clutched at the tug's rail and hauled myself inboard, opened the spitcock and deflated the suit until the weights settled on my chest and back again. It was wonderful. I felt in complete command of myself, and delighted with the success of my submarine Superman act I determined to repeat the performance. Spindle up, flex the knees, away and—clang! My helmet hit an obstruction with a boom that would have done credit to Mr. Rank's gargantuan gong. That sobered me, and I came down on to the deck again and proceeded more cautiously.

Sound travels well under water. I could hear my boots scraping on the deck, an occasional clank as my brass toe-cap connected with a ring bolt, and even my tools jangling in their canvas pouch as I moved. They made a comforting, companionable noise as I fumbled my way along.

In the lower deckhouse there were several open ports, and partly shrouding one was a rotten curtain still sagging forlornly in its place, drenched in fuel oil. This was our first clue that the tug was an oil-burner. Then I found a rounded-top steel door standing ajar and wedged myself through it. At once all light was cut off. In the darkness I lost my balance and began to flounder, and as my sense of direction fled with uncanny suddenness, panic flared up in me. My heart lurched and thumped, and fear increased my respiration. I heard my breath rasping fast and noisy in my helmet. As I scrambled with groping hands outstretched, not sure whether I was making my way across deck or bulkhead, afraid my distance rope had got snagged on something, and desperately uncertain of being able to find my way out of this dungeon, I felt my lines tighten. I followed the drag and with unspeakable relief saw an oblique shaft of thin light marking the partially opened door. I squeezed out through the door and clung to the rail of the ship while I waited for self-control to return. As I sagged there the insistent pull on my line drew my attention again, and I realised that while I was in the grip of my panic my helpers on the launch must have signalled and, getting no response, started to haul me up. I telegraphed hastily that all was well.

Then I climbed laboriously over the rail, lowered myself down as far as I could, and dropped. That was another mistake. Instead of floating down gently as I had expected, I dropped sharply for ten feet or more. My buoyancy was wrong. Adjusted to keep my feet solidly on the deck, the air in my suit was insufficient to meet the rise in pressure at the greater depth. A giant hand closed on me, squeezing. The tremendous pressure rose in a wave starting at my ankles and travelling up to my chest. It held the promise of exquisite pain, but far more than that it was utterly terrifying. Stories flashed through my mind of divers caught in this squeeze: forced up in their suits until all of them that could be hauled up was a soggy mess of pulp in the helmet, the suit trailing emptily below. These were no old wives' tales as I was later to discover for myself, and the squeeze I endured as I dropped down from the tug's side was in any case sufficient indication of the fate awaiting any diver who went forward too boldly.

I got off with a fright. As I stood groggily on the bottom, trembling from the shock, I realised I was breathing my own CO_2. I spindled some more air into my helmet and, as the oxygen revived me, gathered my wits sufficiently to continue my fore and aft inspection. I found what I was looking for: the opening which housed the condenser intake valve and, thrusting my hand in, I could feel the fragments of the valve which must have been shattered when the tug was scuttled. Now we knew where we were; if the tug had been sunk in that way it was unlikely that her Italian crew had inflicted any further damage. When you scuttle a ship with charges of H.E. you do not first go round taking a heavy hammer to the inlet valves; and if all we had to do to get the tug back into service was to clean her off and replace a valve in her condenser, the sooner we got on with the job the better.

I was now in a pretty poor state. Apart from the jarring my nervous system had had, I was working in water with a temperature of nearly ninety degrees. This, plus my under-water clothing and my unwonted exercise, produced a volume of perspiration well beyond any limit I had reached even at Massawa. I was bone-weary and giddy; my flesh crept with prickly heat, my hands were numb and sore and my ears ached. And I had still to get back up top. As far as I was concerned that meant another Martian leap to the deck of the tug—now a much less joyous prospect—then awkwardly picking my way over to the other side, finding the shot-line again and following it up to the surface. Had it been Sodini he would simply have spindled up from where he stood and allowed his helpers to pull him in to the launch's side from wherever he broke the surface, but this was a feat I was unwilling to attempt in my weakened condition. It takes an alert mind and an experienced hand to control pressure in the suit on a 'free' ascent like that, and if nothing worse happened to me the odds were I would take in too much air, shoot to the surface and find myself spreadeagled as if crucified in an over-inflated suit, giving a fair imitation of the little man used to advertise Michelin tyres. When this happens, as it often does to novice divers, it is impossible to bend one's arms to get at the outlet valve and release the pressure. One waits hopelessly and ignominiously to be pulled alongside like a harpooned whale.

So wearily I made my frog-leap to the deck, followed my distance rope back to the shot-line and with a bit of fishing coaxed the shot-line into reach. I signalled with four pulls on my breast rope to be taken up, and when the answering four pulls came down the line spindled air into my suit and gladly let myself be drawn to the surface. The strong sunlight breaking into my helmet revived me for a moment, but by the time I had got my boots on the lowest rung of the ladder I was completely spent. I clung stupidly where I was and waited till Sodini

and Sinfield scrambled over the bulwarks and hauled me bodily
over the side on to the deck. By the time they had dropped my
weights, unscrewed my front glass and wrenched my helmet off
I felt a lot better. I sat, literally steaming, on the stool and drank
God's air. It was good. When they tugged my boots off and
stripped me of the suit it was delicious. I crumpled like a five-
miler after breasting the tape and gave myself up to the throb-
bing ache that enveloped me until fresh energy ebbed slowly
back and I looked up at Sinfield standing by in sympathetic
silence.

'How long?' I asked.

Sinfield flicked open the log in which my travail had been
recorded. 'Twenty-one minutes, Sir. I dare say it seemed longer.
It *was* a bit long for a first dive, really, but it comes easier as
you get on.'

Twenty minutes! Well, maybe it wasn't much; but I had the
deep satisfaction of knowing it hadn't been wasted. Whether I
would ever become a proficient diver was still open to question,
but I could go down again, warily perhaps, but with some confidence. And I knew that we should get that tug. I started to
outline my plans to Sinfield while I towelled the muck-sweat
off my greasy body, and as one of the natives cast off from the
wreck and the launch nosed round towards the base my spirits
rose. I had been blooded.

We tied up alongside the jetty, and I climbed stiffly and painfully up the iron ladder and limped off to my quarters for a
shower before getting back to the signals piling up in my office.
Massawa might not be the Navy's favourite watering place, but
I was looking forward to tomorrow.

The author resting between dives during his initiation at Massawa.

III. DOWN TO WORK

THE morning after was no worse than I had expected. I felt as if I had gone the full distance with Freddy Mills and been given a prize for staying on my feet—most of the time anyway. I had no doubt that before very long I should be able to play a reasonable part under-water, and with this heartening if slightly-founded thought I got down to planning the details of my first salvage operation with Sinfield, on whom the main burden of sub-surface work would fall. In the week that followed, Sinfield found himself going down the shot-line as many as seven or eight times in the course of a day's work. My own contribution was limited to the afternoon watch when I could escape from my First Lieutenant's duties, but even I was diving three or four times daily. After the first dive of the day, neither of us took off our suits until it was time to go home. When we came up Sodini would ease our helmets off and slip our hands clear of the tight cuffs of our suits and we would flop out on the deck until the next call came. For me it was a drastic initiation, but it served to push the mere mechanics of the dive into their proper place. Every time I went down now it was to do something positive. In the shallow waters of the harbour there were few complications to be feared, and quite soon I found myself moving easily and almost naturally in my suit, achieving the right balance of pressure quickly and without dif-ficulty. The fact that I had an objective beyond getting back to the surface in workmanlike manner turned my concentration outwards, and I learned quickly and largely subconsciously. It was an admirable if brief apprenticeship.

Having decided that we were going to raise the tug, the first job was to seal her off, and this had to be done thoroughly. In a larger ship with more freeboard, it might have been enough to pump out two or three compartments and let the resultant buoyancy force her to the surface, but every opening in the tug had to be stopped up before we could hope for success. We raided the Regia Marina stores for timber and combed the beaches round Massawa for flotsam the natives had been too tired to pinch. There was plenty of it, washed ashore from the wrecks.

Sinfield measured up the assorted holes which had to be sealed off. We decided that the engine-room skylights could be closed with their own steel hatches, which were still operable, but the condenser inlet, a door, several ports, ventilators, the stokehold fiddley and other similar openings had to be dealt with. The shipwrights ashore, along with the handier P.OW's., were set to prefabricating patches which one by one were forced into place. We had to make our own hookbolts for the fiddleys, the gratings leading to the stokehold. This we did by forging mild steel bars, circular in section, into the shape of a question mark and threading the straight end to take a nut. The home-made hookbolt could then be clamped on to any suitable projection, such as the bars of the fiddley, and secured to the patch by a nut. Once the patch was lightly held in place, external pressure of water forced it down immoveably.

Between us, Sinfield and I knocked down the ventilators and stopped up the trunks with wooden plugs caulked with oakum and tallow. We even unshipped the funnel and beached it. The work went ahead steadily and quickly until the time came for us to instal the cofferdams.

These products of much thought were square wooden chimneys, built in sections ashore and assembled and secured *in situ*. They were attached to the fore and after hatches and rose up above water level to provide drains through which the tons of water nailing the tug to the bottom might be pumped out. The fact that the Red Sea is virtually tideless made this method of attack possible: if we'd had to cope with a rise and fall of water of ten or twenty feet the cofferdams would have been useless; as it was they provided their own problems.

The wooden walls of the cofferdams, each of which was installed separately, had a natural but distressing tendency to float. They had to be weighted with fire bars and dropped down to the diver standing below, who made them fast as best he could to the hatch coaming, and when all four sides were in place braced them together with a steel hoop made for the purpose. Then the cracks and joints had to be caulked. It was heavy work, but when Sinfield signalled to be brought up after the last side of the second cofferdam had been secured, it looked as if it was all over bar the afternoon in my bunk which I had promised myself in celebration of the tug's recovery.

My scavenging of the dockyard had produced one solitary salvage pump, Admiralty pattern, 1914 vintage. In its day it might have been an admirable instrument, but its day was now well past, and no amount of cajolery would persuade it even to turn over. We abandoned it and for all I know it sits in a shed at Massawa still. The Army provided us with some gallant substitutes—N.F.S. fire pumps, the kind which had saved London in the Great Fire of 1941. Five of these game little machines, which disposed of some twenty-five tons of water per hour, were mounted on a barge moored hard by the tug.

On a hopeful afternoon five days after we had started sealing off the tug, we shackled up the suction hoses to the pump and led them down into the mouths of the cofferdams. I gave the order to start the pumps and stood by complacently for the tug to bale herself out. In an hour the head of water in the cofferdams had failed to drop by a centimetre.

It was to be expected, really. The whole of the Red Sea was waiting to replace every teaspoonful of water we pumped out of the hull, and the sea, much more easily than we, could find

every cranny that we had left unstopped. There was nothing for
it but to defer the celebratory sleep, get back into a diving suit
and go below again to investigate. Sinfield and I dressed mourn-
fully and lowered ourselves over the side.

We took with us brushes made from teased-out oakum and
advanced over the tug holding these out in front of us like sappers prospecting a minefield with detectors. When we got near
a leak, the suction of water caused the brushes to 'point'; we
took the hint and got down once again to patching. It was remarkable the number of things we missed: the port to the
lamp-trimmer's caboose, for example. Ports had to be closed
from inside, and since we felt it was risky to wedge our way into
this tiny, cluttered store, we had to smash the hinged port off
from the outside with hammer and chisel and plug the opening.
Another leak which took a long time to trace was eventually
run down to a voice-pipe. The brush didn't pick it up until it
was virtually over the pipe and then the oakum—and almost
my fist with it—swooped down the voice-pipe and was gone
for ever.

It took us another couple of days to overcome the more
serious leaks and then the levels in the cofferdams began to drop.
After a bit, as pressure within the tug decreased, what leaks
were left became stronger and easier to trace. But every day,
using the cofferdams as our barometer, we had to go down
and stop one or two more gaps.

In just over a week the wreck began to stir. From the angle
she was heeled over at, slowly she began to come upright. We
redoubled out efforts and towards the evening of the ninth day
the tug was clearly on its way up. We worked straight on
through that night and were rewarded, in the first rosy streaks
of dawn, by the sight of the tug's upper-works breaking the
surface. But with this evidence of success came a new snag.
The cofferdams, rising with the hull, pulled the hoses out of the
water, broke suction, stopped the pumping and threatened to
drag the pumps off their seating on the barges. We threw ourselves frenziedly at the wooden columns and hacking madly

with axes and any other instruments blunt or sharp we could lay our hands on chopped raggedly through the tops of the cofferdams. Three times we repeated this performance, and by eleven o'clock in the morning the tug was afloat.

This was the first time I had allowed myself to break my routine as Number One, and when the initial exultation died down and I could look soberly at the tug I began to wonder if it had been worth while. The hulk had risen through the oil patch formed on the surface from escapes which had taken place while we worked under water. The weird marine growth which encrusted the ship and what yellowing enamel was left on her showed dirtily through the oil in streaks. The stench from dead fish trapped in her and the weeds decaying fast in the oven-like atmosphere of the harbour struck like blast from a bomb. Patched all over the place with rough wooden plugs, faintly absurd without her funnel, she looked very, very second-hand to me.

But Sodini, who was used to these uncouth apparitions, was delighted with her. We towed her off with the diving launch and berthed her alongside one of the spare parts of the quay, conveniently close to a workshop, and I left Sodini in charge of an unhappy bunch of Eritrean natives deputed to clean her down. A little digging proved that she was in good condition, and as work progressed a brass plate emerged on her bridge which told us she had been completed as late as 1938. Within a month the tug was ready for service, and most useful she proved to be. We re-christened her, with rather a lack of originality, *Bull I*, and as my stay at Massawa lengthened, recovery work became so much a part of routine that I often saw her about her business in the port without pausing to reflect that here was the first child of my growing love for salvage. *Bull I* would never be pretty, but thinking back I feel a paternal affection for her which didn't grow entirely from the afternoon of blessed sleep which I duly awarded myself when I was satisfied she wouldn't sink at her moorings.

*　　*　　*

While I was working on the tug it was perhaps natural that my vision should be focused like a spotlight on this job alone, but with the prospective *Bull I* safely alongside and in the hands of the Base Engineer, I could look around me again—and for the eager salvager the port provided an embarrassment of opportunity. I discussed with N.O.I.C. the direction which our next step should take and he suggested that I might have a look at the larger of the two floating docks lying on the bottom of the north harbour in forty to fifty feet of water. She was certainly worth tackling. Little short of six hundred feet by two hundred, she would take ships of up to nine thousand tons burthen. If the dock could be returned to service, it would be a most useful acquisition, a handsome supplement to the port of Massawa, and in all probability a refuge for some of the cruisers of the Mediterranean Fleet which were queueing to have their bottoms scraped in Alex.

The great horseshoe-shaped dock lay almost on an even keel, twenty feet of rust-streaked side tanks showing above water. On one runway a crane pointed dismally towards the sky. Massive, looking as if she had grown out of the sea, a fairly cursory inspection from the surface suggested that it was well beyond our powers to raise her. Sinfield volunteered to drop down and scout round, but since the decision to work on her or not would depend on my report, I thought I'd better have a look for myself. We took the diving launch through the portals of the dock and moored it to one wall and I went over the side.

Forty feet down, in the deep shadow of the side tanks, visibility was limited. I could see, in the narrow field of my front glass, about six feet ahead when I concentrated; but I was steadily acquiring the diver's habit of working as much by feel as by sight. Hands in front of me, arms moving in a sluggish swimming motion, obstacles revealed themselves by touch as I picked my way through the tangle of wire hawsers, manilla rope, twisted angle irons and other debris on the dock's bottom. The great difficulty, working almost blind on the enormous floor-area of the dock, was to make sure of not missing anything. I knew roughly what I was looking for, and I started by making a quick examination of one side of the dock—quick in the sense of cursory, for across the bottom of the dock at roughly three-feet intervals were hefty, chest-high bilge-blocks, the timber ribs of which could be raised or lowered, extended or retracted, to support ships of varying sizes, and for every three feet of wall I inspected I had a Cook's tour of some fifty or sixty feet of rib before I could get at the next short stretch of side. As I made my slow progress along the wall of the dock Sinfield followed me on top with the launch.

I was also looking for the heavy joints, indicated by a cluster of rivets on the floor of the dock, which would tell me that I was at the junction of two bottom tanks; when I found the rivets I traced them back to check that this particular compartment at least was intact and, apart from pumping out, would not need our attention. The first two compartments I covered in this way appeared to be perfectly sound, but on the lip of the third I almost impaled myself on a wickedly sharp tongue of metal thrown up by an explosion and growing out of the deck like a submarine succulent. It was on the perimeter of a sizeable hole which I thought I'd better investigate and moving gingerly, fearful of ripping my suit on the razor-edge of the sliver of steel, I dropped down into the interior of the tank. It was pitch dark, and I hadn't quite got over my fear of working inside a wreck. The prospects of escape in an emergency when one is working totally blind in an enclosed area seem to recede with frightening speed, and the utter loneliness which is the most nerve-wrecking feature of diving closes in stiflingly, almost paralysing the will to go on. But I forced myself to pace the compartment and, once satisfied that the charge had blown upwards and left the bottom of the tank intact, I spindled thankfully upwards to the comparatively friendly gloom above, closely followed by my inevitable escort of garfish.

On the other side of the dock, directly opposite, I found a second jagged hole. This time when I went down I went straight through the floor of the compartment and on to the sea bed.

The doubly-holed tank was going to present us with a particularly sticky job of patching, and my hopes of being able to salve the dock, never very high, were now diminishing fast.

I had been down for a solid forty minutes on this inspection, and in Massawa anything over half an hour below the surface was sheer cruelty, so I gave the customary four pulls on my breast rope and had myself hauled inboard. That, when I thought about it afterwards, was a distinctly risky thing to do, for though the hole in the ceiling of the tank was a good ten feet in diameter and I could have 'blown' myself through it with ease, by electing to be hauled up from the bottom I took a chance that the launch was not directly over my helmet and it was quite on the cards that I could have been wiped against one of the steel fangs which surrounded the hole. I was later to discover what it meant to gash my suit, but if it had happened at that early stage in my career I doubt if I could ever have talked myself into making another dive.

A rest with helmet off in the shady lee between the walls of the dock restored me enough for one more dive that day, and I went down again to have a look at two more compartments before knocking off. Neither compartment had been damaged as far as I could discover, but in one of them I found a manhole big enough to admit me. As I lowered myself down through it my boots glanced off an object that rolled gently away before my feet touched bottom. I didn't have to run my hands over the cylinder I'd stumbled on to know what it was, and I recoiled in instinctive horror at my proximity to what could only be an undetonated charge. There was no danger from the charge itself. The wires I found running from it indicated that it had to be fired electrically, and there was of course no power on the sunken dock; but it was not impossible that the engineers who had scuttled the dock had left a booby-trap for inquisitive innocents like myself, and even if the charge itself was harmless, I could never be happy in the presence of something like a hundred pounds of high explosive. As far as I was concerned this was something for my report. I had already done more than enough for one day, and between the usual muck-sweat induced by diving in the tepid waters of Massawa and the nervous perspiration brought on by my first encounter with H.E. under water, I felt pretty wobbly.

I touched the spindle and floated up, clawing for the rim of the manhole above me, found it and eased myself through. On the floor of the dock again, I halted trembling, waiting for the jitters to pass before I signalled to be taken up. For a long moment I stood with my eyes shut. I seemed to be swaying back and forth in a sickening arc which I traversed at increasing speed and then, suddenly, I had the impression of myriads of white lights streaking upwards from the back of my eyeballs through the crown of my skull and as consciousness drifted away I knew, just before the black pall descended on my mind, that I hadn't the strength to reach for my breast-rope.

* * *

My slow return to consciousness was confused by the strangest sensation. I had the impression that I was dead, and indeed there was little to contradict that feeling in what I could recollect of my last moments before the blackness came down. I seemed to be stretched out on a cold, wet pavement with my head propped on somebody's doorstep and, though I knew my eyes were open, I could see nothing, nothing but a vague blurry whiteness wavering above me. A shudder ran through my body as the coldness penetrated my mind and struck through my flesh to the bones. And with the coldness came fear of the unreality and a greater fear of discovering the truth. It took me minutes, in my weak and muddled state, to make an effort to find out where I was—or even if I was. Then, raising one hand, I felt a damp covering and pulled at it. It was a wet sheet, draped over me from head to toe. When it slithered off, I could discern a dim blue light burning above my head. My eyes settled to its glow and the surrounding darkness, and I struggled on to one elbow and looked around me. Running the length of the long, cold room were not the hospital cots I had half expected to see, but a line of marble-topped slabs; and on the one next to mine, under a sheet, lay what was unmistakably a body. Somewhere between hysteria and the heartiest laugh of my life I realised I had fetched up in the mortuary.

I sat abruptly upright, sweeping the headblock on to the floor with a tremendous crash that brought Pilkington, the base M.O., bustling on to the scene, full of professional heartiness. He seized my wrist to feel the pulse. 'How're you doing, Peter? Better now? Sorry about the sordid surroundings. Had to get your body temperature down somehow, and this is the coolest place in Massawa. Not too uncomfortable, I hope?'

I gibbered.

He dropped my arm. 'Hm. Still a bit rapid. But better that than this . . .' He nodded at the still form on the adjacent slab. 'That's Thompson, poor old chap. He collapsed this morning and he'd gone before I could get to him. Not that there was much I could have done. He hadn't your bovine constitution.'

Thompson had been our Sea Transport Officer, an elderly, kindly man who'd been finding the going at Massawa a bit hard, although he never complained. Two days ago I had had a couple of drinks with him before dinner. I took another look at the heap under the sheet and almost had a relapse. It was obviously high time I got out of this place, but when I started to swing my legs off the slab, Pilkington put a restraining hand on my knee.

'Take it easy, Peter. You're a long way from being as frisky as you think. Sinfield told me that when he fished you out he thought you were a goner. I wasn't too confident myself when I saw you—you've been deep blue for hours. Heat stroke. Just hang on a jiffy and I'll get somebody to give me a hand with you.'

I wasn't going to stretch out on that slab again, so I sat up and shivered until Pilkington returned with a couple of Italian P.O.W. orderlies. Between them they got me off the marble and carted me across to the hospital. There I was billeted in a pleasant, air-conditioned ward and a few days later was fully restored. I never

got heat collapse again, although, of course, I went on diving—
possibly it was the thought of a return to the morgue, in one
condition or another, that kept me on my feet. At that time
the mortality rate in Massawa averaged out at one man per
day, mostly from heat stroke or, an even stickier end, prickly
heat.

Whilst I was in hospital Sinfield came in to tell me that he
had completed the inspection of the dock I had started. He said
that the dock walls seemed to be in good condition, but that of
the twelve tanks in the bottom of the dock, four had been blown
up and another four housed unexploded charges.

Sitting up in bed I drafted my report and, when I was up and
about again, took it along to the N.O.I.C. It was quite obvious
that this was a salvage job well beyond our present resources.
We had none of the oxy-hydrogen torches needed to trim the
jagged holes in the tanks preparatory to patching, nor had we
anything like enough steel for the patches themselves. In addition, cutting and welding steel is a skilled job, and I questioned
if we had an artisan at the base capable of doing it. In any case,
if we were to get the dock up in a reasonable time we would
need a squad of welders. My conclusion was that we could do
nothing for the moment, but given the equipment and a few
men the dock was by no means beyond redemption.

N.O.I.C. told me, when I saw him, that he'd had a signal
warning him to expect shortly the long-promised help from the
United States, a fully-equipped salvage ship, manned by artisans
and under the command of Captain Ellsberg, U.S.N.R., to be
followed in time by a salvage tug.

Ellsberg I knew of. He was the famous figure of the 1926
U.S. submarine salvage triumphs, and as a youngster I had read
the books he had written on marine salvage. I admired his
achievements and I expected to like him; and when he flew in
he was, indeed, a joy to work with. His aggressive approach to
the job in hand was in sharp contrast to McCance's reserve, and
in fact I thought there might well be trouble between the
two of them. But if the burly, vigorous American and the

well-groomed, courtly Englishman were in any danger of falling out, Captain Lucas, suavely diplomatic, was able to keep the peace.

When Captain Ellsberg's ship arrived off Massawa, forty-eight hours after her skipper, I went out to pilot her into the harbour. She was a perfect example of American engineering ingenuity and resource, compact of every salvage device ever thought of. She was a ship to make the most sour salvage officer sing in his bath, but coming alongside I was astounded to see that she had no portholes or scuttles, no visible means of normal ventilation. This was explained when I stepped into the bridge house and had to borrow a jacket from her captain just to keep my teeth from chattering. The ship was entirely air-conditioned and even colder than the morgue of which my memories were still vivid.

This dream-ship's civilian crew was composed largely of college boys, longshoremen, and technicians from the studios of Hollywood. Some were thoroughly efficient, practical men, as they had claimed to be when they were recruited for the work, and some, as we were to discover, were not; but as I guided their ship into our heat-ridden port, even at this early stage of their initiation, they declaimed loudly, bitterly and with one voice against the bleak inhospitable aspect of the place. I couldn't help grinning to myself at the thought of what they had yet to discover about Massawa, and I wondered how long their air-conditioning—which seemed to double the blast of heat outside —would continue to be a comfort to them.

As it happened, through an error on the part of one of their amateur engineers, the ship's air-conditioning plant broke down completely and we had to burn holes in her sides to let some air in. The entire crew hurried ashore into the new quarters which the contractors hurriedly threw up for them, and for weeks the Americans were ready to take on the entire Royal Navy in hand-to-hand combat if any member of the service so much as smiled at the failure of their home comforts.

Shortly after this Captain Edison Brown arrived from the States bringing with him his small but game diesel-electric tug

Intent, whose welcome power was duly added to the scrum. We now had a considerable salvage force in action. Brown, an experienced West Coast salvage man and a genial soul always willing to impart his knowledge, was allotted the sunken Italian ship *Brenta*; McCance and his energetic assistant, Youill, were hard at work fairing and patching the holes in the bottom of the German steamer *Gera*; and, while with the Naval party I got down to some of the smaller wrecks in the port, Captain Ellsberg began to vent some of his savage energy on the dock which I had been surveying.

The dock was the biggest and toughest assignment, and the most important. I watched progress on it with interest and a faint sorrow at the job's going out of my hands, but Ellsberg tackled it in a most businesslike way. He had a pair of expert divers who quickly confirmed my general findings and Ellsberg himself, although he was really about twenty years too old to be diving, went down for a look around.

First they cleared the wreckage on the floor of the dock, including a massive crane, counterpart of the one still standing on the runway, and started to trim and clean off the ragged holes in the tanks for patching. The Americans had a great deal of trouble in getting their under-water cutting apparatus to work, and it was then that Ellsberg in a volcanic rage discovered how many of his self-declared experts had never before held a torch in their hands, or if they had, that their performance showed no evidence of it. But his few good men trudged sturdily on and the cleaning up continued. One problem was finding steel for the patches and this was eventually solved by taking plates from the less likely wrecks strewn around the port; but it was clear that outside help would be needed to complete the work. I got permission to signal to General Theron, the South African C-in-C Middle East, asking for twenty experienced boiler-makers, platers and welders. Within three days we had a reply saying that twelve artisans—all that could be raised—were on their way to us by air. It was a magnificent response and much better than I had hoped for, and in a few days' time a dozen surprised sappers who had been dug out of the hot sand round Mersah Matruh found themselves collaborating with the American salvage force and sharing the usual liberal American rations.

These South African sappers did tremendous work. They made templates and showed the divers how to use them. The divers went down, marked off the shape of the holes in the templates and then the Engineers cut, drilled and welded the plating exactly to fit the holes. Some of the prefabricated patches had to be made in sections so that they could be lowered through the smaller holes in the top of the tanks to fit over the greater holes in the bottom. Bit by bit the damaged tanks were sealed off, and as it had been decided that there was a good chance of getting sufficient buoyancy by sealing off six of the eight punctured tanks, the Americans worked on this assumption.

While the patching proceeded, surface crews installed compressors on the sides of the dock and ran air-tubes to the tanks under repair. At the bottom of these tanks spill-pipes were fitted to allow the water driven down by compressed air to escape into the sea. The tanks in the sidewalls of the dock were checked and seemed to be airtight, and after three weeks of toil, sweat and oaths, the time arrived for a test 'blow'. Ellsberg gave the order, and the compressors were started. Immediately the spill-pipes vomited oily, rust-stained water from the depths of the dock into the surrounding ocean which was stirred to a devil's cauldron of bubbling, frothing, swirling turbulence; but inside the dock itself could be seen almost innumerable streams of tell-tale bubbles as the air was applied. Leaks! The divers went down again to begin the long, tedious job of making good the bigger leaks while Ellsberg stood impatiently by, waiting to find out if the dock would lift.

In time he was satisfied that the leaks were sufficiently slowed, and he recalled his divers. About five o'clock in the afternoon the dock began to move, but while one side came up slowly, the other refused to budge from the bottom. The compressors were stopped again and down went the divers once more to look for the undiscovered leaks which were responsible for the list. They worked all night and in the early hours of the morning Ellsberg blew the dock again. This time she started to come up more readily, although she was still leaking in a dozen places, and by three o'clock in the afternoon she was high enough out of the water for the manholes in the tanks of the sidewalls to be opened. A handful of men boarded the dock and disappeared into the walls, searching for hand-valves with which the side tanks could be sealed. The lift was in its critical stage: if to the buoyancy produced in the bottom tanks by the furiously pumping compressors could be added the potential lift of the undamaged side tanks there was a good chance that the dock would come up cleanly, bringing with her the many tons of water still trapped in her two unpatched compartments. It was a colossal juggling act, put on without rehearsal, and Ellsberg was dashing about his ship almost berserk in an effort to make sure that everything and everybody was working flat out.

The situation looked good. The dock was coming up ever faster and on an even keel. If Ellsberg could get the water out of the side compartments which were still flooded, nothing could stop the salving of the dock. But while his men were working inside the walls, a sudden sibiliant explosion shot a column of water from one of the upper tanks and in a second that side of the dock sank like a stone to the bottom. And inside it were two of Ellsberg's crew. Almost at once one of them came up to the surface unconscious in an air bubble and was quickly hauled out of the water. His companion was less fortunate; in the bubbles welting up from the sunken side there was no trace of him.

Three of the salvage ship's hands dived over the side after their mate and swam down to the manhole, groping through it and actually touching the trapped man before they had to surface for air. But they couldn't get him out. Ellsberg, peering down, saw that they had failed and throwing off his gold-laced cap dived in, boots and all, straight through the mouth of the manhole. It was an enormously courageous thing to do, for the chances of his being able to find the manhole again, once inside the compartment, and fight his way up to the top while the oxygen in his lungs lasted were not good. Ellsberg got his man right up to the opening, but still couldn't get him through; at his last gasp he kicked his way up and broke surface, half fainting, and would have gone down again had he been able to stand. Instead, others went down and eventually succeeded in coaxing the limp body through the manhole. They worked for hours on the man, but life was gone. It was the first fatality at Massawa from salvage operations.

All this time the compressors continued to hammer away, and weary divers followed each other in quick succession over the salvage ship's side in a disheartening repetition of the monotonous pursuit of leaks. I came aboard Ellsberg's ship just after the unfortunate sailor had been hauled in and found the captain padding about the deck, still in his sopping uniform streaked in fuel oil, and exhorting his men, for once in undertones, to keep going. The floodlights, rigged for the previous night's work, were blazing and the group worked on very fast and unusually quietly, as though it mattered more to them personally than it had before. By morning they had the dock afloat and level, with the Stars and Stripes flying at half-mast on an improvised flagpole.

For three days they held her like that, the compressors still blatting away. Divers, now able to get right underneath the floor of the dock, went round making good the compartments one by one in a final, searching overhaul. Meanwhile, on top, men were swarming all over the dock, stripping her gear. Her motors were hauled out and sent to Alexandria to be rewound; all her electrical equipment was removed for repair or replacement, either on the spot or in the Middle East; and the dock was kept afloat at her moorings by two of the dozen compressors originally used to pump her out.

Ultimately the motors came back in good running order, the whole vessel was rewired, every valve was checked and tested. The dock was switched over to her own power and some three months from the time I blacked out on her bottom, she could flood her tanks, submerge to take a ship, pump herself out and rise with her great bay emptying of water: a floating dock in full commission, ready for her first Allied vessel. And there was a ship waiting to be docked in her.

In the months that followed each of our three cruisers in the eastern Mediterranean, *Dido*, *Cleopatra* and *Euryalus*, were taken into her for repairs that were by that time long overdue. Captain Ellsberg and his followers had every right to congratulate themselves on a most valuable job well done, and the enemy had made one more unwitting contribution to our strength at sea.

IV. MOPPING UP AT MASSAWA

URING the weeks spent in recovering the dock, Edison Brown was engaged on *Brenta*. She was almost completely submerged, her hatch coamings under water and her upperworks only just awash. Brown's diving team went down for the usual preliminary inspection, but before they could set to work in earnest, one of the divers came up with a report that he had discovered in No. 2 hold of the eight-thousand-ton ship a cargo of live mines, smallish but nasty looking, and some torpedo war-heads. The Americans were a purely civilian outfit, and rightly decided that the disposal of this unpleasant cargo was no part of their job. So the Navy took over, and in due course I was hauled off my current task of checking up on the smaller wrecks and detailed to investigate the position. At the same time a signal was sent to the Middle East asking for a mine-disposal officer and we were shortly joined by Sub-Lieutenant Cox, a cheerful and courageous Australian whose dangerous duties cost him his life not long after I left Massawa.

My first descent to the *Brenta* was memorable. It was pitch dark in No. 2 hold, and all I had for company as I groped my way across the floor was the gentle hiss of air in my helmet—we still had no telephones. I suppose I was careless and over-confident, for taking the first half-dozen paces too fast I walked smack into a mine. It was sitting up on its sinker mechanism, and involuntarily I flung my right arm up and crooked it round one of the mine's stubby, leaden horns. I do not know if I actually stopped breathing, but certainly I froze like a statue and then began to mutter the Lord's Prayer. Perhaps it was as well that telephones were not provided.

But nothing happened. I withdrew my arm with painful slowness and edged back off the mine. Gingerly I groped around it and, treading with the utmost care, sidled along checking on the others. There were about thirty altogether, some on their sinker pedestals and some resting on the deck. A number of them were connected together by electric leads, and I assumed that these had been intended to constitute the main demolition charge. The rest of them, together with some torpedo war-heads which I found in the wings of the hold, had no doubt been expected to explode in sympathy with the wired ones. It could still happen, too, I reflected every time I stubbed my lead-soled boots on a projection on the deck.

A search along the bilges revealed no damage. If it is the same in the other holds, I asked myself, what has made this tub sink? With my confidence flowing back, I turned my attention to the connecting wires on the mines and one by one pulled them out. They came away easily enough when I jerked hard. Then turning to the centre of the hold, under the hatch, I closed my exhaust valve to let the suit fill with air. Soon I was riding up the shot-line, and tilting my head back I could see the welcome flashing silver of the surface. A moment later my helmet was flooded with light. I clambered up the ladder to the deck and sank on to my stool while Sodini twisted the helmet off and unhitched the front and back weights.

As soon as Cox arrived I described the underwater set-up. When I told him about the mines, their shape, size and fittings, he identified them without hesitation as the Italian type 'C'. There and then we decided to lift them out one at a time into a lighter and then beach them in some remote spot where Cox could explode them in safety. Cox loved bangs—I suppose that is why he went in for this particular job—and his eyes glistened at the prospect of no less than thirty shattering *whumphs*, all in one session.

We made up some wire-rope slings with shackles joining the legs, rigged one of the ship's derricks over the flooded hatch and connected a compressed-air hose to a winch that was above water. Cox sent someone ashore to get the lighter while Sodini got me ready for another dip.

Presently I slipped down the shot-rope, dragging the sling and the derrick's wire with me. On my second descent, when I reached the floor of the hold, I moved more slowly and this time found the first mine with my finger-tips instead of embracing it as I had before.

Working with great caution, I shackled on the sling, then retired to the shelter of the bilges and passed the signal to the men up top to heave in on their winch. A moment later I felt the down-line running gently through my fingers and knew that the mine was on its way up. I could visualise it rising out of the hatch and swinging over to the lighter which ought, by now, to be waiting alongside. A few minutes passed before they gave me the all-clear signal, and then I dragged the empty sling down again. I found the next mine, shackled it fast, and stood clear again while it followed its predecessor up into the light of day. In this way we cleared all the mines out of the hold. It had been decided to leave the torpedo war-heads where they were until the ship was lifted and the hatch drained. The war-heads could reasonably be expected to be less temperamental than mines, and it would have been a tricky business to lift them out now.

Our Australian friend soon had his lethal cargo landed on a distant beach, and that evening the whole port rocked and trembled to thirty earth-shaking explosions.

A survey of the *Brenta*'s other holds disclosed no more mines or charges of any sort, nor was there any damage to the ship's hull, but in the dark and oily engine-room I found the answer. The condenser intake valve and every outlet valve in the ship's skin had been withdrawn or smashed. Obviously the Italians had planned to fire the mines and destroy the ship *after* she was on the bottom, and certainly if it had worked *Brenta* would have been a total loss. But something had not worked, and here, by this happy mischance, we had a practically intact ship to raise.

Edison Brown and his men started work now, plugging the broken inlets and shutting off the bilge lines. They built wooden cofferdams round the hatch coamings, and set the *Intent*'s powerful salvage pumps to work. Throughout days and nights the pumps thundered and gushed discoloured water by the ton until eventually *Brenta* stirred on her coral bed, and, listing heavily with the weight of slack water in her 'tweendecks, rose—and floated. Men toiling in these oil-slippery 'tweendecks ran compressed-air pumps into the wings, and soon had them dry. In tow of the little *Intent*, and with only a slight list, another prize slid away into the north harbour. All that remained to be done now was to clean her up and get her engines and boilers back into commission, which was achieved by the increasingly efficient dockyard people in good time. A merchant service crew from the Pool in Alex. came down to take her back to the Middle East, where she was formally seized in prize, renamed, and set to work as a cargo vessel flying the Red Duster.

*   *   *

Meanwhile I had returned to my scrabblings on the floor of the harbour, deciding which of the small craft, the destroyers, tugs, coasters, minelayers and minesweepers scuttled by the Italians were worth recovering and which should be disposed of as a danger or a nuisance to ships using the harbour. For the most part it was dull work, but the time wasted in dressing, the ponderous descents and the many lets and hindrances attached to diving in full gear, drove us to an innovation which saved many man-hours and much relieved the monotony of the job.

I don't remember whom the idea struck first, but it was an eminently simple and practical ruse. We turned some of the

Italian gas masks, with which the stores were well stocked, into crude diving masks. There was little difference between the Italian pattern and our own British gas masks. We removed the canister containing the filter along with the corrugated tube leading to the face of the mask and substituted instead a non-return valve and a union, to which was attached sixty feet or so of ordinary light gauge hose such as is normally used to feed oxygen from bottle to oxy-acetylene cutter. Air was fed down the hose from a compressor on the deck of a lighter or diving boat and the exhaust air, escaping round the side of the diver's face, jetted out by the back of the mask. With air supplied at a more or less standard pressure of sixty pounds, the diver absorbed more than he required for breathing purposes and had nothing to fear from pressure at the modest depths in which we were operating.

Our usual rig for this skin diving was a boiler suit to protect us from barnacles and the sharp coral, a pair of tennis shoes, sometimes weighted with lead, and a weighted belt which provided us with a ten-pound sinker. It is surprisingly easy to swim about under water with an extra ten pounds round one's middle, and we were saved all the delays attendant on the preliminaries to a full-dress dive. If we felt in need of exercise, we swam down to descend. Otherwise, all that was necessary was to exhale and sink. The reverse course brought us to the surface.

Naturally there were drawbacks to our improvised equipment. The eye-pieces to the masks, which were not optically co-ordinated, gave us double vision and some thumping great headaches from working with one eye shut to correct this; we also picked up the spines of the infamous sea-urchins in every exposed part of our bodies. Nor could we rely entirely on our diving masks for the work we had in hand. It was dangerous to enter a wreck in this rig, for if the air line snagged anywhere, as it could without being immediately noticed, one step forward was enough to snatch the mask from the diver's face and leave him trapped between decks to drown. But the advantage of being able to swim freely and quite swiftly around the hull of a sunken ship, and the relief from stifling immolation in a twill and rubber suit, more than outweighed these disadvantages.

Swimming was not a popular pastime at Massawa. In the course of my formal duties as Number One of the base I had had torpedo nets rigged in the water as an anti-shark measure, but the sea was too warm to be refreshing, and there were few takers for this form of relaxation. The threat of sharks, emphasised by a recollection of the purpose of the nets, was at the beginning a great source of worry to our face-mask divers. Contrary to popular belief and the highlights of numerous yarns of under-water adventure, a shark will not attack a dressed diver, and in fact the *Naval Diving Regulations* expressly lists the creatures as one of many excuses not acceptable to authority for a diver's surfacing before his time. Nevertheless, facing a shark with the protection of suit and helmet is one thing; squaring up to him in a boiler suit and gas mask is quite another. But whether the bright plumes of bubbles streaming from behind our ears as the air exhausted out scared them, or whatever else, we were never troubled by them and soon lost our fear. As familiarity grew, we even baited them a bit, encouraging them to come and have a good look at us. But they were not to be tempted. Thirty feet or more was their range, and probably it was a good thing, for there were more sharks of many varieties in Massawa harbour than we had divers to provide for them.

The garfish stayed with us of course, and we met a good many octopuses lurking in the darkness of explosion holes. But they were lethargic creatures and provided no amusement. What we were most scared of were barracuda. They are as lethal as sharks, although they take more time over the job, and at Massawa they were bolder than their big brothers. Often they would swoop down on a diver, who would raise a flurry of bubbles, kick up the sand if he was on the bottom, and beat a hasty and respectful retreat. However, we suffered no casualties.

Damage was confined to the poisonous rash provided by the sea-urchins, some cases of ear trouble and the innumerable cuts, abrasions and gashes we suffered through barging against sharp projections of one kind or another—the badge of a face-mask diver at Massawa was a great splotch of iodine. On the other hand, frequent and prolonged immersion without a suit checked and eased the prickly heat which was the bane of everybody's life, and there was a large element of sport in the work. Some clown, working under-water with a mate, had the bright idea of taking a deep breath, snatching his mask off and swopping it for his opposite number's, and then an astonished helper on the surface had the shock of pulling in the wrong fish. Soon everybody was playing the game; but a great deal of useful work was done at the same time. With as many as six unencumbered divers working together on a patch or making fast a cofferdam, progress could be rapid, and both McCance on *Gera* and I on my diverse jobs were able to use gangs of divers when necessary.

We were a little ahead of our time with our gimcrack masks. Units specially constructed for salvage work, with tight-fitting masks and a demand valve as well as a non-return valve, were afterwards manufactured in America and some were in time acquired by the Navy. I had one myself, and it was possible to use it as deep as a hundred feet, although this required the highest degree of physical fitness. Ever after my first experiences of skin diving I felt faintly aggrieved if I had to don a regulation suit.

*   *   *

We were not the only people in Italian Somaliland complimenting ourselves on our powers of improvisation. Three Italian naval officer prisoners of war were surreptitiously engaged in a piece of construction work which would have astonished even Heath Robinson in his prime—and they, much more than we, were prepared to risk their lives to prove their contraption.

The Italian prisoners of war were allowed a good deal of latitude; most of them regarded their war as being over and were well content with the thought. During the hours of daylight they wandered at will through the streets of Asmara, the capital of Italian Somaliland situated about ninety miles from the coast, and reported back to their camps only at curfew hour. Some, even, were able to continue almost uninterrupted their family life which had for a time been rudely disturbed by the Allied invasion.

But not all the prisoners were satisfied to spend an indefinite part of their lives in captivity, although escape, if British territory were to be avoided, could only be to Abyssinia or by sea; and the treatment meted out by Abyssinian natives to any of their colonial masters whom they could lay their hands on was no encouragement to hopeful escapers. Having regard to this and to their proper calling, the three naval officers, who had decided to make a break for it, decided to go by sea.

In an Italian-owned underground garage in Asmara they began to build a boat, filching their material from the many dumps of scrap which Italian armed forces seem to delight in accumulating —and from which I myself had greatly profited. They built the boat in sections, using sheet metal, sheet brass and even oil drums opened up and flattened out. They must have had a good deal of help from their companions who were still permitted to run garage businesses, for parts of the hull were welded together and other parts were bolted, although some of the joints were actually soldered. Their standards of shipbuilding would not have satisfied the Board of Trade, but somehow they contrived to put together a hull eighteen or twenty feet in length, decked fore and aft, with a crude canvas awning to keep the worst of the sun off.

The great difficulty was to provide motive power. Their craft was far too unstable to make sailing a feasible proposition and they had no hope of being able to cast a propeller or of hewing one out of the rough. But they did succeed in laying hands on two Italian motor cycles—there were scores of them abandoned about the place—and stripped and reconditioned their engines and gear-boxes. These were bedded side by side into the boat and the gear-box shafts coupled to pumps which, when I saw them later, appeared to be the kind used in conjunction with agricultural windmills for pumping the many wells dotted about Asmara and the hinterland. Propulsion for the boat was to be drawn from the sea itself. The naval officers' plan was to pump water in over the side of the boat and then, by pumping it out again through the stern by way of a much narrower pipe, to get their momentum from a primitive kind of jet. The extraordinary thing was not so much the ingenuity behind the idea —at a time when liquid jet propulsion was virtually unthought of—but the fact that the scheme worked.

The sections of the boat were smuggled, presumably by Italian lorry drivers working for H.M. Government, down to Massawa, and then to an isolated stretch of coast surrounded by bush. The escapers strolled out of their camp one morning and, evading the controls which were pretty slack anyway, contrived to rendezvous in safety with their boat.

Their story ended in anti-climax. We got intelligence of the attempted escape, and although the Italians launched their boat under cover of darkness and made some twenty miles out from the coast in their first night, we sent a tug out to look for them and they and their craft were picked up early in the morning.

How they would have fared without our intervention is open to question. In the still, calm weather prevailing in the Red Sea at the time, they were pushing steadily ahead at a gentle walking pace. The food and water supplies found aboard the dinghy were not abundant, and the petrol, which must have been painstakingly stolen and stored a pint at a time, was stowed in a weird assortment of small containers all round the boat: it could not have added up to more than twenty or thirty gallons. The cockleshell had ridden out its first night in safety, but it was a precarious craft with about as much stability as a racing skiff, and ahead lay a journey of some two hundred miles to the dubious safety of the Yemen. Everybody appreciated the sporting element of the venture, but the general feeling was that if the cruise had not ended in bathos it would have ended in tragedy. The three officers boarded the tug quietly, possibly with relief, and on their return to the base were easily persuaded to give a demonstration trip round the harbour. We packed up the dinghy and sent it off to the Middle East as a curiosity; but at the same time we increased

our watch on the scrap dumps and all road controls were sub-
jected to a much-needed and little-appreciated tightening up.

*   *   *

Any break from routine at Massawa was welcome, and when
I was working on a job on Dahlak Atoll, a forlorn, volcanic
island just off the coast, I gladly seized the chance to inspect the
palace on it which the local sheik shared with a few disgruntled
wives and a bunch of miserable-looking pearl divers. It was an
enormous place, crammed with marble lavatories and bath-
rooms, radiograms and electric chandeliers. There was no drainage system on the island and no electric power, so that none of
the elaborate fittings ever worked. The sheik just liked to have
them around. And stored in old pickle jars in the palace was
the finest collection of pearls I have ever set eyes on. Everything
about the sheik and his palace united to form an extravagant
monument to uselessness; and the old man was perfectly happy.

The job that had taken me, with Edison Brown, out to Dahlak
was the raising of the Italian steamer *Tripolitania*. She was one
of several ships that had taken refuge in the natural harbour
provided by the islands, a narrow inlet which swelled suddenly,
in the bosom of the island, to a circular stretch of sheltered water.
Here, before abandoning her, the Italians had opened the *Tripolitania*'s intakes and smashed her valves. She was sitting on a
shelf of sea bed that ran right round the atoll under no more
than forty-five feet of water. Her recovery gave us little difficulty, but fascinated by the topography of the island, I decided
to stay behind after *Intent* had towed her quarry into Massawa.

From the scrub-covered knoll under which the *Tripolitania*
had lain I looked across the mile of glinting, placid, sun-dappled
water to another knob of scraggy rock and coral on the other
side. The water was crystal clear, and on an impulse I decided
to have a look at the shelf which lipped the almost land-locked
anchorage. I called away the diving boat and before long was
dropping down to the bottom. Shuffling along over the white

sand and coral, my path was illumined by the sun slanting down and spreading in refulgence as it glanced off the bright bottom of the sea bed. My magnified brass toe-caps stirred the fine sand into little milky clouds; furry brown sea slugs hurried out of my way and garfish darted electric-blue across the glass of my helmet. I could see ahead for thirty yards or more, and I trudged on enjoying what was in effect an afternoon stroll in another world.

Gently at first, and then more sharply, the shelf on which I was walking tilted down towards the centre of the atoll. The coral bottom gave way to harder, rockier ground, and ahead of me loomed suddenly a blue-black cloud, stretched across my visibility like a velvet curtain. I slackened my pace, moved cautiously forward, feeling an unaccountable dread of this dark barrier ahead. I hesitated, half-deciding to turn back, and then I noticed that of a sudden the fish, my constant companions, had disappeared. I took a few more faltering steps, peering into the gloom that seemed to have drifted around me and there, at my feet, the shelf ended abruptly and left—nothing. A great black void. It was a heart-stopping experience to be confronted without warning by this pitchy, ominous-looking chasm with its silent promise of extinction, and I signalled hastily to the surface for all slack to be taken up on my lines. I felt myself being drawn backwards, and with immeasurable relief I stumbled into translucent water again, comforted by the sun's penetration.

Back on board the diving boat I looked at the inviting waters of the atoll with new eyes. This was no gentle mill-pond: the island, growing out of the sea, held here in its core the heart of a volcano, long since extinct, but plunging down heaven knew how far into the depths of the Red Sea, a rock-encircled shaft leading nowhere. In spite of the bright sun I shivered as I turned my back on it.

Later, we tried to take a sounding from the launch. Three thousand feet of piano wire went over the side and down into the dark pit without finding any bottom.

*   *   *

These alarms and excursions, not specially significant in themselves, helped to engage our interest, and at intervals to jolt any feeling of complacency that might have been settling on us in the course of the daily round at Massawa. I was fortunate to be the only naval officer working with the English and American salvage teams, for I was regularly hailed in by each of the skippers to lend a hand with tricky jobs and to commandeer any bit of equipment that was hard to come by through civilian channels. My steady task of clearing the harbour and cleaning up the small ships which cluttered its bed could always be left for a time in emergency, and I was glad, occasionally, to get my teeth into some really tough assignment. But there was one operation which, had I been given the opportunity at the critical point, I would have given my teeth to be out of. It was my last job at Massawa and the most gruelling of the lot—the raising of the minelayer *Ostia*.

The *Ostia*, which had capsized in sinking, lay completely submerged in fifty feet of water alongside one of the most useful quays in the port. We needed the quay, and so *Ostia* had to move. She was a minelayer of the *Lepanto* class, something under a thousand tons, and she still had a full outfit of mines in her. As with the *Brenta*, the enemy's plan had been to use the mines to destroy her, and to scuttle the ship they had smashed the engine-room inlets.

Cox was of the opinion that all the mines in *Ostia* would be 'armed'—that is to say, that they would be fitted with their primers, so that any contact with their horns would immediately detonate them. Naturally, to detonate one would be to detonate the lot. It wasn't a very happy picture, as we thought about it from the surface, because with the ship on her side we imagined that the mines would be in a heap and jammed together on the lower side of the mine-flat.

I decided to lift *Ostia* with 'camels'. A 'camel' is a sort of tank which can be sunk, flooded, to the level of the wreck, attached to it with heavy wire strops and then blown with compressed air to give the necessary lift. The technical aspect of this operation is worked out in advance by balancing the submerged weight of the ship against the lifting-power of the camels and the size and number of them necessary to take the ship off the bottom. But figures on paper are often proved liars when it comes to the testing moment.

There were no pontoons in Massawa that could have been adapted for the job, but by a stroke of luck we found a number of big petrol-storage tanks underground on the airfield. These were dug up, and the American contractors modified them for us, fitting heavy struts inside and strong hawse-pipes to take the lifting-wires. And, of course, the tanks had to be fitted with vents and air connections.

While this work was in progress, Sinfield and I investigated the *Ostia*'s mine-flat. To our surprise and delight, we found that the mines were still in position on their racks. But they were, indeed, 'armed'. On the jetty Cox explained with the aid of rough sketches on a signal-pad how we should go about the job of removing the primers from the mines, and, in low spirits, we dropped down again to the wreck and began the task of disarming the whole shipload. It was not a thing that one could do in a hurry, particularly in the dark where one false move might—well, might save us the trouble of disarming the others —and the slow, nerve-racking job seemed to take months. But it was only a couple of weeks later that we fixed the last mine, and, practically exploding with relief, surfaced with some sensation of surprise at still being alive. The 'camels' were ready, and the Port Said dockyard had delivered the seven-inch circumference lifting wires we needed.

The thing now was to get these wires under the ship's hull. She was lying in mud, grit and rubble and through all that we would have to tunnel our way under her keel so as to get the wires into a sort of cradle for the 'camels' to lift. The tools for tunnelling were high-powered hoses led down from the surface. With me and the other divers guiding the hoses' nozzles, their powerful jets would drive passages through the muck of the harbour bed, and the plan was to pass the wires through these tunnels under the ship and out on her other side.

As I had more than half expected, this soon turned into one of the nastiest jobs I have known. After the initial cave-like opening had been made in the silt which was piled up against the wreck's side, Sinfield and I had to lie flat directing the jets ahead of us and, as we worked the tunnels farther in, the ground ahead would sink and with our helmets lower than our boots the exhaust valve would cease to function. Then we would struggle round on to our backs in the confined space and try to use the spit-cock, in the helmet's front, as an exhaust valve. Wriggling back again with helmet held up, some of this grit regularly found its way into the valve chamber, preventing the valve from sealing properly and thus causing a leak through which our suits would begin to fill with water. We would find the tunnel growing deeper and producing a fast backwash from the hose's power that was full of flying grit. And on top of that—worst of all, and really very unpleasant—when we were well and truly into those narrow tunnels of our own making, the backward stream of water would weaken the tunnel's sides and the whole thing would cave in behind us so that we were completely buried with our helmets scraping on the ship's hull. This is the sort of nightmare which does not often come true. But a diver who wants to live has to face it with planned thought and purpose instead of with the panic which is always close at hand and often fatal. Our solution was to fight the hose around and back between our legs to reverse the tunnelling process and wash ourselves out again. This happened to both of us more than once, and eventually we came to the conclusion that we were inviting either a very sticky end or a passage home in a strait-jacket. We were not getting anywhere as far as the wires were concerned: only digging holes and—so far—getting out of them when they filled up again. I had to think up some other way of getting the wires into position.

Before long I had a system worked out. Some rigid sections of hose pipe were made up, with couplings at the ends of each section so that they could be joined to the main hose and to each other, rather like the parts of a chimney-sweep's pole. The idea was that with the hose's considerable power forcing water through those lengths of pipe we would be able to force or wangle them in under the hull, adding other sections as the first ones went in. We ourselves would not have to burrow in and repeat the beastly experiences of the last few days.

A light pilot wire was seized to the extensions, so that it would go with them under the ship, and at the front end of the leading section we left a free loop of wire which would be jetted ahead in the stream of water. We had a diver waiting on the other side to grab the wire and haul it in as soon as he saw it, after which we had to unscrew the connections from the main hose while the waiting diver pulled the whole lot through. At the end of the light wire we proposed to shackle on the heavy lifting-wire and that, in its turn, we hoped, would be hauled through under the ship.

The scheme worked. Within a very short time we had all six wires under the *Ostia* and triced up to the surface, ready to be passed through the hawse-pipes in the 'camels'. Much depended now on how those 'camels' would behave. Like their real-life namesakes, the best of them are inclined to be tricky, temperamental beasts. The usual procedure is to flood them down through their Kingston valves and vents with their level maintained by a system of balancing valves. But our 'camels' were by no means thoroughbreds, and it seemed to me that to adopt such a method would be to ask too much of the makeshift gear. So I decided to use the Italian eighty-ton floating crane which we had salved earlier to lower the 'camels' down with their vents open. Edison Brown, with the *Intent*, brought the crane over and moored it where we wanted it.

We lifted the first 'camel' on the crane, ran the lifting-wire through its hawse-pipes and let the weight come down on the crane brakes. Slowly the improvised pontoon sank with its vents bubbling cheerfully and the wires rendering easily through the hawses. Once it was bottomed, Sinfield and I went down after it to bolt heavy toggle-clamps hard against the hawse-pipes' rims.

It was hard work, down there, but we got all six 'camels' rigged in their places and just before dark finished screwing-on the air leads and checking the vents. That was that! All that remained was to find out, in the morning, if this rough-and-ready lifting system was going to work.

I didn't get much rest that night, and it was still dark when I left the mess and hurried down to the jetty, long before time. I paced up and down the stones, visualising the assembly of wired pontoons down there round the *Ostia*, three of them on each side of her, and wondered whether in these contraptions we had the lift, the buoyancy that would be necessary to shift the wreck. In feverish calculations I balanced one figure against another, gave it up and wondered whether in any case the pontoons' improvised fittings and strengtheners would stand up to the strain.

The next hour or two would answer those questions. Soon we would know whether our weeks of work and planning would bring results or whether perhaps by lunch-time we would be starting all over again. One way or another, I was anxious to know. The sun came reaching cautiously out of the sea to the east, and I heard the lorries rumbling down through the dock-yard. They stopped at the end of the jetty, and as the sailors came straggling up past me I saw that many of them were still half asleep. At times like this I envied them their carefully pre-served irresponsibility.

But I turned my mind back to the job and soon we had the compressors running. The air was pungent with diesel fumes as I waved 'Ready' to Edison Brown, who was watching from *Intent*'s bridge, and he waved back to start the air on its way. We were all set. The thunder of the compressors rose as the pressure came on at full blast. Some way out from the quay wall the harbour's calm surface turned suddenly into a crazy madness of bursting air bubbles and frenzied, leaping water. I held a light line in my hands—its other end was secured to *Ostia*'s rail—held it taut, waiting and feeling for the first slight movement from the wreck. But there was no movement. The whole area out from the quay was a chaos of jumping sea and the noise of the compressors was deafening, overpowering, but from the line in my hands came not the slightest tremor. Time passed, and I began to feel sick with the thought that I had bungled it, forgotten or miscalculated some damn' thing—wasted weeks. But suddenly the line in my hands went slack and at the same time the compressors' angry roar settled down to a steady beat. The line came in as fast as I could gather it and, far sooner than I expected, some of the 'camels' broke surface, black and shiny like a school of whales. And, in the turmoil of flying white between them, the encrusted superstructure of an Italian mine-layer rose unevenly and hung—*afloat*!

I yelled to the men who were waiting in a dinghy, and they sprang on to the pontoons to shut the exhaust valves and vents. Crawling over the slippery and still violently heaving 'camels', they swung off on the heavy vent handwheels, and as they dragged the vents shut the chaos died. The wreck rose and fell gently in its slings. It seemed to have crept into an almost up-right position. I regarded the wreck with affection for a moment, and then climbed aboard to supervise the tightening of the toggle-nuts. Brown got his towlines aboard, and soon he was edging *Ostia* away from the quay. From the jetty I watched anxiously, dreading the sudden snap and spring of parting wires, fearing disaster at this moment of triumph. Edison must have seen my alarmed expression. He leant out of *Intent*'s wheelhouse with a wide grin on his sunburnt face, and called,

'Relax, Lootenant—we *got* the sonofabitch!'

*　　*　　*

It would be quite untrue to say that I did not welcome the end of my time at Massawa, but my ten months there had given me a stimulating introduction to the practice and problems of salvage. There had been compensation for the vile climate of the place in the companionship I found: the self-possessed McCance, the rugged American skippers with their informality and tremendous drive, the steady, reliable Sinfield and the omniscient Sodini admitted me to a brotherhood which in the seafarer's world is unique and select. But now that I could consider myself to be in some small measure qualified in salvage, I was eager for fresh fields, and when a signal came through in December '42, recalling me to the Mediterranean, I packed my traps and returned to my old hunting-ground without regret or misgiving.

V. HOLOCAUST IN TRIPOLI

THE air in Alexandria when I got back there had a new smell. The fruity atmosphere of any Middle Eastern city was still present and uppermost, but something new had been added. It took me a little time to identify it as the lovely scent of victory. Our own aircraft filled the skies and one recalled with faint surprise that only a little time ago our lookouts and A.A. gunners had been warned that any formation of more than two aircraft could almost certainly be regarded as hostile.

When I reported at Naval Salvage Headquarters the talk was all of our advancing army and the need for close support from the sea. To keep the land forces' lines of communication functioning with maximum speed and efficiency, ports recently in enemy hands would have to be kept free to allow convoys to discharge supplies as close to the fighting front as possible. But the Germans were not going to make us presents of serviceable ports, and the role of the salvage force had changed in short order from coping with losses suffered under the shadow of defeat to backing up successes in the field. Over eighty per cent of enemy shipping plying between Italy and Tripoli had been sunk by submarines operating from Malta and by our new strength in the air. But all of that and the Army's brilliant thrust would be brought to naught if we couldn't bring supplies in fast enough through captured seaports.

*   *   *

Wheeler had now been relieved as Fleet Salvage Officer by Wilber Rippon, an R.N.V.R. Commander who was later awarded the O.B.E. for his salvage work and promoted to the unusual R.N.V.R. rank of Captain, Special Branch. Rippon was a marine engineer whose peace-time job had been ship repair; he had been brought up in Italy and worked for years in France and had, I suspected, although I never got confirmation of it, done a bit of salvage during the Spanish Civil War. He was full of energy, highly competent and given to the aggressive pursuit of daring salvage methods. They were to be needed in Tripoli, to which we were both now posted. The Germans were expected to pull out of the port at any moment, and in preparation for our move in, Rippon and I attended a series of technical conferences. After our briefings had been brought to various vague conclusions, Rippon left westwards, followed by the Fleet Salvage train, which included *Gamtoos*, and I followed a few days later. As we steamed across the top of the Gulf of Sirte, with fleet sweepers clearing the Italian minefields ahead of us, we heard that Tripoli had fallen to the Eighth Army.

That night, in search of a little entertainment, we tuned in to Lord Haw-Haw's evening broadcast from Germany. Announcing the loss of Tripoli, Haw-Haw said the port was so well blocked that the Allies would not be able to get a ship into it for months. The following morning, when we closed in towards the harbour entrance, it looked as if for once the propagandist was not very wide of the mark. Outside the harbour growing daylight showed us that the roadstead and anchorages were crowded with landing craft, tankers, store and hospital ships, all deep-loaded with supplies that ought to have been on their way to the front. But across the narrow entrance to the harbour between the tips of the eastern and western moles, lay no les than seven blockships, jammed close and sunk to their upper works. At first sight it looked as if they represented a routine if prolonged clearance job, but I was shortly to discover that they formed probably the most thorough piece of port blockage in history.

I was quickly ashore on a scrounging expedition, hoping to pick up some useful stores before competition from other branches of the Service became too keen. I first reported to Rippon, who told me that his chaps had made an almost fatal attempt to take over a motor launch tied up to one of the quays. It looked in fine condition and, after tinkering for a few minutes with the engine, an E.R.A. had started her up. The resultant explosion and the flame-tinged blast that swept down the boat nearly cost the working party their lives—and gave us a sharp warning to be on the look-out henceforward for booby traps.

I thanked Rippon for his tip and, borrowing a few hands, made for the Regia Marina Stores where, through the window of a locked shed we saw a whole row of Italian diving dresses hanging neatly on hooks. It looked a bit too good to be true, and instead of dashing in we tossed a hand-grenade at the door, standing well back and hoping that the grenade might set off any booby-trap the Germans had left behind. But nothing happened, and I pondered on the prospect of walking in and helping ourselves. I decided it was still too risky and instead sent some men scouting round for long poles with which we could do some preliminary fishing. They returned with a couple which would allow us to reach the dresses from outside the store, and we broke a window and poked gingerly at the tempting suits. First one, then another, then a third was fished off its hook and dropped on to the floor without damage. But the fourth was wired to a charge. A sharp, cracking explosion sent us reeling back from the shed with glass tinkling about our ears and when, after the smoke had cleared, we ventured cautiously into the store, little was left of the beautiful diving equipment for which we had been window-shopping. So much for German generosity.

I salved what I could from the debris and returned to confer with Rippon. He was supervising an underwater inspection of the *Giovanni Battista*, the biggest of the blockships, from the *Battista*'s sloping upper deck.

'This one's all right,' he told me, gesturing downwards at the eight-thousand-ton hulk beneath his feet. 'We don't have to move her to let traffic into the harbour; it's these other little sods that are going to give us trouble.' He indicated the remaining six blockships with a wave of his hand.

'They don't look too bad to me,' I ventured.

Rippon snorted. 'Just wait until you've had a look! The Jerries have been working on this lot for months. They've filled every one of these ships with steel reinforcing rods, old machinery, bits of trailers, unserviceable lorries, even motor-bikes—any old junk they could lay their hands on. Then they've poured thousands of tons of concrete—literally thousands of tons, I tell you—in on top. Thorough bastards. There isn't a hope of getting the ships up, and if my guess is right we'll have to blow our way through about a shovelful at a time and get *Gamtoos* to drag the bits apart. You'd better check up for yourself.

'Oh—and another thing. We've already discovered a couple of booby-traps in this old tub.' Rippon kicked the *Giovanni Battista*'s deck. 'So be careful. Hundred-pound canisters of explosives with spring-loaded detonators joined with a trip wire. You know what'll happen if you fall over one of these.'

I did. If a diver fouled one of these wires and detonated the charges at either end of it the hammer force of water flung at him from both sides would squash him as flat as his own shadow.

While I was still talking to Rippon an air-raid warning changed from yellow to red. Within a minute we heard the drone of aircraft engines from the direction of the coastline and soon we saw the first flights, groups of dots rising and growing into the familiar shapes of Stukas. Flight followed flight and all of them were coming down this way. Rippon and I dropped down under the shelter of the *Battista*'s steel bulwark and watched each successive flight breaking up as the planes peeled off and came screaming over the harbour area. Our shoreside A.A. gunners were ready and willing, and a grey-black rash of bursting high-explosive spread itself across the path of the dive-bombers. It was probably a stiffer opposition than the enemy had bargained for, and certainly it must have spoilt their aim. A couple of fires were started in the dockyard and several bombs fell in the harbour, but not a single ship was hit.

Flat on my face I looked out through a washport and saw one of the ugly little raiders trailing thick black smoke as it vanished over the land. The noise died as suddenly as it had started. Our divers were still at work under the ship and the pumps were still pushing air down to them.

Later, we repaired to the Italian villa which Rippon had taken over as Salvage Headquarters—he used it for some days before discovering the presence on his roof of the bodies of fourteen Germans who had formed an Ack-Ack unit wiped out by the R.A.F.—and continued our talk. I was told that Command wanted the port entrance cleared within ten days, enough for large ships to be able to use it. The advancing Eighth Army needed eight thousand tons of supplies each day to keep the wheels turning in the right direction, and any shortfall in that rate of supply would slow the advance and give Rommel a chance to dig in along the Mareth Line. If the enemy were allowed that breathing space the whole campaign might well be wrecked, certainly braked.

It was strangely satisfying to think how much difference our small efforts here could make to the outcome of the desert war. But this was no time for ruminating on the wider issues of the campaign; our task was to get on with the job under our noses, and we discussed it from every angle.

*   *   *

Before dawn the next morning we drove down to the docks and boarded the *Battista*. Since she was not our prime target and

Photograph by T. F. Devonshire

A section of the line of blockships that barred the entrance to Tripoli Harbour. The gap permitting Allied vessels to enter the harbour was blasted between these two ships.

the tideless Mediterranean respected the privacy of her upper decks she was being used as a quarters ship for part of the salvage team and as a base of operations against the other blockships. Groups of men were already squatting on her decks, packing explosive charges into lengths of canvas hose and fitting them with detonators, ready for the divers to take down to the bottoms of the smaller ships. I togged up to go and have a look at the job for myself, and very quickly confirmed Rippon's violently expressed opinion. Since we were as usual short of divers and Rippon could look after things on top, I kept the heavy harness on and went to work with the under-water party. First we placed necklaces of gelignite round the rock-like formations of concrete in the holds, for we had to break up these before we could achieve anything with the ships themselves. It was slow and heavy going—slipping down into the murk, making our way through the holes in the bilges blown by the scuttling charges, alert for any indication of a booby-trap, fitting and setting the charges, then coming up to wait for the explosions. While we waited, glad of the short rest, the wrecks heaved and shuddered under us. Then, armed with another lot of charges down we went again to check up on results and plant more gelignite where it would do most damage. At the same time artisans with acetylene torches were hard at work in the partially flooded higher decks, cutting the steel apart, while exhausted working parties staggering around in the foul air with oil and water up to their waists dragged wreckage clear as the burners cut it loose.

Ashore, our lorries scoured bombed and burnt-out sheds and stores, rounding up tools and materials and the always scarce oxygen and acetylene bottles. Soon we had built up a considerable stock, but it was composed mainly of French, German, Italian and American equipment, and in *Gamtoos*'s machine workshop engine room artificers had to make adaptors to fit all the different types of gas-bottles to our own equipment.

There was no time to relax, not even during air attacks. The divers spent hours in their dresses, and even slept in them, flat on the deck with bundles of woollen stockings under their heads to keep their necks off the corselet rims. We were all of us deaf, stiff, sore and just about witless from hard work and loss of sleep.

By the fourth day we had made enough of a gap for the smaller craft and lighters to pass through, and some supply ships began off-loading into lighters. Five days later, with one day to go before our time limit expired, we had blasted a passage one hundred and thirty feet across—wide enough for anything. But it was only eighteen feet deep. The concrete was reduced to heaps of rubble at a harmless depth, but the pliant reinforcing rods jutted up from it like a petrified forest of bamboo. We could not blow the rods up: explosion after explosion had only worsened the tangle of steel, and to cut through the rods one by one with burners would take to the end of time. The blockage stolidly resisted every attempt we made to shift it, and our divers went mad with frustration as time after time their airlines fouled and jammed in the maze of steel.

When all normal methods had proved futile, Rippon and I, in anxious consultation, resolved on a new and desperate approach. With my chief's blessing (which he had no right to give), I went out in our launch and boarded an L.S.T.—a Landing Ship, Tanks—in the anchorage. Laden down with tanks and heavy trucks, her draught was just what we needed, and I informed her skipper with a suavity I was far from feeling that he had been singled out for the honour of bringing the first deepdraught ship into the port. He even stood me a gin on it. I told him that he would be getting a signal soon from the Senior Naval Officer and suggested that it might be as well if he shortened in right away in anticipation of the signal's arrival. I also told him that there were a number of wrecks close inside the entrance and that consequently he would be wise to have plenty of steerage-way on his ship when he came through the gap.

With the C.O.'s thanks for all this helpful advice burdening my conscience, I dropped back into my launch and chugged into Navy House jetty. Reporting to the Senior Naval Officer,

I told him that we were ready to bring the first ship in and mentioned that one L.S.T. was already hove short. Might she not, I suggested, be ordered in immediately while the others prepared to weigh anchor? S.N.O., delighted at the prospect of getting the port working again, made the signal at once.

I doubled back to the launch and was on board the *Giovanni Battista* when the landing ship headed up to the entrance and came pounding in at a good eight knots. Her crew and some Army passengers cheered happily, and our salvage team yelled ruderies back at them, but in the midst of this celebratory cheerfulness Rippon and I stood speechless with anxiety, waiting to see if our preposterous gamble would pay off. If it did not—but we dared not think of the consequences. . . .

The L.S.T. struck the tangled steel. Her bows rose, the whole ship heaved, hesitated, then that heavy bow came down hard like a huge hammer. She snored her way through and a moment later, safely inside the harbour, turned on her helm to her allotted berth. Rippon and I silently and surreptitiously shook hands. The L.S.T.'s flat bottom had steam-rollered out our channel and deepened the gap to twenty-six feet. We needed no more. The job was finished, and only Rippon and I knew that it had been done by using a valuable ship as a flat-iron.

*   *   *

Now the port was open, and an avalanche of supplies began immediately to pour through that hundred-and-thirty-foot gap in the blockships. All day and night the jetties seethed with activity as convoy after convoy arrived deep-laden. The moment one ship cleared her berth, another was ready waiting to take her place. Army stevedores toiled incessantly, and from the gates of the dockyard an unbroken stream of trucks, lorries and fighting vehicles growled away to the west along the desert road. By night the jetties were floodlit so that the work could go on without pause, and under the protection of what must have been one of the most concentrated and powerful A.A. defences any port ever had, the lights were not even doused for air-raids. This stream of supplies was the lifeblood of our advancing army. But just when we were beginning to relax a bit, the Luftwaffe slipped in a blow we had not bargained for.

It happened at about sunset on a day in the middle of March. Under low cloud there was a light drizzle falling. We were working on the *Giovanni Battista*, patching her for'ard in the hope of being able to pump enough buoyancy into her fore compartments to lift her bows and allow us to pivot her on her stern clear of the harbour entrance. Close by, *Gamtoos* lay secured to the boom gate. There had been no air-raid warning of any kind, but suddenly we heard the rising note of approaching aircraft engines and a flight of JU–88's came streaking in out of the seaward mist. They were flying at mast height and by the time I had realised what they were I saw the flicker of their cannon firing. As they roared in over the port I watched in horrified surprise and saw the bombs fall clear, shooting out ahead of the planes as they rocketed steeply up and vanished into the low cloud.

I jumped for the ladder, and ran up it to the *Battista*'s boat-deck. Just as I reached it we were bracketed by bombs and the wreck shuddered and bounced to the close shock of twin explosions: spray fell heavy and drenching right across the ship. Fearful for *Gamtoos*, which had served us so well and was still invaluable to our work, I peered through the smoke and spray and was relieved to find her still afloat, apparently intact, spitting fire from her meagre A.A. armament. As I watched, a second screaming wave of Junkers tore in from the sea, and one plane, hard hit, burst into flames and dived straight for the salvage ship's foredeck. I saw men running aft from her forepart, then the bomber hit the windlass on her fo'c'sle and broke up into blazing fragments which scattered and cascaded into the sea. A third wave of Junkers was on us, and it was at this point that the shoreside A.A. batteries opened up with everything they had. They were a bit late, though, because the raid was over.

By flying in along the surf-line at nought feet the raiders had

kept themselves under the effective radar zone, and not a single
echo had shown itself on the warning screens. Now the air was
quiet, but the harbour was in chaos. The big *Ocean Voyager*,
fully laden with ammunition and R.A.F. bombs, had been hit
several times and was afire fore and aft. At any moment we
might hear a really gigantic bang. Near her a small tanker, also
badly hit, was listing and burning furiously while the 100-octane
aircraft spirit from her tanks was spreading out in a sheet of
white flame over the surface of the harbour. The port was
brightly lit from the flames and would soon be ablaze from end
to end. With the bombs, the Germans had dropped some circling torpedoes, and one of these hit the Hunt-class destroyer
Derwent. She had been turning, out in the centre of the harbour,
and the torpedo smacked right into her boiler-room. She stopped
in a cloud of steam and drifted slowly round with a heavy list.

I ran down the ladder and jumped into our launch, which
was moored alongside. The crew, who had been sheltering on
Battista's for'ard well-deck, joined me, and we shoved off. There
were burning oil-patches all over the place and we had to cut
this way and that through the lanes between the fires. It was
as light as day, and the ammunition in the *Ocean Voyager* was
beginning to explode, showering sparks into any oil that was
not already alight. We ran the launch up alongside *Derwent*,
and I hauled myself aboard over her guard-rail. After a brief
conference with her C.O. we set to work running out an anchor
and wire to the near-by shore and soon we managed to warp
the destroyer on to the beach, where she could sink no further.
I put a salvage party and some pumps aboard her and left them
there to shore up bulkheads and pump out the damaged compartments.

As soon as the first fires had started, S.N.O. had ordered all
ships to clear the harbour forthwith. Now, one after the other,
they surged out through our narrow gap to the comparative
safety of the anchorage outside. Soon in the burning port we
were left with only the casualties. The tanker had sunk, leaving
her cargo alight and turning a vast area of the harbour's surface

into an inferno as the burning oil spread. The *Ocean Voyager* was still afloat and blazing like a torch, now and then shaken by internal explosions. Her crew had been disembarked in anticipation of her sudden and inevitable end.

Another motor-boat arrived with our acetylene cutting gear, and I boarded her and gave instructions to close the *Voyager* in order to try to burn through her bow mooring cable as a preliminary to towing her to a spot where she could go up without endangering other shipping. We nosed past the islands of flaming octane, tense and sweating less from the fire than from the urgent likelihood of the *Voyager*'s cargo going sky-high as we approached and taking us with it. I peered apprehensively at the blue-grey smoke writhing about the doomed ship, cut occasionally by a streak of gold as a round of tracer exploded in her deck cargo. Then, as I watched, the *Voyager* seemed suddenly to swell like a toy balloon, a photographic impression that barely touched my brain before I hurled myself down in the bottom of the launch. In that split second the world changed into roaring, writhing orange flame. Two giant fists buffeted my ears and a huge and unseen force lifted our boat and whirled it away at terrific, dizzy speed. After what seemed minutes of incredibly violent motion we crashed and bumped and were abruptly still. All around us pieces of what had been the ammunition ship were raining down. One by one we sat up, dazed, and marvelling to find ourselves alive, and by the brilliant light of a dozen fires we saw that we were hard up on the shingle under the Ceremonial Jetty, near Navy House—six hundred yards from where the tidal wave had seized us! Of the *Ocean Voyager* there was no sign: seven thousand tons of explosives had blown her into small pieces. One of her fifty-ton boilers came to earth three miles inland, and a complete Oerlikon mounting dropped surprisingly out of the sky to punch a hole in *Gamtoos*'s foredeck.

Yet from all the destruction and chaos of that night, we had only seven dead and thirty wounded.

*   *   *

About this time Commander Rippon was transferred to the staff of the Commander-in-Chief, Western Mediterranean, and in his place I was promoted to Lieutenant-Commander and appointed Senior Salvage Officer, Levant and Eastern Mediterranean. My territory would include Italian and Greek waters, the Levant, the Suez Canal and the Red Sea, but promotion made little immediate difference to my daily routine and, in point of fact, coincided with an experience that might have written me off altogether.

One day our diving boat, holed by a splatter of bomb-splinters from an evening blitz, sank quietly alongside one of the quay walls, in about forty feet of water. It went down with the compressor in it, and a lot of other valuable tools, and I decided to get it up again without delay. My divers were all engaged in various jobs about the port, so I got hold of a Petty Officer Shipwright to look after things topsides while I went down to shackle a crane-wire on to the boat's slings. The shipwright knew nothing about diving, so I had to show him how to get me dressed and how to work the pump. There was plenty of willing if inexperienced help available from the crowd of interested soldiery that had congregated on the jetty, and soon I was clambering down a bank of rubble into the dark water, dragging the end of the crane wire with me.

I found the boat easily enough and had no difficulty in finding its slings and shackling the wire on to the swivel-piece at their apex. Then, abruptly, my air supply stopped in sudden silence after the friendly hissing in my helmet. More puzzled than alarmed, I reached up and thumbed the valve shut in order to retain what air was already in the suit. Then I grabbed the airline and jerked it four times, demanding to be taken up. To my horror it came drifting down to me, yards of slack hose coiling loosely at my feet. Now seriously worried and breathing with some difficulty, I staggered back towards the jetty. I bumped against something that lay ahead of me, something that had not been there before. Bringing my face glass close up to it, I realised in speechless dismay that the object was my pump, lying on its side at the foot of a heap of stones instead of working up top feeding me with essential air. Seeing it there on the bottom was like looking at my own tombstone.

There was no time to sit down and think the situation out. With my air supply cut off and breathing my own nitrogen forty feet down, I knew I couldn't last more than a few minutes, and if I had been faced with the sheer wall of a jetty I would have been finished there and then. But before the Germans had pulled out they had blown up the quay I was working from, along with the others, with spaced charges, so that instead of a clean wall to tie up to, they had left us a continuous steep slope of broken concrete and stone. I started grimly to climb the seeming mountain of rubble in front of me.

It called for an effort I could never have made without death as the certain alternative. Fighting for breath, with daggers of pain stabbing at my chest, I inched my way up the slope. My hands were lacerated from the flinty corners of broken masonry, and every now and again I would lose a little height as a section of loose rubble slid from under my boots and avalanched down to the bottom. I had actually got about a quarter of the way up by my reckoning when I realised I was still wearing my front and back weights. I fumbled for the hitches that secured the weights, thanking God that I had made them myself, and tugging at the loose ends threw off the burden of lead. I forced myself on, driven by stark terror to impossible physical effort.

Then, suddenly, amazingly, my front glass cleared and light broke in. I was on the top. As I lay slumped over the rough edge of the jetty, panting like a gaffed fish for air, I saw the infinitely sweet and comforting sight of a pair of stout Army boots inches away from my helmet window. I gestured feebly for my front glass to be removed and then in a last paroxysm of rage-inspired strength seized the unknown hand that started trying to screw the glass the wrong way and roughly corrected its direction. The glass turned, loosened, and in a moment I was drawing deep into my lungs the unforgettable relief of clean, fresh air.

When, later, I got shakily to my feet I looked for the P.O.

Shipwright who had been in charge of the pump. He was little less shaken than I, as indeed he deserved to be. With his Army assistants he had set the pump on a sloping block and when they had started to work the handles, the pump had gradually edged its way forward until the whole issue had toppled over the edge of the quay into the harbour.

I felt deeply grateful to the German who had blown up the jetty. If it had not been for that slope of rubble, I would never have seen daylight again. Even as it was it had been a pretty close thing.

*   *   *

The promise of victory in North Africa turned at last to reality, and the next move was the invasion of Sicily—'Operation Husky', as the planning staff had named it. I was to provide Advance Salvage teams to go in with the fleet sweepers and establish a headquarters in Syracuse. But as it turned out, there was no work for our men to do there, and we were all soon back in Tripoli. Shortly after this a signal ordered me to report forthwith to the Senior Naval Officer in Benghazi. A Free French destroyer, the *Leopard*, was hard aground to the east of the port, and Combined Headquarters in Algiers were anxious for a determined salvage attempt to be made. It was probably more a matter of diplomacy than anything else, because with guns of a Continental calibre and machinery of a type for which spare parts were unobtainable, the French destroyer was of little use to our operations: in fact, from a maintenance point of view, she was regarded as a damn' nuisance. However, orders are orders, and within a few hours I found myself in an aeroplane flying east across the Gulf of Sirte.

VI. THE FIGHT FOR 'LEOPARD'

My plane landed at Benina airport, and I was driven in to Benghazi, to an ornate building which had been the Royal Italian Bank and now housed the Senior Naval Officer, Cyrenaica, Captain John Campbell, D.S.O., D.S.C., and his headquarters. Well wined and dined in these baroque surroundings, I went early to bed and woke feeling fit and rested, ready to take a look at the stranded Frenchman. From the few facts I had been able to gather about her I knew she was a flotilla leader of some two thousand tons, and local opinion was that she was hard enough up on the beach to stay there for good and all.

After an early breakfast I set off by car along the coast road and followed the ribbon of tarmac as far as it went, which was not nearly far enough for my liking. When the road petered out, we ditched the car and took to our feet across miles of undulating desert, pinkish white like icing sugar and reflecting a blinding brilliance from the sun beating up off the baked sand. Eventually we topped the rise of the last dune and saw the ship lying within a hundred yards of where we stood. She was high and almost dry on the beach, listing heavily to port: not a happy thing for a seaman to look at. Standing there I visualised what had happened—the destroyer zigzagging on the convoy's inner wing, knifing through the dark sea; then suddenly the white flash of the breakers, frantic helm orders given a moment too late and two thousand tons of fighting ship driving into the sand at twenty-odd knots, urged on by fifty thousand horse-power behind the screws that motivated her; a split second of silence and then a sudden roar of high-pressure steam, white hot, lifting the safety valves to ease the fury of the ship's stilled turbines. And on the bridge the captain standing, solitary in responsibility, sick at heart at this thing he had allowed to happen, casting up the reckoning.

A beached ship is a tragic sight and this one had ploughed in far enough to be nearly high and dry. She was almost on her beam ends, listing heavily to port, and already the active sea had started to build up a sandbank outside her so that soon she would be completely engulfed. The tricolor still flew bravely from the destroyer's gaff, but under it she looked shabby, forlorn, dying if not dead. As I stood watching, a couple of sailors moved slowly for'ard along her steeply sloping deck, echoing in their own attitude the dispirited appearance of the ship. The whole scene was one of such hopelessness that I had to stifle an inclination to turn on my heel and leave the shifting sand to complete its work.

But instead of retreating I scrambled down the steep side of the dune and walked across the beach to the water's edge. A line rigged from the destroyer led to a tripod on the shoreline, and soon a Carley float was being hauled across the short stretch of water on an arrangement of pulleys. It contained Lieutenant Geoffrey Barton, R.A.N.V.R., an Australian from the Benghazi salvage team. He had brought down pumps, compressors, and a generator from Benghazi, and had been engaged since a day or two after the *Leopard* had stranded in rigging an emergency lighting system and making a preliminary inspection of the damage. I joined him in the float, casting a speculative eye over the ship's side as we pulled ourselves out to her. At least her back did not seem to be broken. There was a rope ladder slung over her quarter and Barton held the float alongside while I climbed inboard. As I vaulted over the rail on to the quarterdeck, I was seized firmly by a small dark Frenchman with burning eyes, embraced dramatically and soundly kissed on both cheeks. It struck me as an unusual way to be received aboard a warship, but I put it down to Gallic fervour and stood back to let Barton make formal introductions in French so anglicised that even I could understand it. I learnt that my assailant was the *Leopard*'s Commanding Officer. In his shiny, oil-stained reefer, his face smeared with grime and a nervous tic twitching his cheek, he had the same down-at-heel appearance as his ship. The first moment Barton had me alone he told me in a whisper that the captain was on the verge of nervous collapse and had twice tried to shoot himself. On the Australian's advice the *Leopard*'s First Lieutenant had now dumped or hidden all the small-arms in the ship. All in all, the background to the task could hardly have been gloomier.

Barton led me down a canted ladder into a wardroom smelling strongly of bilge, stale wine and Caporal cigarettes. We propped ourselves up on the high settee and wedged ourselves in against the list with our feet against the edge of the table and began to discuss the problems involved in refloating the ship. The French captain, who knew no English to speak of, followed every word and gesture with quick, eager glances. The oppressiveness of the atmosphere was unendurable, and I took Barton on deck where we could talk on our own without those dark, anxious eyes darting to and fro between us. I had already come to the conclusion that the job of getting the destroyer afloat again was nearly impossible, and I had not the heart to say so in front of the Frenchman. He was a man in pain.

Barton had done the sensible thing in laying out anchors to seaward to prevent the destroyer's being driven farther ashore: with them holding her, only a gale could have shifted the ship. But the value of this move had been discounted—with the best of intentions—before Barton's arrival on the spot. The day after they had run aground the Frenchmen had landed most of their ammunition, some of the guns and nearly all the stores, and the lightened ship had in natural consequence been driven much farther ashore than she need have been. I now gave instructions to flood all the lower compartments that had not already been flooded through holes and leaks so that the added weight would hold the ship where she was for the time being. If we ever got her ready to attempt refloating, it would be simple enough to pump out the compartments.

I had brought my new American face-mask kit with me and, linking it up with one of Barton's compressors, I went down over the side for a preliminary survey of the underwater hull. There was surprisingly little damage to the hull plating, and I felt pretty sure that however difficult she might be to refloat, repairs would present no serious problem. Back on deck I voiced this opinion to the French C.O., and at once felt still more depressed at the sudden joy which lit up his strained face.

Now we had to have a look at the ship from the inside. The engine-room and gear-rooms were both flooded up to sea level, but the boiler-rooms could be kept dry by constant pumping. To inspect the damage from inside the ship was going to be no easy task, for the *Leopard* had the typical French *torpilleur* cross-section, wedge-shaped with hardly any turn of bilge, no 'double bottom' and thus no easy access to the bilge-space—just a shallow area under the deck plating divided by vertical frames known technically as 'deep floors'. But we had to get in there to assess and pinpoint the damage and so, since movement in a cumbersome regulation diving dress would have been impossible, we had to don boiler suits and face-masks and risk snagging our lines at every twist and turn of our inspection of the ship's bottom. We started diving in the filthy, oil-bound water under the engine-room, forcing our bodies down between the frames and deep floors and through the small oval holes in the frames. Several times we got ourselves jammed down there in the heavy black oil that had escaped from the engine-room and ruptured fuel tanks. Each time we just managed to wriggle out and up for a lungful of greasy air. The French C.O. insisted on helping, game as a terrier, and twice he got himself so badly stuck that

Barton and I had to get down in the narrow space and drag him out, manhandling him in pitch darkness, trying desperately as we pulled and wrenched at him to keep his face mask from being torn off. The second time he was almost unconscious before we got him clear. Fanatically eager to see his ship off the sand, he was entirely without fear and gave no thought at all to his personal safety—in fact, thinking back on it, I sometimes wondered if he was possessed of some deliberate intention to finish himself off in these stinking bilges in expiation of his fancied crime. But by this time I knew enough about the extent and location of the damage to call a halt to the proceedings and I had a plan roughly formed in my mind for effecting the necessary repairs.

Barton, the Captain and I were all of us filthy with black fuel oil, and the only thing we had to take the muck off our bodies was the wardroom butter. It had already turned rancid because there was no power to keep the refrigerator going, and although the butter removed most of the oil, its own stench mingled with the pungent smell of fuel and left us reeking to high heaven. The wardroom had to be blacked-out at night, and the ship's ventilation system was out of action, so that in the confined space of our quarters the below-deck atmosphere rapidly worsened. I tried not to notice it that evening while I sat awkwardly at the slanting table and drafted signals to Benghazi and to Alexandria, giving them technical details of the situation and of my plans for an attempt at refloating.

The signals had only just been dispatched when we were visited in our lonely outpost by a single enemy bomber which made a preliminary run, dropped a few flares, circled and came in again to get rid of its bombs. Some of the destroyer's light A.A. weapons were brought to bear, and despite the awkwardness of working from tilted platforms the French sailors shot well enough to discourage any very close attack. The bombs fell near, in sand and shallow water, but not near enough to hurt us. The enemy's engine noise trailed away to the west and seawards.

The Captain was now in a most cheerful and effervescent

frame of mind. The sound of his own ship's guns and the fact that I had formulated some rather sketchy plans of salvage had convinced him that he as good as had his command at sea again. As soon as the raid was over he insisted that Barton and I should join him in a celebration. We followed him down to the wardroom, and in that foetid closeness he offered us wine which was white, warm and vinegary. I detested the very look of the stuff, and anyway I did not feel that as yet we had anything to celebrate. But I supposed that this nervous optimism was better than having the C.O. relapse into his previous mood of self-destruction, so we forced cheerful smiles on to our faces and drank as though we really liked it and there was in fact something to drink to. But the slender chances of salving this ship depended more than anything on luck and good weather, and it would have been a long shot to count on both. I was torn between dampening the Captain's hopes here and now—with possibly disastrous effects—and letting his half-demented gaiety run its course with every danger to his stability if, later, our best efforts should fail. As it was, I put off the decision and helped to finish that horrible wine.

I had the navigator's sea cabin to sleep in, and lying there with the after-taste of acid wine in my mouth I racked my brains for a method of dredging a ten-foot channel to seaward through the heaping sand. With a suction dredger it would have been simple, but the nearest was operating between Port Tewfik and Ismailia and its presence was vital to the maintenance of the Suez Canal. Even if it could have been spared for a short time on this job, the salving of one single ship could never have justified risking our only dredger on this unprotected coastline.

Everything else I had already thought out. For the damage to the hull I would build a concrete-pump, in Benghazi, bring it here and use it to pump cement down into the bilge-spaces and seal the leaks without risking divers' lives in the deadly confines of the destroyer's bottom. I was quite confident that in this way we would make the hull watertight. All we needed after that was a channel ten feet deep that we could float her out in. If it could be done at all it would have to be done quickly, before the sizeable sandbank built itself up much higher and thicker, and before the weather changed. Met. reports were favourable, but although I was no expert on meteorological signs and conditions I had a nasty feeling that this calm was not going to last for more than a few days.

I lay there half dozing and still thinking out ways of shifting sand without a dredger, but none of the ideas that came to mind could possibly have worked, and I was falling asleep with Lewis Carroll's lines about seven maids with seven mops sweeping for half a year drifting through my brain when running feet on the deck outside and the drone of aircraft overhead brought me suddenly awake. I hauled myself over the high side of the bunk and up the sloping deck to where I had left my clothes in a heap on the chart table. It sounded as if we were about to be bombed again. Dressing quickly and haphazardly in the dark I went out on deck wondering why the enemy should be wasting his time on this wreck when the Mediterranean and its ports were full of live targets. They must have been rather more hopeful of its recovery than we.

Flares were drifting down overhead, and in their pale light I saw the French gunners standing to their weapons and searching for a sight of the target. Then came a new sound, the high drone of fighters hurtling over from Benina. We waited in silence while the flares died and suddenly to my delight I heard unmistakably the hammering of cannon-fire. Looking up I saw a flicker of tracer and in less than a minute a streak of fire showed us part of the bomber before it was all flame, a comet streaking down towards the sea outside us and perhaps three miles away. One Junker the less, but instead there was the *vin ordinaire*, and more of the Frenchman's jubilation to be reckoned with. Anyway, sleep was out of the question that night, and at dawn I was making do with an uncomfortable doze in the staff car as it bumped and crashed its way along the road to Benghazi. The road was rutted by lorry wheels and ribbed with tank tracks, and with the vast stretch of desert reaching away for miles to our left, empty and silent, it was strange to think that only a few months ago it had been loud and deadly under one of the grimmest campaigns in history. Now and then we passed burnt-out fighting vehicles, or a patch of graves marked with simple wooden crosses.

As we bumped over the numerous potholes into the outskirts of the town, I noticed from the car the red shoulder flashes of a South African regiment. Stopping to investigate, I learnt to my delight that they were being sported by sappers from my old friend George Cowling's Engineer Company. Now wide awake, I soon located their H.Q. and surprised George at his breakfast. I say 'surprised', but George only looked up from a plate of cold meat, swallowed and grinned. Judging from his cheerful greeting he might have been expecting me. George was not an easy man to surprise. Over a cup of coffee I told him about the *Leopard* and of ways in which I thought his unit might be able to help us. As I had expected, he immediately promised his best assistance, and a moment later we were joined by his C.O., Major Ussher, who confirmed that we could count on their co-operation subject to the C.R.E., Colonel Archibald, giving his approval. We arranged to meet later, in Navy House, to talk over the details, and, much heartened, I drove on to report to Captain Campbell.

He listened closely to my detailed report and plans, but although he nodded from time to time and seemed agreeable to all that I proposed, I soon got the impression that he had something on his mind—something he did not find easy to mention. When I had finished what I had to say, he showed me the replies to the signals which I had sent off earlier. One, from Alexandria, was simply an acknowledgement, but a second message, expressed the opinion that the *Leopard*'s situation was hopeless. Then Captain Campbell handed me a long signal from the Fleet Engineer Officer. It had come through the office of Flag Officer Levant and Eastern Mediterranean, and pointed out that there were no further stocks of French calibre ammunition and no spare parts at all for the *Leopard*'s machinery. Reading between the lines, this was F.E.O.'s advice and prayer to leave the ship where she was and save everyone a lot of headaches.

It seemed that *Leopard* had little chance of ever floating again. I looked at Captain Campbell and in the back of my mind saw a picture of that desperate-eyed French captain fighting tooth and nail for the life of his ship. I did not want to be the man to tell him that we were not going to try to refloat her. My expression must have shown some of the dismay I was feeling, because Captain Campbell smiled comfortingly and handed me the last signal. It was from C-in-C at Combined Headquarters in Algiers. With a tense situation developing between Generals Giraud and de Gaulle, and with the feverish desire of the Free French to take some part in the great operations which lay ahead of us, it had been 'deemed expedient' to make every effort to get the *Leopard* back into operational service. We were ordered to proceed with all dispatch towards this end, and I, still thinking more than anything of the mercurial C.O. on his lonely, silent ship, forgot the dismal time behind and ahead in my relief.

Yet the S.N.O.'s manner was still peculiarly restrained, and the glances he shot at me were uncertain, questioning. I stayed silent so that he would have to come out with it. After an awkward pause, he cleared his throat in an unnecessary cough, raised one hand to pull at his right ear, and began, gruffly:

'Er—Keeble——'

'Sir?' He paused, and avoided my eyes by staring out of the window at nothing in particular.

'You're—er—welcome to use my—that is, I dare say the facilities up there weren't altogether adequate, and if you'd care to use my—er—my bathroom . . .'

I burst out laughing. I'd completely forgotten that I still reeked of rancid butter.

*　　*　　*

Now that we were committed to the task, there was not a day that we could afford to waste; any bad weather would write off our already slim chances of success. This sense of urgency was the keynote of a conference later in the day, when the sappers arrived, the C.R.E. with them. Rapidly I outlined my proposals. I wanted to build a suction sand-shifting plant on a flat-bottomed 'Z lighter', a type of shallow-draft barge built for river work in the Middle East of which there were several in Benghazi, manned by units of the Indian Army. The sand-pumps would have to be standard naval salvage pumps, the eight-inch variety, and their flexible hose sections could be fitted with steel nozzles to be thrust into the sand by attendant divers. A flow of sand through those pumps, which were made to handle only water, would soon ruin their impellers and destroy the suction, but we had plenty of spares and it would be worth the cost. I estimated that eight pumps would shift up to three hundred tons of sand an hour, passing it out through discharge pipes to the shoreline. The sappers at once produced a number of original and highly practical suggestions. They knew where they could get hold of some salt-pan pumps specially designed to cope with abrasive material, and they could lay hands on all the rigid steel piping we could possibly need by the simple expedient of digging up the drainage system under the town streets. Damn it, said George, as we stared at him in amazement, the place was so badly knocked about already that a little addition to the chaos would hardly be noticed. Nobody argued.

We selected a 'Z-lighter'. Within a few hours its deck was alive with toiling sappers and thunderstruck Indians. The local salt factory, deserted anyway, was denuded of its pumps and these were stripped for the wear in their much-used impellers to be built up by hard welding and fixed into prepared positions on the lighter's steel deck. Heavy diesel power-units were coupled up to these pumps and the first pipes, which were to convey the sand from the bank blocking the *Leopard*'s exit to the shore, began to arrive from excavation parties in the streets. The local populace were now convinced—if they had ever been in doubt —that the British were stark staring mad.

Throughout the hot days and clammy nights the South African engineers worked like fiends and the crazy dredger grew as we watched. The sappers overcame every difficulty by sheer red-eyed determination. They broke every rule and precept of engineering practice and got away with it. George and I designed and built a double-barrelled cement-pump from short lengths of what had recently been sewer piping. Into one barrel of this comical machine we poured ready-mixed cement, closed the lid and provided a blast of compressed air from a compressor coupled up to the gadget. By means of a rough-fashioned flap valve we controlled the ejection of the cement mortar through a three-inch flexible hose in such a way that as one barrel emptied we could fill up the other barrel and so ensure a continuous supply. By all the laws the contraption should have exploded in our faces, but it did not—it worked. Luck or fate or genius was on our side in these highly empirical operations and when, fearing the worst, we tried out our pump we were as delighted to see the mortar shoot from the nozzle of the hose under high pressure as a couple of children exercising their first pair of water pistols. We loaded the whole issue into a lorry with two sappers perched on the top of a high load of cement bags and sent it away down the coast.

With Captain Campbell, I left in an A/S trawler, and next morning we dropped an anchor and transferred ourselves by boat to the *Leopard*. We were welcomed by her C.O., who was now heavily bearded and absolutely filthy. His eyes blazed excitement at our arrival, and I kept well in the background and left the reserved and very English Senior Naval Officer, Cyrenaica, to be soundly hugged and kissed on both cheeks. If he had been upset by my odour of butter, he had something much more solid to cope with now—at least, I had not pressed myself to him. As Captain Campbell shook himself free, he looked like a man in a diplomatic nightmare.

Soon Barton had the cement-pump aboard, and he assembled it on the high side of the upper deck. Down below, oil-covered Frenchmen directed its nozzles into the bilges, and in a few moments the home-made pump was grunting strangely as it thrust sealing cement into the damaged areas between the bilges.

The scene alongside the listing hull of the French destroyer *Leopard* as the improvised suction dredger goes into action.

Frequent stops were necessary, to clear solidified cement from the valve-box, but the contraption proved its worth and in less than twenty-four hours all the holed sections had been sealed. A test pumping showed that we could get the ship dry as soon as we were ready. The weather, God bless it, held fine.

As soon as we knew that the sealing had been successful, Captain Campbell and I embarked in the trawler and returned to Benghazi. There we found that work on the lighter was almost complete. George had conducted tests and found that the power-units were well able to handle the pumps. We still had to find out how those pumps would fare on a diet of sand, though, and next morning we tried them out. The lighter was shifted off the quay and moored over a sandy section of the harbour. A diver went down and we lowered the suction and nozzle to him. The discharge pipe was triced out over the side, and in grim silence we started the pump. At once the flexible suction curving over the lighter's side began to throb and jump. The pump's power picked up the load and the discharge started to vomit a jet of water. But no sand. I called the diver on his telephone, and in reply got a volley of language only slightly diluted out of respect for rank.

'Flaming thing nearly got me boot off!' he yelled. 'Give us a chance, Sir—haven't had time to get the blasted nozzle into the sand yet!' Nobody else heard the vigorous complaint, and I told the waiting officers gently that the diver was not quite ready.

I turned to look at the discharge—the glistening jet of white changed gradually to yellow, and soon the water overside was covered in a spreading patch of sand. The machine worked! We changed to the other pumps, and as soon as the diver got the hang of managing the unwieldy suction nozzle, down on the bottom, sand came up fast—by the ton.

Elated at the success of these experiments, we began to get the lighter ready for its sea passage down coast. Major Ussher told us that he had had a request from his men that they be allowed to come along and handle the lighter's equipment. We

were only too pleased to have them, and they rushed on board
with their kit and rations like a pack of schoolboys on an excursion trip. An hour or two later, the 'Z-lighter's' two feeble motors
edged her slowly out of harbour and down the swept channel
between the minefields. She was escorted by an A/S trawler
and a motor launch, in which were Major Ussher, George
Cowling and the naval divers. I went happily ashore for a hot
bath and some of Captain Campbell's whisky. It was a good
evening, because for the first time we had some reason to believe
that if the weather stayed on our side we would get the *Leopard*
off her beach.

*   *   *

Early in the morning I left in the car and we bumbled noisily
back along the rutted coast road. We stopped in the same place
as before, and I set off across the dreary waste of sand towards
the sea. From the top of the shoreside sand-dune there I looked
down on a scene much more hopeful than the one I had witnessed from this same spot a week or so ago. Our lighter was
already moored in position on the *Leopard*'s seaward side, and
instead of a couple of slouching sailors there was now a throng
of men, brisk and purposeful, on the Frenchman's upper deck.
Out of a group on her quarterdeck a slight figure moved clear
and waved at me with both hands, like an old-fashioned sema-
phore machine out of control. Even at this distance I recognised
the French captain, and although I waved back and was glad to
see the man still alive I quailed at this manifestation of his un-
bridled exuberance. Suppose we failed? We did not intend to,
and our confidence was gathering, but one good stiff blow would
carry all our hopes away.

I slithered down the sandy slopes and as I neared the sea rejoiced to hear the hum and throb of our pumps' power-units.
A French sailor brought the boat across to meet me, and a minute
later, climbing aboard the destroyer, I found, to my intense relief, that the captain was too preoccupied to greet me. He was
deeply involved in what he probably regarded as a conversation

with his Number One, screaming at the top of his voice and gesticulating madly. From the look on his First Lieutenant's face I reckoned that we had arrived in the nick of time.

I crossed the *torpilleur's* upper deck and went over the plank on to the lighter. Flying jauntily from her stumpy mast was the South African flag, and on her rusty side someone had christened her in big white letters, *Sarie Marais*. Her pumps were running smoothly and the divers were ready dressed, waiting to start. Looking up, I saw a clear and threatless sky, and for all a sailor's natural caution I could not for the life of me suppress the feeling that nothing now could stop us getting this ship back where she belonged, in deep water.

The divers went down, and it was not long before the pumps were sucking sand out of the bank that had piled up to seaward. As the bank dwindled, the stream of sand from the discharges built up a new one along the beachline, inshore of the *Leopard*. Hour by hour and day after day the pumps spewed silt, and *Leopard*, ballasted as she was by the weight of water in her flooded lower compartments, gradually eased herself into an almost upright position. The channel deepened and widened, and we began to shift the lighter out seawards on her mooring wires, laying buoys behind her to mark the edges of the dredged passage.

It was a slow process, but there was no faster way of doing the job. Various small technical problems arose from time to time, and we dealt with them as they came. We had to modify the suction-ends, and after a time we found that by slinging them from derricks we could position them on the bottom with only occasional attendance by the divers. And dozens of times we had to stop the pumps to fit new impellers. But for all the snags—and there were plenty—our home-made dredger moved on seawards, leaving behind her a fairway ten feet deep and sucking up, as she edged forward, about 250 tons of sand each hour. The motor launch had laid out a set of anchors and, using the six wires with which they were now holding the *Leopard*, we worked the destroyer round so that she faced down the channel. I was certain that when we pumped her out she would float. Given a stay of this weather, we could hardly fail.

*　　*　　*

The French captain was feverishly and needlessly active. None of his diverse activities materially assisted our operations, but they seemed to give him a great deal of satisfaction, and we preferred to have him occupied to celebrating each step forward in sour wine. He spent hours in a small, leaky raft which he had had brought out of its stowage in the tiller flat and crouched in this coracle talking rapidly to himself he took countless soundings of the channel we were dredging and jotted down figures in a little book. We kept a friendly eye on him, in case he should get himself caught up in the dredger's suction. It would have been a most unfortunate thing to explain in Algiers if the captain had disappeared into what had been the backbone of Benghazi's drainage system, and there was some real danger of this happening. But, over all, a spirit of optimism was beginning to prevail. The destroyer's First Lieutenant even set his men to work with paint-brushes and scrapers, and cleaning the brasswork. At first sight of all this I felt it was a bit premature, a tempting of the fates —but then, the *Leopard* might have kept her brass bright anyway.

Things looked good, but a constant anxiety to me was the possibility of enemy air action messing up everything that we had done. One chance bomb, after all this effort, would be enough —I could just about see it happening. We had had several visits from high-level reconnaissance planes, doubtless taking photographs, and it was obvious that the enemy were taking a close interest in us. I for one could have done without it. It spoilt my sleep. I still had vivid memories of that raid on Tripoli, and I was highly allergic to the sound of aero engines in the dark. During the daylight hours we had constant fighter protection, but it went home at night, and there were no shore batteries to look after us.

Contrary to my morbid expectations, we were left in peace, and there came a day when we were close enough to success for me to drive down to Benghazi and arrange for a couple of 'Double-L' sweepers to stand by for the tow. Our channel was ten feet deep, about a hundred wide, and stretched for several hundred yards out to sea. In a day or two we could start pumping the water out of *Leopard* and then warp her out.

That evening, just back from Benghazi, I sat in the wardroom with Barton and a now grimly silent C.O. gnawing at his fingernails, when the R.N.V.R. liaison officer joined us and, as he sat down, casually handed me a signal. The captain pushed a fresh bottle of bad wine and a used glass across the table, but the liaison officer declined the offer with a polite smile. Disappointed that the captain was not going to claim another victim, I started to read the signal. My expression must have changed, for Barton asked quickly 'Bad news?'

I handed the flimsy sheet of paper across the table, trying hard to control an enormous disappointment and rising disgust. Tomorrow or the next day—within the week, anyway—*Leopard* would be given her chance to float, and this signal ordered me to proceed forthwith to Tripoli. I should not be here for the launching. No reason for my recall was given in the signal, but there was nothing for it but to get on my way again. As I said good-bye to the single-minded Frenchman, now agitated again, and wished Barton luck, I felt sure that a good deal more *vin ordinaire* would be spilt over the destroyer's refloating. I was not sorry to miss the party, but I should have dearly liked to see the captain restored to normality by having a sea-going ship under his feet again. He had worked for it.

However, he was to be spared nothing. Days later in the mess at Tripoli, I learned the end of the story. Off Benghazi the weather broke. A gale blew up, and although our lighter got clear and safely in tow, the *Leopard* was breached and damaged beyond hope. The order was given to abandon her, and as I thought sourly about my first failure I remembered how much greater was the little Frenchman's loss. The keenest cut of all, illogically, was the feeling that we had let him down. I hope he got another ship.

VII. MAKE AND MEND

THE signal which had dragged me away from the last hours of the *Leopard* had not, as I had half feared, been the product of a bureaucratic flap. The blockship parties had worked faster than I had imagined possible, and their assault on the *Giovanni Battista* had reached the point where we were able to consider moving her. If we could raise her for'ard enough to slew her round on her heel, the narrow gap which we had blasted during the hectic days in January and which represented the harbour entrance would be greatly enlarged. So we put aboard her every pump that could be mustered until her groaning decks were solid with them—six-inchers, eights, tens and even twelves. But for all the months of back-breaking work that had gone into preparing her for this move, I had little confidence in the strength of the much abused hull, and I dreaded the moment when she would come lifting off the seabed. She had been resting on it a long time and it was the main support of her weakened frame. The chances were, I felt, that when we started hauling on her she would break off in chunks and leave us an unholy mess of bits and pieces to sweep up.

With every pump roaring, water rushed out of the discharges all round the *Battista*, and the levels in her holds fell steadily.

But I knew well that when a certain level was reached the leaks might start and then the rate of emptying would slow, perhaps stop altogether—and, sure enough, stop it did. But divers on the bottom, working round her sides, stuffed bundles of tallowed oakum into any spot that would suck it in and gradually we reduced the leaks, plugged the edges of the steel-plate backed patches and sent down more oakum. The pumps began to gain mastery, and the filthy water crept down in the rickety holds. I signalled to the tug to get her lines on to the blockship's bows and to take the strain: in every hold the water level was still falling. I called up the divers and got them inboard.

Grudgingly, like a bad loser, *Battista* gave up the long fight. She stirred, listed a bit, groaned all along her spine. I signalled again to the tug and the heavy towing wire came up out of the water and strained taut and quivering as the tug churned the sea under her stern into foam. And the blockship moved! Slowly her bows turned off from where they had lain for months, and as she swung, her stern still fast on the rubble of the demolished mole screamed in protest as the plates rent and buckled. But the bows slewed further and further round and soon the *Giovanni Battista* lay with her nose up the shelving beach outside the entrance. We stopped pumping. Slowly her holds refilled and she flopped gently down on the bottom again as the tug eased herself astern venting steam in a torrent of triumphant sound. The task was done. We had a clear entrance now, five hundred feet across and deep, and I went happily ashore to report to N.O.I.C.

*   *   *

But there was little time in Tripoli to put our feet up. While we were coaxing the *Battista* into her present harmless position, signals had been humming into the base from a convoy of Liberty ships proceeding under British escort from Malta to the port. About a hundred miles off Tripoli one had stopped a torpedo, and I was under orders to go to her assistance as soon as she made port—assuming that she did. It sounded like a routine

and rather dull job, but two things gave it an unusual twist of
interest.

The full and sorry story of the crippling of the Liberty ship
I learnt only after I had played out my part in her salvage. In
calm weather the convoy was plodding along on what promised
to be a quiet voyage. On the bridge of one of the covey of
escorting destroyers a full watch jostled one another in the
limited space and an American naval officer, on passage, found
himself wedged into a corner of the wing of the bridge. Loung-
ing there and chatting easily to the Sub. of the watch he somehow contrived to poke his elbow through the protecting covers
of the torpedo-firing keys. Down below in his caboose the leading torpedoman on duty was startled by the sudden buzzing
which was the signal to fire. He knew his tubes were trained
amidships ready for action, and he very properly took the flashing light in front of him and the rasping buzz to be his order to
fire. Fire he did, and with a muffled thump the torpedo arced
out of its tube and splashed gracefully into the water.

On the bridge the familiar sound brought half the watch
rushing to the port wing, and a line of strained faces watched
in consternation the wake of the torpedo arrowing through
the water. The torpedo is a temperamental instrument. In the
most critical circumstances it will run shallow or deep, or it
will manœuvre in concentric circles to the peril of the ship that
launched it. But this one, with all the perversity at its command,
ran true—straight across the intervening quarter-mile of water
to the Liberty ship surging along dead on the destroyer's beam.
It buried itself in No. 4 hold, and the horrified watchers saw
the ship lurch under the hammer of the explosion and come
quickly to a standstill as the way fell off her and the sea poured in.

It was no time for nail-biting, and at a signal from the Senior
Officer the destroyer went at full speed into its towing drill,
often rehearsed, but never before called for in these dismaying
circumstances. A wire was passed astern to the Liberty ship and
bent on to her anchor cable; the destroyer took the strain and
ploughed on towards Tripoli with her victim listing heavily and

A typical example of torpedo damage to a ship. On the plating at the left are signs of welding carried out under water to isolate the damage and to allow the ship to be raised and towed 1,500 miles for repair.

showing with every roll most of a fifty-foot hole in her side. Aldis lamps flashing from bridge to bridge brought some comfort with the news that at least the torpedo had missed the engine-room and nobody aboard the American vessel had been injured.

The sad cortège reached the roadstead at Tripoli without further incident, and I had the *Gamtoos* standing by to make a first survey, above and below the waterline, of the casualty. Shortly afterwards I arrived and, after sympathising with the skipper on his undeserved misfortune, noted with silent delight that a good part of the Liberty ship's cargo consisted of jeeps, which in our particular theatre of war were at a premium. I made a private decision that some of this cargo was going to get lost—it was, anyway, necessary to shift some of the transport units to get at the damage.

We patched the damaged sections of No. 4 hold with practised speed and well enough to let us pump the for'ard deep tank and pull the ship on to a more even keel. But she was still drawing a good deal of water, and I stood tensely on her foredeck as the *Gamtoos* drew her steadily through the now wide-open harbour entrance. I didn't want another ship sitting fast between the moles after the fun we had had clearing the gateway. We made it all right, though only just; I felt a shiver run down her back as the ship's head ploughed into the tangled iron remains of the blockade and then scraped through. Probably we had deepened the channel by a couple of feet, which was all to the good, and the danger of providing ourselves with a gratuitous blockship was past.

I dropped over the side into my launch at the first opportunity, and we stood off while the *Gamtoos* struggled on with her lame duck. It was the end of the war for this unlucky vessel. These Liberty ships were beasts of burden that nobody expected to last very long, and if one got mauled, it was mercilessly cast aside. The main thing was that her valuable cargo had been saved; some of it, I observed from the shrouded humps on *Gamtoos's* deck, for Fleet Salvage. From that little exploit we were quite unofficially leased or lent several brand-new jeeps, another couple of damaged vehicles, and quantities of spares. They served us well, not merely for the purpose for which they had been manufactured, but as useful bargaining counters when we were after equipment with which the current owners were reluctant to part.

By this time I was overdue to move down to Alex in order to take over formally my duties as Senior Salvage Officer, but I decided to postpone the shift for a few weeks while I had a shot at clearing Benghazi. There wasn't much in the way of shipping there that was worth salving. Most craft that had been sunk in the harbour had been plastered and plastered again during the repeated bombing raids and even sitting on the bottom had received further damage that made recovery pointless. One such vessel, which had stopped several direct hits after going down in the deep water of the outer harbour, was, however, a pronounced menace to navigation, and she had to be disposed of. In conference with the Base Staff I hit on a method of putting her out of harm's way which later became the standard approach to similar problems in our area.

With the help of a Warrant Torpedo Officer and scores of heavy depth charges, still effective but of obsolete pattern, we laid a ring of explosives on the bottom right round the wreck and at a respectful distance from it. These charges were wired together, and the fuse led to a detonator rigged on a remote point of the mole. One thrust of the plunger and the whole series of depth charges went up in a single, shattering explosion. The harbour bed in the immediate area was lifted and spread around and the wreck settled feet deeper into the crater, and at the same time thousands of tons of water, incompressible and driven in on the ship from all sides by the explosion, crumpled the vessel like a paper bag. When the sand subsided, we went down again and laid another chain of charges round the ship, closer this time, and exploded these, too. The crater deepened, the ship was pulped still further, and the submarine obstruction simultaneously shrank and buried itself in the harbour's bottom. Again we went down and again we laid a ring of explosives round the battered mass of metal and when the plunger went down for a third time and the water cleared sufficiently to let us see the results, all that was left of the hulk was a mis-shapen heap of scrap-iron protruding a few feet above the harbour bed. The wreck's beam had actually been reduced in places to ten or fifteen feet, and there was no possible danger to shipping passing directly above it.

The system, of course, would not work on a rocky bottom, but on sand, mud or limestone it provided an admirable method of getting rid of rubbish by pulping and burying it, and this marine scavenging was only one of the many tricks we had to devise to meet new problems that beset us almost daily in the course of our work. The entire job at Benghazi was of this order, improvisation largely taking the place of excitement, and when a signal arrived urgently demanding my presence in Alexandria I complied with it without regret.

It was good to be back in Alex and to see the progress that fleet salvage had made since my last visit. But the task in hand was an unpleasant one. A U-boat's torpedo had got the cruiser *Birmingham* square in the keel, just about in line with 'B' turret and right under the seamen boys' mess-deck. About seventy men had been killed in that compartment when the torpedo struck the keel and blew a wedge-shaped hole upwards through the plating. The cruiser's damage control team isolated the flooded parts and with her bow almost severed the ship dragged herself towards Alexandria. I went out in *Prince Salvor*, the latest salvage ship we had acquired, to meet her.

As we first saw her, bow-on, she looked pretty normal—perhaps a bit down by the head. But when we closed, and turned to steam abeam of her, I saw that from the second turret her fo'c'sle sagged at least six feet and was moving to the sea quite independently of the rest of the ship. I could guess at the shape of the damage by the way the plating was wrinkled at the water-line. Aldis lamps clattered from ship to ship, and I soon had a fairly clear picture of what had been done in the way of first aid. It would be a waste of time to board her or to transfer a salvage party; the main thing was to get her into Alex harbour

before the bows dropped off. All went well, and her captain
nursed her along until eventually she was berthed in calm water
in the outer harbour.

As soon as she was secured I brought *Prince Salvor* alongside
her, and at once we started passing our main pump suctions and
compressors aboard. Investigations showed that the for'ard section was in fact six or seven feet lower than the rest of the ship,
and in that state we would never get her into dock. A four-foot
sag would be the most we could cope with, so the task ahead
of us now was to lighten the bows. We slaved at it for three
days and nights, welding and patching above and below water,
sealing off every bit of buoyant space that our pump suctions
and compressed airlines could reach. After those three days of
continuous work we had enough buoyancy for'ard to allow us
to open up the hatches which had been battened down over the
flooded messdecks. Under the hatches we looked down on a
dark, oily surface where, a week ago, the seamen boys had lived
their off-watch lives, eaten and slept and written their letters
home. Then came two more days of work best forgotten. The
divers, and I with them, worked by feel alone in the flooded
compartment, recovering the bodies of those seventy-odd. The
smell of death lingered and haunted the *Birmingham* long after
a destroyer had steamed slowly up the swept channel, taking
those sailors, shrouded in Union Jacks, on their last journey.

Sealing the messdecks again, we kept a good pressure of air
in them, and soon had the cruiser settled on the blocks in the
floating dock. When the dock was up and empty of water we
saw the enormous hole. It was something to wonder at that a
ship could take such tremendous damage and still float. Her
survival was due mainly to fine work, within minutes of the
explosion, by the ship's damage control team. Now she was
high and dry, and dockyard engineers started straight away to
patch her so that she could be taken off to some port where she
could get more permanent repairs.

*   *   *

We had in Alexandria, undergoing refit, the salvage tug *Max Barendt*. A German vessel with a distinguished pre-war career of long-distance tows, she was trapped in the Mediterranean when war started, and joined the Italian fleet. Just after the 1942 Tobruk *débâcle* she went to work again with her German crew —but not for long, because the R.A.F. scored a direct hit on her, in Tobruk harbour, shortly before we recaptured the port. The bomb went clean through her foredeck, right through the double bottom and ended, still unexploded, in the sea bed. The *Max Barendt* sank by the head in shallow water. When we were back and work started on clearing the harbour, the wreck excited the interest of the Port Salvage Officer, an Australian reserve lieutenant by the name of 'Jumper' Collins. In between Stuka raids he filled the section of double bottom where the bomb had gone through with reinforced concrete and, although it sadly reduced the tug's boiler-water capacity, 'Jumper' was able to refloat her on his pumps and put her machinery into some sort of order. Unfortunately, he was no engineer and, ignoring leaky joints and brack water and an absence of boiler-lagging, he decided to raise steam. The result will long be remembered by those who witnessed the performance. White-hot steam gushed from every joint, roaring like thunder, the whole ship shook and shivered from the fright of its life, and 'Jumper' and his unqualified assistants retreated in haste and horror to a safe distance where they waited for their prize to blow up. It wasn't their fault that it didn't. The fires died down before things reached explosion point and after an hour or so they crept cautiously back on board to find the ship practically red-hot and her boiler tubes finished for good and all.

As soon as we could we brought the tug down to Alex in tow, and the dockyard authorities were persuaded to give her refit a maximum of priority. She would be a most useful addition to our salvage fleet. Ignoring somebody's suggestion that she should henceforth be known as *Jumper's Folly*, we renamed her *Captive*. Meanwhile, as we had a tremendous amount of ship repair work on hand, and as in any case we did not expect her to have a very long life in our future operations, we left the concrete plug in her bottom and did only what was absolutely essential to the rest of her. We were anxious to get her into commission as soon as possible, with the result that some of the work was over-hurried and her trials developed into a series of hilarious and unseamanlike incidents. The Captain of the Dockyard, Captain Coppinger, a precise and dignified officer, decided to attend in person, and with a naval crew and an R.N.R. commanding officer, we cast off from the quay. Little did we know what we were facing.

We were hardly off the jetty when the C.O. gave a sharp tug on the lanyard operating the steam whistle. There was a loud screaming noise overhead, followed by several peculiar, shorter notes, then a crash and the sound of escaping high-pressure steam as the siren, complete with some of its mounting, fell off the steam pipe and dropped among the gold braid on the bridge. While a stoker turned off the steam valve to where the siren had been, the C.O. reached out to the engine-room telegraph and moved it to the position for 'Stop Engines'. He let go of the handle, and there was a rattling noise and a shower of rust, the telegraph chains parting and falling away down the pipe. Now we were really out on a limb—still moving ahead, no siren, no communication with the engine-room, and the harbour crammed with ships. We tried shouting down the voice-pipe, but this had no effect—because, as we later discovered without surprise, the voice-pipe was blocked halfway down.

A runner took a message to the engine-room to stop engines, but the ship still had a certain amount of way on her and at this point her helm jammed, hard over. We circled, slow and helpless in the middle of the harbour. By some miracle we hit nothing, and the First Lieutenant managed to unfreeze the windlass so as to let go our only anchor. This would have solved our immediate problems, if only someone had remembered earlier to clench the inboard end in the cable-locker. As it was, the rusty cable roared out in fine style, and did not stop. The end rushed into view and with a defiant crash disappeared over the side. I took a cautious look at the Captain of the Dockyard. His normally reposed features were a mask of frozen horror, but he made no comment and very soon the big Admiralty tug *Respond* saw our plight, lashed herself alongside and took us back to our berth.

So *Captive*, no less shamed than her captors, went back into refit. We dived to recover her anchor and cable, and the dockyard staff no doubt encouraged, or at any rate enlivened, by whatever Captain Coppinger would have had to say to them, made sure that for her next trials she would be in better shape. The new trials went off without even a laugh, and in the nick of time too, because she had only just been signed over to us when we had urgent need of her. A convoy passing through the Straits of Pantellaria had been attacked by enemy torpedo-bombers, and the Liberty ship *Thomas Masaryk* had been hit in her No. 3 hold and stopped, on fire and settling by the head. She had a valuable cargo on board, and in her 'tween decks was carrying drums of acetone—aircraft 'dope'—which was highly inflammable, and, with a fire raging over No. 3, deadly. Her crew had taken to the rafts and been picked up by the escorting destroyers. One other of the convoy, carrying ammunition, had blown up; the remainder had reformed and moved on, leaving the burning Liberty ship behind them. In Alexandria we had the story by signal, and wasted no time in getting *Captive* to sea. This was what she was for. It was the job she was used to, and as we cleared the boom and felt the first lift of the open sea, I let myself think that she was feeling her power again and liking it. Once again the famous ocean-rescue ship was bound on an errand of mercy.

We ran our distance to the estimated position, and it was not difficult to spot the *Masaryk*—the bright glow from the flames that were consuming her stood out clearly on the horizon. We altered course towards the blaze which was still only a pinpoint at this distance, without glasses, and as we pounded through the swell our crew got the heavy towing wires ready, warmed-through the towing winch and had the line-throwing guns laid out ready on deck. We had no heavy fire-fighting equipment, and I had already decided that if we could keep her afloat our best chance would be to tow her to the nearest sheltered bay. I studied the chart, and selected Menelao Bay: it was well protected and had just the shelving beach we would need.

As we closed in, we were joined by two motor launches, and I was delighted to find that one of them had aboard the *Masaryk*'s Chief Officer and Chief Engineer. We called the ML alongside, and hauled the Chief Officer aboard. He told me that the cargo consisted of aircraft (we could see some of them on deck aft), transport vehicles, aircraft engines, tanks and various items of machinery—plus, of course, that acetone in Nos. 3 and 4 holds. The idea of boarding the wreck became far from attractive. Her plating near the burning hold was literally red hot, and as she rolled her sides down into the trough of a wave, the sea hissed and rose in clouds of steam. The roar of burning acetone was deafening, punctuated by sharp explosions as now and then a drum burst and sent a sheet of white flame high over the hatch opening. From aircraft which had just about disintegrated on the deck above, streams of molten duralumin trickled through the scuppers and ribboned the ship's side. Exploding drums sometimes showered us with white-hot metal, and we had to be ready with fire extinguishers to deal with the small flare-ups which it started on our own decks.

It looked to me as if the ship was certainly afloat on her bulkheads and that with any luck she would stay afloat under tow. The only way we could have got the fire under control would have been to flood the holds, and with No. 3 already open that would have sunk her. So we could only let her burn, and get her in tow without wasting precious time. Getting aboard to rig the towlines was going to be a tricky operation, but there was only one way to do it, and we decided to lay *Captive* alongside the wreck's bows. Under any circumstances it would not have been easy, with the two ships rising and falling in the fast-running swell; and with the head of the Liberty ship like a blazing torch in our faces the problem was, to put it mildly, disconcerting. Time and time again we edged our bows up under the flare of the *Masaryk*'s fo'c'sle, only to be thrust off violently as the great nose came down like a vast swinging hammer that flung us sideways, lurching with our bow damaged and the sea bursting up between us through the gap and hissing on the hot steel. Once we settled for too long against her side, and the wooden belting of the tug began to smoke. But after what seemed hours of these attempts, we rose on a crest of swell that was higher then usual, and our fo'c'sle party succeeded in getting a couple of grapnels over the *Masaryk*'s bulwarks.

Thus encouraged, our skipper drove *Captive* hard alongside and held her there, ignoring the murder that was being done to our fo'c'sle and rails, while with my heart in my mouth I led a boarding party up and over the side. Once there, we danced about like cats on hot bricks—the deck was too hot for a man to stand still on. *Captive* backed away and lay off, licking her wounds, and we set ourselves to the task of hauling over the heavy towlines. There were only six of us and as we strained on the ropes I soon realised how unfit I was for exertion of this nature. But we did it—we got the lines inboard and belayed them to the heavy bollards for'ard and then again, to make sure of it, round the heel of the stump foremast. By this time we were black with smoke, singed here and there, and our hands were bleeding from burns and other lacerations. But we had the lines fast, and I signalled to *Captive* to take the strain, praying that she would not take it up too fast and part the wires so that we would have that gruelling job to do all over again. I need not have worried. The tug's skipper pointed his ship off and worked up his revolutions as he eased back on the towing winch. Juggling, the two dripping wires came gently up to take the weight, and the *Thomas Masaryk* paid off and moved ahead.

But I soon realised that this tow was going to be a very slow affair, because the *Masaryk*'s rudder was about ten degrees over to port, and weaving against the slant of the wreck's uneven progress *Captive* could only nurse her along in a series of wide, slow arcs. To work our way aft and correct the rudder was impossible—we were trapped here, with no chance of getting over the red-hot deck on No. 3 hold. But something had to be done, and I decided to leave the fore deck and try to reboard aft. I hailed one of the MLs, and told her C.O. that we would jump overboard and expect him to pick us up before we were drawn in against the hot plating further aft. We stood, looking hesitantly at the lifting water, then at that moment the *Masaryk* made up our minds for us. With a series of violent explosions, releasing sheets of flame, the hatch covers of No. 2 hold blew open, and we, as one man, went over the side. With commendable promptitude and no little skill the young officer commanding the launch worked her in between us and the ship's side, and one by one we were dragged aboard. Then he slanted clear again, with the paint on his launch's side alight.

They dosed us with rum, gave us dry clothes and doctored our cuts and burns. At the same time I detailed my plans for reboarding the ship over her stern, which, fortified by another issue of rum, we succeeded in doing.

After a struggle we uncoupled the power steering and switched over to emergency control so that we could steer by hand. Soon we had the rudder amidships, the speed of tow rose to a respectable rate, and the tug could steer a straight course. We were fairly comfortable aft, but although the fire in the midships superstructure had burnt itself out, the deck was still too hot for us to do any exploring and we stayed where we were on the poop throughout the night, watching an intermittent firework display from the for'ard part of the ship and hearing the crashes as one after another the acetone drums burst open and blazed. Soon after dawn we raised the coast at Menelao Bay, and *Captive* started to work her tow into a steady run towards the beach. From the top of the *Masaryk*'s afterhouse we watched her ahead of us as she closed the land, and then, with a toot from her siren, sheered off and dropped the towline. Our ship ploughed steadily on and presently we felt the hull under us take the sand. We had arrived. Calling the launch alongside, we dropped thankfully down the lines, and were soon back aboard *Captive*. I ordered the launches to shell the wreck along her waterline, to flood her and kill the fire; and this they did with great enthusiasm, with their three-pounders. When, in the heat of the moment, the ML's field of fire began to widen dangerously, I called the party off and they ceased fire. The *Thomas Masaryk* was now well grounded, and slowly her fires spluttered out. I left in one of the MLs for Tobruk, flew from there to Alex, and suggested that another Liberty ship, light, should be berthed alongside her to take her war cargo. This was done, and all the extremely valuable material that had not been destroyed by fire was brought off in the other ship. It was a simple task to repair the shell-holes; the torpedo damage to her keel was not great; and a few weeks later I watched *Captive* bringing the *Masaryk* into the Old Harbour at Alexandria to wait her turn for surgery with the other casualties already there.

VIII. TOP SECRET DIVE

WITH news of fresh casualties pouring in almost every day, we were kept steadily on the hop in Alex. A swift excursion to sea would be followed with a few days' hard labour in the office to bring myself as nearly up-to-date as I could ever hope or contrive to be. During one of these spells of clerical convulsions, just after the *Birmingham* job, I was sent for by Vice-Admiral Sir Bernard Rawlings and instructed to take a quick trip to *Medway II*, the submarine base at Beirut. I was promised 'something of interest'. It turned out to be the toughest and certainly the most dramatic operation I had yet embarked on.

I had a quick run round the establishment at Alex and then took passage by air to Beirut and reported to Senior Officer, Submarines. He called a conference within the hour.

In the Operations Office Captain (S) quickly outlined the position. The corvette *Gloxinia* and destroyer *Petard* hunting together had depth-charged a U-boat and forced her to surface. She had wallowed for a minute in a heavy swell, long enough for about half her crew to scramble up on deck and throw themselves overboard, before dipping at the head and sliding down to the depths in a welter of flotsam-spotted air bubbles.

Whether her last dive had been caused by damage from depth-charging, or whether one of her officers had performed his ultimate duty to the Reich by opening the vents and scuttling her, was not known; but, Captain (S) said, *Petard* had got a pretty good fix on where she went down. He laid a finger on the chart the base navigator had pinned down on the chart table:

'There, Keeble. She's pretty deep.'

I looked over his shoulder and whistled. The soundings marked nearest to the circle and dot indicating the position of the sunken U-boat read thirty-eight fathoms—about twice as deep as I'd ever been. 'And you want us to raise her, Sir?' I asked.

'Well—yes. We'd like to have her up, of course. But more than that we want something out of her.' Involuntarily Captain (S) lowered his voice. 'This is top secret, Keeble. If the enemy get wind of what we're up to, the operation doesn't stand a chance. D'you understand that?'

I nodded.

'Jerry's been getting on top lately with his U-boats. Our backroom boys think they know why, but they're not sure, and from what we've gathered from the survivors from *Petard*'s victim, U-307 can probably give us the answer. Our guess is that the new technique is for the U-boat to surface at night and lie awash, presenting a cluttered or negative radar echo, and wait for a target to present itself. There'd be no point in this if they had to depend on ordinary night vision for seeing it, and so the boffins have deduced that they are using some sort of infra-red gadget which will pierce the darkness and give them a clear view of what they're shooting at. Survivors have admitted that U-307 is fitted with something of the kind. We've got to get it.'

I interrupted with a question. 'Do we know what the thing looks like, Sir? Where it's located, how it's rigged? We'll be working absolutely blind down there—assuming we can find the sub. in the first place.'

'Oh, yes. The boffins have given us a good conjectural picture of the machine, and they've flown one of their chaps out to advise on the spot. You'll be thoroughly briefed. And you realise, of course, that there will be an explosive charge embodied in the gear?' The Captain smiled shortly. 'The diver will have to remove that before dismantling the instrument. Any questions, Keeble?'

'Rather a lot, Sir, I'm afraid. We'd better bring *Prince Salvor* over from Alex. I'll send a signal for her at once; but she's an extremely valuable ship, and I'd like to know what our chances are of getting air cover for her.'

'That's all right,' Captain (S) answered. 'I'll take care of that. We'll give you an air umbrella and an A/S escort. The escort'll help you to sweep for the wreck.'

'Good! Now what about the interior of the U-boat? Can you provide any dope on her layout? The less we have to discover for ourselves the better our chances of getting what you want. Working time at that depth will be strictly limited.'

'Pilot's thought of that,' the Captain said. 'The gadget's in the U-boat's control space, and he's got together a good collection of photographs of the layout of the space while we were waiting for you to arrive. We're making a mock-up of the whole issue for you to practise in. I take it you'll be doing the job yourself? Understand you're an experienced diver.'

'I was going to ask you about that, Sir. Naturally, I'd like to have a shot at it; but one ought to be pretty fit to work at two hundred feet. More fit, probably, than I am. I've been turning over in my mind whether it would be better to send my chief diver down instead of me. C.P.O. Devonshire is a first-class man, younger and fitter than I. What do you think, Sir?'

The Captain looked at me and said slowly, 'There must be no leakage of any kind about this operation, Keeble. I think you'd better go.'

*   *   *

During the week that followed I spent many hours 'working up' in the caricature of a U-boat's control room the carpenters and engine-room artificers had rigged for me. It was built of plywood, lifesize, and followed accurately the layout of a submarine—sawn off a few feet fore and aft of the conning tower. The first question was whether it would be possible to get a fully dressed diver, complete with front and back weights, through the two hatches leading to the control space. We decided it could be done. I had innumerable dummy runs, with a bandage round my eyes, groping for the reputedly cylindrical gadget that was the object of our exercise. Lowering myself solemnly through the conning tower hatch, down through the lower hatch, I would inch my way along inside the belly of the 'submarine'. Broom handles, lengths of hose, blocks of wood, anything that had caught the chippies' fancy, simulated the miles of piping, the valves, manifolds and the thousand and one parts of a submarine's gear that I had to know by heart before I penetrated the U-boat. Quite soon I could find my way about by touch alone and almost without thinking.

Meanwhile, *Prince Salvor* had arrived. At once the First Lieutenant set about checking on all equipment. Main and secondary compressors were tried out, all the diving gear, suits, helmets, communication sets were tested. The diving hose was ranged up and down the fore-deck, and the sections coupled up and joints minutely examined. Pressure and depth gauges were checked and rechecked. The recompression chamber was broken out from under the mass of stores that normally engulfed it.

Careful checking and testing of equipment was a routine preliminary to any operation, but when a working party was turned to for the disinterment of the seldom-used recompression chamber, the mess-deck hummed and buzzed. Obviously there were some deep dips ahead, and this was quickly confirmed by a steward's report that the young Quack had been seen brushing up on 'the bends' over a gin in the wardroom. Rumour reached fantastic proportions and must have greatly excited enemy Intelligence, for security was always rocky in the Levant.

But we went steadily on with preparations, and I made a point of inspecting the recompression chamber personally. This was an elliptical-shaped tank about six feet high, ringed with portholes and having access through a small door in the bottom. The tank was hermetically sealed when closed and coupled to a compressor so that pressure inside could be built up to equate with the pressure a diver endures when working deep. Where there is time for a diver to ascend slowly from the depths, resting at intervals for considerable periods, there is no need for a recompression chamber, but a swift ascent causes the nitrogen bubbles his system has absorbed from the tremendous pressure of air in his suit to expand rapidly and an hour or two after he returns to the surface his whole body will be convulsed from the excruciating pain of it. Hence 'the bends'.

But with a recompression chamber available the diver can be hoisted up and popped into the tank without the periodic delays his body requires to adjust itself to varying pressure. There, he himself, or observers watching through the ports, can adjust the pressure in the chamber to the depth the diver has just left, and then taper it off to atmospheric pressure over a period of two or three hours. The use of a recompression chamber has the additional advantage of making interrogation of the diver easy; and he can have his inevitable cuts and bruises dressed as he talks.

When I was satisfied that the equipment was in order and that I should be able to find my way about U-307 if we were lucky enough to strike her, I hauled Walters, our tame boffin, on board, and we pushed off. Less than a day's steaming brought us to the search area and our rendezvous with the anti-submarine escort Captain (S) had laid on for us.

We went at once into a pre-arranged box sweep, crossing and recrossing a great square of ocean on parallel courses a quarter of a mile apart. With our fathometer searching the ocean bottom, we watched its stylo trace an undulating line across the graph paper, following every lift and fall of the sea bed. If our luck was in, if *Petard*'s navigator was as good as he should have been, if the floor of the ocean wasn't strewn with great rocks, if all our calculations were correct, a sudden lift of the stylo, a sharp peak on the graph, would pin-point the U-boat we were looking for. Or some other wreck. Or some submarine obstruction. Taking the great waste of the sea bed and the fallibility of men and their instruments, the odds against our getting on to U-307 seemed colossal; and as the hours passed they lengthened.

*   *   *

Throughout the long night as *Prince Salvor* traced the monotonous pattern of her sweep I dozed on the chart room settee or paced the narrow bridge house, stopping at intervals to peer at the scrawly line on the fathometer's graph. It pursued its placid course, echoing the roll of the ocean bottom, but never for a moment lifting to the peak which might indicate the sunken U-boat. It clattered indifferently on as hour followed hour.

Then, towards dawn, when I was flat on the settee drawing dispiritedly on a cigarette, the even clacking of the fathometer changed to a quick fretful clatter that told of a sudden change in depth. I leapt to my feet and almost collided with the Officer of the Watch as with one mind we sprang at the graph. There it was: the jump in the spidery blue line that meant *something* on the bottom. Something! But what?

'Stop both,' I yelled into the wheel house, and out of the corner of my eye saw a hand go to the engine-room telegraph. The Officer of the Watch darted to the bridge telephone and cranked rapidly. 'First Lieutenant! First Lieutenant! Wanted on the bridge—right away, please.'

The stylo had resumed its steady line. Forty fathoms—just about right. From the wheelhouse the quartermaster called, 'Ship's losing headway, Sir.'

'Right!' Action Stations were shrilling through the ship, and the watch below burst up on deck. I nodded at the First Lieutenant panting at the head of the bridge companion: 'Get a dan buoy over the side as soon as you can while the way is off her, Number One. And Yeoman—make to S.O. Escort: "Have contact—proceeding with sweep".' A Signalman jumped to his platform in the wing of the bridge and the Aldis clattered its message to the destroyer just beginning to show in the dim morning light on the horizon.

I drew Number One into the chart room and together we inspected the pinnacle. 'Could be,' I said. 'Looks too sharp for a rock. Might be another wreck, of course; but it could be what we're looking for. Now that the buoy's planted, get your sweep over the side and start praying.' The First Lieutenant slid joyfully down the ladder bellowing for the P.O. of the watch.

I went thoughtfully out on the bridge and called to the Officer of the Watch: 'All right, Sub—midships the helm; slow ahead starboard; half astern port.' I leant over the binnacle. 'When she's round, steady on 090, Quartermaster.'

Prince Salvor's head swung slowly to port, gathering speed as the screws took hold. 'Stop port!' I ordered. 'Meet her, Quartermaster. Slow ahead port.' The helmsman spun the wheel and the Cox'n conning him answered: 'Both engines slow ahead, Sir! Steady on 090, Sir.'

I moved to the wing of the bridge and stared aft through the thin grey light. 'Sub! You can stream the sweep now and get another dan buoy ready to drop at the end of the run.'

'Stream sweep, Sir!' acknowledged the Sub-Lieutenant and bent over the telephone panel.

The sun grew steadily out of an almost calm sea. Hull down, the silent escorts carried out their Asdic patrol and up in the void above three Spitfires wove their effortless patterns, the roar of their engines rising and falling. Under my feet *Prince Salvor* wove her own pattern, the sweep wires vibrating to the pull of the bight on the sea bottom far below. Nobody spoke on the bridge as we steamed back on a reciprocal course. I faced the fathometer again, staring at it in mute appeal while I waited for the rise in the trace line as the invisible pulse fled to the object on the bed of the sea and ricocheted back to the receiver. I saw the stylo lift sharply, hesitate for a split second, then swoop down again to the mean line. With my head cocked I waited for the shout from aft that would announce the sweep's being caught and held on the anonymous object below. Nothing came.

We went about again, and again the blue line lifted and fell without result. Four times I watched the fathometer record our passage over this lump on the bottom and four times my heart sank when I realised the sweep was still trailing free behind us. Then the fifth time it happened. Simultaneously I felt the slight tremor run through the ship and heard the bridge telephone rattling. The Signalman, stammering in his excitement, gasped: 'S-s-s-sweep's fast, Sir!'

'Stop engines!' I ordered, and gripped the bridge rail hard in my hands as if I could slow the ship with my personal strength. Slowly, all too slowly, *Prince Salvor* lost way and eased quietly to a standstill. A hoarse voice from the bottom of the companion called 'Captain, Sir! We've got her, Sir! The First Lieutenant's compliments and she's taken nearly all the wire, but we're well fast and nothing's broken!'

Then began the slow, nerve-wracking manœuvring of the ship into position for further investigation. Working with strained care we recovered the kite at the end of the light-wire sweep, gently easing it up, coaxing it towards us so that it would not snap or break free from the obstacle on the bottom it had wrapped itself round. With the kite safely inboard, we bent on a light but strong flexible wire rope and, hauling on the sweep, ran the heavier wire down and round the obstacle. I eased *Prince Salvor* astern, taking the strain on the wire, aiming at getting the ship right over whatever was lying on the bottom. When the wire had straightened to an angle of seventy degrees or so I felt we had tempted fate far enough. I stopped engines and sent Number One away in the launch with a mooring party. The four three-ton anchors *Prince Salvor* carried were lowered into the boat and one at a time carried out and dropped in a square at a respectable distance round the wreck, if such it was. With the ship spreadeagled by her anchor cables I was then able to work her right over the point where the sweep had snagged. Easing off on two cables, shortening in the wire on the third mooring, we inched the ship into position. When the line from the wreck had righted itself almost to ninety degrees, I decided we could start diving. Six hours had passed since the fathometer had recorded our first contact with the obstacle.

Devonshire, working with his diving party in the waist, had a shot-line with a two-hundred-pound sinker attached rigged to one of the derricks. The weight was swung outboard and the chief diver, hanging on to a stanchion, stretched out over the water and hacked with an axe at the marline lashing racking the wire shot-line under the derrick snatch-block. The lashing parted and with a twang like a bowstring the heavy weight disappeared into the ocean, the coils of wire on the deck snaking over the side after it. Devonshire leapt nimbly back inboard, and with his elbows on the rail thoughtfully watched the white painted marks on the descending line steadily telling off the depths through which it was plummeting. A sudden slackening in the shot-line showed that the sinker had reached the bottom, and Devonshire's hand went up to stop his party paying out more wire. 'Hold it,' he ordered. 'Take in the slack. Make fast.' He squirmed over the rail to see the reading on the wire.

I joined him in the waist. 'What's the score, Devonshire?' I asked.

'Two hundred and thirty feet, Sir.'

We looked at each other for a minute. They weren't far wrong, I thought to myself. 'All right, Devonshire, get dressed and go down and have a nose round. As you may have guessed, we're looking for a wreck. It's a sub. If you can find it, we'll lower a second down-line to you. Shackle it as close to the sub.'s conning tower as you can. When you've positively identified whatever's down there, come up and we'll recompress you. I want to free the sweep, but not till you're clear.'

Devonshire and a stand-by diver dressed quickly, while his team coupled up the necessary lengths of diving hose. Once Devonshire's helmet was on I tested out the telephone set. We were working with a combined mike and speaker in the helmet connected to a loudspeaker on deck. Remembering the secrecy of the operation, I substituted a pair of headphones for the amplifier and clamped them over my cap. I settled down on a canvas chair while Devonshire, standing on the steel diving grid, was lifted clear of the deck and swung overboard. In a few minutes

Devonshire's voice rasping over the roar of air in the telephone told me that he was on to the shot-line. We waited tensely as he descended.

The telephone came to life again. 'All right, Devonshire?'

'O.K., Sir. Visibility not bad. Wreck of some kind not far off.'

Minutes passed.

The line crackled. 'Captain, Sir. This is . . .' The words that followed were drowned in a splutter of atmospherics. Probably a leak in the telephone cable. I leant forward, bellowing into the mouthpiece on my chest, asking for the message to be repeated. Devonshire's voice came through at intervals, unheeding.

'. . . dark blue sides . . . damage not extensive . . . nearly on even keel.'

'Devonshire,' I shrieked. 'For Christ's sake, *what is it?*'

'Whassat, Sir?' The voice was faint, wandering away. It came back. 'It's the sub. all right. I'm on her deck now. . . . Conning tower hatch's open. . . . Permission to enter, Sir?'

'No. I'm lowering a shot-line to you. Make it fast and come up.'

Devonshire's voice trickled through plaintively. He didn't want to come up. Instead, he was trying to get his distance rope round the bight of the shot-line he had gone down. A running commentary interrupted by bursts of static told us that he was hauling it in now to the conning tower; had lashed it up; was asking for a shackle.

We lowered the shackle to him and he made the shot-line fast to the U-boat's gun platform. We had a direct line from *Prince Salvor* to U-307. It was almost incredible. I relaxed in my chair, sweat breaking out with relief.

Devonshire came through again, giving instructions to warp the ship right over the wreck, guiding us steadily, calmly, as the capstan rattled and hissed and the anchor cable groaned under the strain. When he was satisfied the ship was in the most advantageous position he consented to come up.

I looked at my watch and at the sky. By the time Devonshire had been recompressed and I had had a chance to talk to him it would be dark. The crucial stage of Operation X-ray would have to wait till tomorrow. I thought with loathing of the dragging hours ahead.

*   *   *

The next morning Devonshire and I dressed side by side in silence. The Chief Petty Officer had been speechless with fury when I told him that I was going to enter the sub. 'At your age!' he had said, his eyes telling me plainly that there was no fool like an old fool. And of course he was right. Two hundred and thirty feet was no depth for a man of almost forty, of not better than middling fitness, to be playing about at. The fact came home to me very clearly during the hours of waiting. I was fatalist enough not to worry about the effect on me, but I was desperately worried lest physical weakness on my part robbed the operation, brilliantly successful so far, of a triumphant ending. So was Walters. The scientist had spent hours the previous night going over the routine of dismantling his precious device, and always I had felt his eye on me, coldly calculating. He was standing by now, waiting to help if I got into difficulties down below. He was especially anxious, and not for my sake, about the demolition charge. I shared his anxiety fully.

I spat out a cigarette and jerked my head at the attendants. They lowered the helmet over me and it settled heavy on my shoulders as they twisted and locked it into position. Resting my head back against the inside of the copper dome I waited as a hand thrust in through the four-inch opening and plugged in the lead for the telephone set. The mike crackled deafeningly and then the noise wore off to a low irritating buzz, and I heard Number One's voice testing the set. I raised a hand, thumb up, to let him know it was working.

My crew hooked the big front- and back-weights on to me, over the corselet lugs. I braced myself against the weight and felt them tightening the lacing around my waist. Under that load it needed the usual effort to get off the stool and on to my feet, which felt as though my enormous boots were anchoring hem to the deck. I signalled for the compressor valve to be opened, and while the air hissed into the helmet I squinted hrough the opening at the gauges on the instrument panel. In front of me somebody held up the small tools which I had elected for the job of getting the gadget off its mounting on he bulkhead: I nodded and felt the tools being slipped into the ag lashed to my belt. Here goes, I thought without appetite.

I raised one hand, and a couple of inches in front of my nose he thick glass of the front port was screwed into its place, leaving me alone with my hard breathing coming back noisily off he curved walls of the helmet. Out of the side glass I could ust see Devonshire. His half sulk had worn off and he was on his feet grinning in at me, holding up two fingers in a jaunty Victory sign.

*   *   *

My suit was bellying out with the pressure building up inside. I fumbled awkwardly for the exhaust valve and opened it a couple of turns. Then I shuffled to the steel grid and grabbed hold of the wire bails. Number One's voice crackled in my headphones.

'Hold on, Sir. Taking you over, now.'

'Go ahead,' I told him. It was a relief to be on the move. The grating trembled under me as the winch took the weight and swung me up high enough to clear the rail; then I felt the swing sideways and I was being lowered gently towards the sea, gently down. I watched the sea as it rose and suddenly my boots were out of sight and the water was creeping up my legs, bulky in the twill suit. The twill pressed in against me as I sank and the pressure rose sharply. Opening the exhaust valve another turn and a half, I felt more comfortable as the helmet's weight lifted slightly off my shoulders. The waterline trembled silver up across the glass in front of my face and then it was green, gentle gloomy green and I was on my own, and on my way down and more alone with every foot of the grid's lowering.

The platform stopped; it swung slowly under me while I

checked my suit for leaks, and tested the valve. Everything seemed
to be as it should be. 'Lower away,' I said into my microphone
to the men up top.

The shackles began to grate again on the wire down-line, and
as I sank deeper into the sea the light from the surface faded and
the deep green closed in. Suddenly, so hard and sharp that I
almost cried out aloud, a stab of pain shot through my head.
I gasped into the microphone urgently, 'Hold on—hold it!' At
once the platform stopped, and panting under that savage pain,
never less for being expected, I closed the exhaust valve a bit
and rose slowly up the wire bails with my feet clear of the grating. I yawned hard and swallowed, grimacing, and with the
click of the distending tubes the pain left my eardrums. Clawing
down the wire, back to the platform, I bent my knees and
shook my head, swallowed, inviting the pain to return. But it
held off and I told them up top: 'All right, surface. Lower away.'

Once again I was on the move downwards with the pressure
increasing every second and that greenish dark closing in to
match it. The only sounds were my own breathing and the creak
of the shackles. I kept my eyes on the down-line and presently
the white-painted ninety-feet mark rose to the level of my
helmet and the platform stopped. This was where I got off.
I manœuvred my air pipe and the telephone cable clear of the
sling, grabbed hold of the slimy wire shot-rope with both hands
and swung myself off the grating. As I went on down I gave
the platform one last look. Each part of it was outlined in massed
and sparkling bubbles, clear and bright as diamonds. I slid away
down the line, only slowing occasionally to let the air-pressure
build up to counteract the increasing outside pressure. The deep
green was changing now, turning from green through grey to
a blueish twilight, blue-grey, blue-black, and infinitely silent and
menacing in its depth and weight. At the other end of the shot-
line people talked and smoked. They belonged to another world.
I had left them and it for this vast loneliness, this solid void, so
different because of an extra hundred feet that I felt as if I had
never dived before. There was a coldness inside me unconnected

with the temperature of the water, and I shook my head briskly to clear my brain of the terrifying impressions that were edging in on it. No good panicking at this early stage.

One of my boots struck something solid and, forgetting now to be afraid, I checked myself and eased down another couple of feet. My boots slid off whatever it was and found some sort of ledge: peering down, I realised that I had landed on the edge of the U-boat's bridge gundeck. I could make out the dim shape of the mounting with its twin machine-guns swinging loose, unclamped, and looking up and for'ard I could just see the periscope standards and a pencil-thin quiver of black which I knew must be the jumping-wire. Very cautiously I clambered round the A.A. mounting and, squeezing my bulk between the after periscope standard and the side of the bridge, I found the conning-tower hatch standing wide open, the brass hatch itself thrown back. I stared down at the black circle of the hatchway, morbidly comparing it to the entrance to a tomb—which in fact it was. Or it might, for my part, be a trap, baited and set. Whatever way I looked at it the opening seemed excessively uninviting. I rested for a minute, leaning against the after standard, trying to get my breath to come more or less evenly, and the hatch gaped back at me, daring me to enter.

*   *   *

I did not want to let any air go; the pressure was bad enough without that. So instead of reducing my buoyancy to get down the ladder, I left the valve alone and hooked my boots *under* the rungs and pulled myself down. When I stepped into the hatchway my boots looked even bigger than they were. Each one seemed about the same size as the hole, and it struck me that for all our calculations back in *Medway* I was not going to be able to squeeze myself in. I cannot pretend that the idea upset me very much. At this stage I think I might have accepted the impossibility of access as divine intervention, reprieve. I dragged myself hesitantly down into the black hole and sure enough my front and back weights jammed on the rim of the hatch. Without them I could have slipped through fairly easily, but these weights, ninety pounds of them, just did not fit. Well, I thought is this as far as we go? I stopped where I was, panting under the effort of movement which with my heavier breathing was producing a lack of oxygen and a surfeit of nitrogen, and looking down and feeling the brass ring of the hatch about my middle I realised, suddenly, that it was not round but oval. I should have remembered that from my exercises in the dummy. Anyway, it meant no excuses after all. I swung my body sideways turning, and felt the weights come clear in the side width of the hatch. Groping with my feet for the next rung of the ladder, I pulled downwards again, and then I was inside U-307. But suddenly it was bad, worse than it had ever been, although the symptoms were familiar enough. The panting came harder and faster, and I couldn't do a thing to control it. It shook my whole body and I choked for the want of air, and the more I tried to get the less there was to breathe. Specks of light exploded in front of my eyes and shot away in brilliant white streaks. The pound of my own heart was like some detached force which I could not stop in its efforts to drag my chest apart. Sweat ran down my face and the sickness started, too, acid in my mouth and—well, it is not possible to be sick properly against pressure, you just feel sicker and sicker and retch pointlessly and the breathing gets worse and worse. Relax! I told myself. If you don't, you've had it. You won't last another two minutes. Forget that it's hard to breathe. The performance hasn't started yet, and if you don't take it easy it never will. It's not pressure that's bothering you; it's not lack of oxygen: it's plain bloody panic. Just take it easy and save yourself for what's coming.

The panting slowed and my breathing came more gently, although it still jagged. I listened to it as though it belonged to someone else, and I was just trying to help. Still trembling from the attack, I clung to the ladder with my boots and with my left hand, and I brought up my right hand to open the spit-cock on my helmet. Sucking, I drew in a mouthful of salt water, swilled t round to clear away the acidity of sickness and then spat it all out at the inside of the glass port in the helmet's front. It cleared he misted glass as well, two birds with one squirt. Not that it made much difference whether or not the glass was misted. Here in the tower it was pitch black, darker than any night I had ever known. When I pressed one finger against the outside of the glass port, right in front of my eyes, I could only just make out faintly the whiteish blob of my finger-tip. My micro-phone crackled, and a voice which might have been a thousand miles away asked, 'Sir—can you hear me?' It wouldn't have been much use trying to talk back. The chances were that they wouldn't hear me up top, and instead of trying to speak I pressed he chin-switch, and at once the voice crackled back at me.

'Jolly good, sir. You've thirty minutes more. Are you all right?' I wondered what was so jolly good, but anyway I chinned he switch for a second time and that must have satisfied them, because the crackle died out of the speaker. All the same, down here in the pitch dark with the steady hiss of air escaping from he vents I could not help grinning to myself: once I had got myself down and off this ladder into the submarine's control room, what would they be able to do about it on top even if *wasn't* all right? Phone for an ambulance?

I rested again and braced myself once more to go on down. The brass toe-caps of my boots scraped on the rungs of the ladder as I shuffled, extending one leg to hook myself a step further down. Instead of the cheerful clang I had expected to indicate I had found the next rung, something soft stopped my leg as I tried to straighten it. Something so soft that it seemed more like my leg refusing to straighten than anything under-neath in its way. Through the solid weight of the boot there was no question of any sort of feeling, only I had an impression of resilience in whatever it was that I was forcing down on physically. What the devil was going on? I kept the toe of my right boot jammed under a rung and held tight to the sides of the ladder with my hands. Then I raised my left leg in the small space left to move in and stamped downwards with all the force

I could muster. The same soft but determined resistance stopped my foot again.

I tried to feel with the boot, to feel where this started and how wide it was more than in any hope of assessing what it was. I moved my foot sideways, pressing down: it slid over and down and I lodged it under a lower rung, jamming the toe there while I shifted my hands lower on the ladder and pushed my other leg down. There it was again—that soft, solid resistance to pressure. It seemed to be right across the middle of the tower and somehow part of or mixed up with the ladder itself. Pulling myself down still lower I groped out and down with the other boot until I had a leg on each side of the obstruction: I kicked at it from the side, swinging my leg like a pendulum, but that did not budge it either. I got my hands low on the ladder then and dragged myself down astride of the blockage, hooked myself there with my boots locked under the rungs so that my hands would be free to pull the thing out of the way.

Bending was a fiendish effort, and I felt the lack of air again and had to rest where I was for a minute or two. I was wondering how much time I had left and to forget my growing sickness I concentrated on the thing below in childish petulance. I leant downwards and found it with my hands. At first it felt like a mattress in some sort of mackintosh cover. Then the fingers of my right hand moving across it found some small, hard object: my hand was swollen, by now, and insensitive, and it was a little time before I realised what I had found. It was a zipp-fastener. I dragged it open and forcing my hand through the gap I felt buttons—the metal buttons of a naval uniform. This was a dead German I was sitting astride. He was fat with swelling inside his waterproof suit—the sort our submariners call an Ursula—and he was completely jammed-up in the ladder. When the submarine made her final dive with the vents open he must have been starting up the ladder behind the others who had already got out, and halfway up he had met the sea coming in and had been there ever since. Of course, he could have drowned inside and been washed up into the tower

fterwards, but I do not think he would have been as tightly
mixed up with the ladder if it had been that way.

Well, now I had to get past him: no good *thinking*. I opened
he valve as far as it would go and forced myself down. I did
not make an inch. I grabbed hold, and pulled; jerked sideways;
t made no difference at all. Time was running out and the sickness rose suddenly in an overwhelming wave and left me reeling,
half-conscious and fighting the same old white lights. I made
myself rest and my senses told me urgently to take it easy again,
easy, or there'd be two of us for Devonshire to clear.

I knew perfectly well, now, what I would have to do. It was
not a very pleasant thing to ponder over, and I tried not to think
t all as I slid my right hand around my waist to the haft of my
diver's knife. The knife was a heavy weapon designed for anything from sharks to hemp and rope, and it had a serrated back
edge, to saw with. I set my teeth and, reaching down, began to
cut my way through. I was not a human being, I was just a
diver doing a job. Up top there were several hundred men
backing me up: all I had to think about was the object of the
operation and the value of its achievement. Not about the feel
in my hand when my saw-edge got to bone.

The thing began to sag and then it fell away except for something which I kicked, and that went too. I let the knife fall on
ts lanyard and pulled myself down through the lower hatch on
o the control room ladder, then slowly down another ten rungs.
I felt the deck plates under my boots and a moment later I was
off the ladder, standing close to the for'ard periscope where the
U-boat's captain would have been during an attack. I felt the
barrel of the periscope with my hands and it was still greasy.
The wires on either side of it were still bar-taut.

Standing by the for'ard periscope and resting there with one
hand on each of the wires, I summoned into my mind the
sketches which they had shown me of a U-boat's layout and the
interior of the mock-up I had spent so many hours fumbling
about in at the base. Now patience has its reward, I thought.
I am between the ladder and this periscope and its lifting wires

are athwartships, to port and starboard of it. I am square behind
them, so I can only be facing for'ard. There cannot be any mistake about that. Now if I turn ninety degrees right and move
three paces ahead I will come up against the control panel on
the starboard side. I reached up and pulled in a bight of airline
and telephone cable, enough to let me get over to the submarine's side plus another three feet or so to give me enough
slack for the short journey for'ard to where the gadget was
supposed to be.

I turned what I reckoned to be ninety degrees right, and
checked the way I was facing by feeling to my left for the
periscope and its wires. This was the way I had planned to do
it and so far there were no snags. Everything seemed right.
moved straight ahead with both hands stretched out in from
of me. Three normal paces to go—that'll be about six of my
shuffles. All the same I moved more slowly and cautiously than
need have done. I forgot to count, and I could only have covered
about a few feet of the distance before I began to think that by
now I should have found the ship's side, that something was all
wrong and upside-down—my memory or my sense of direction had failed me. I controlled a quick flare of panic, an urge
to turn and try another tack, and in the next moment my finger
touched the steel bars which protected the vent levers. Now i
was all right, I knew where I was. If I had given way to that
pressing, unreasonable urge a few seconds earlier I would probably have ended up circling into the port for'ard corner of the
control room and then I would not have known where the devil
I was. I would have had to follow my lines back to the hatch
and start all over again.

I was close up against the ship's starboard side now, and my
hands ran over the vent levers and the H.P. valve wheels. The
vents were open, all the levers pulled right back and loose.
shoved them in, one by one, thinking of the possibility that they
would decide to raise this wreck and give the job to me. If
could shut the vents now it might save me a second trip. One
excursion of this kind was enough, I felt. But there was no

reaction from the vents; no thumps of their closing, not even a hiss of telemotor pressure. Just the same, I pushed all the levers home, thinking that in any case it would not do any harm to have them the right way. Then I realised that I was dawdling, wasting time, *getting sleepy*. I was losing sight of what I was here for. And this drowsy feeling, my eyes heavy, worries fading, that lovely idea of *relaxing*. Just leaning up against something and letting it all slide. . . .

I pulled myself together. That would have been a quick way out, that snooze. You've overstayed your time as it is, I reminded myself, and if you let yourself slide now you'll be here for keeps. I talked to myself as if I were talking to a child, and with an effort forced my eyes wide open and turned left to face for'ard, which was the way I had to go. . . .

Now this was the chart table. Its top was smooth, greasy, or perhaps my hands were greasy and everything they touched had that feel. After those ghastly minutes in the tower with that knife my hands felt filthy enough to be burnt. I took hold of the edge of the chart table with the fingers of my right hand and as I pulled myself forward the top of the desk rose in my hand. It was hinged at the back like a school desk, and sliding my hand in I felt around—out of curiosity, or perhaps because I was sleepy again and vague in the real purpose of my being here at all—and my hand found a sodden mass of paper, slimy bulk, then a metal parallel-rule, a pair of dividers; something bigger, heavier—perhaps a course and drift calculator or a station-keeper. Where was the man who had used them a few weeks ago?

Just for'ard of the chart table was a short section of thwartships bulkhead. I had expected it, but it was a comfort to find it right here where it was supposed to be. My fingers gripped its edge, and I realised that my hand must be within a foot of the box of tricks I had come to get. I felt no excitement; not even the excitement of fear. I was as sleepy as a baby, and I wondered why the sickness had held off for so long. Out of a dreamy awareness that it was vital to stay awake I heard the voice again in my headphones. I realised suddenly that I had heard it before, but

it had not penetrated. I had accepted it as part of the sluggish
growing sleep, and I had neither listened nor tried to answer.

'Can you hear me? Captain, Sir—can you hear? Chin switch
if you can, chin your switch if you can hear. Do you hear me?'

I couldn't recognise the voice. It was so faint it might have
been Snow White calling long-distance from Buenos Aires.
I bumped the switch with my chin and the tinny jangle of its
bell whispered back out of the telephone. The voice came again
and it sounded less excited, easier.

'Your time's up, Sir. More than up—more better you come
up pronto!'

'More better'—the phrase identified Number One. Stupid
bastard, I thought. Talk English *and for the love of God leave me
alone*! I turned my face to the helmet microphone and forgetting the value of saved exertion I cursed them all, the whole topsides crew; I cursed them personally and I cursed the times and
tables which I had always enforced myself. I cursed the whole
lot nastily and crudely using words I would normally regard
as outside even a seafarer's vocabulary. I didn't know I was
doing it, and I didn't remember doing it, even afterwards when
I was told the whole story.

I dragged myself on, up to the steel partition. My finger
found the junction-box exactly where the scientists had said it
would be, and I traced the thick metalled lead out of that and
through another box and then—how simple!—I had my hand
on the Thing itself! Its size and shape were right and the connections were in the right places, and I could feel the securing
screws. I almost grinned to myself as I reached down into the
canvas bag at my waist and picked out the screw-driver, took
it in my right hand and with the fingertips of my left hand
guided its point into the groove of the first screw. Then everything seemed to slip and before I had realised what had happened the tool was away down there in the dark and of course
I could not bend to pick it up. I should have had the damned
thing on a lanyard, but it was too late to think of that. Much
too late!

Groping among the odd tools in my bag, I found a pair of pliers. Perhaps they would do—with a spanner. Using them was not easy because my fingers were stiff, slow and fumbling. But after what seemed an age of blind effort the nuts and studs dropped away, and as the last pair went rattling down I felt the whole thing swinging loose. Searching above it, my hands felt the unions and the cable-piping stretching up, exactly as the scientists had sketched it in that drawing that I had been shown —several ages ago—in *Medway*. Now—last lap!

Bit by bit the spanner loosened the union nuts. I battled on at them, and then something broke in on my concentration, tapping on the back of my helmet! I'd ignored the first couple of raps, but now it happened again, and I began to feel angry to the point of losing my temper. A silly thing to get heated about, but I suppose under circumstances like these a man's thoughts and feelings get to be exaggerated. I stopped work and turned sideways to feel around for whatever it was up there behind my head. At once my hand closed on what was unmistakeably an arm. Less angry now but somehow not shocked or surprised I ran my hand down along the arm: the hand at the end of it was puffy, obscene to the touch. On one finger was a thick metal ring, the sort of ring that our own stokers used to file up out of odd bits of metal when they were off watch and had nothing better to do. I realised that this was what had been rapping on my helmet—almost as if the owner of the hand had been trying to attract my attention. But I had no time, now, to be sociable; I reached up with both hands to the body floating face-down with its hunched back brushing the deckhead and its arms drooping out and down like a bat's wings, and I moved him a couple of feet for'ard, where we would be out of each other's way. He moved easily enough. And he was probably more comfortable than I was. I forgot him, went back to work on that blasted pipe.

Another minute's work, and the nuts were free enough for me to be able to move them up the cable. I dropped the spanner back into the toolbag, and wrenched at the piping. It moved a

little way, then stuck fast. I tugged again, but it would not budge.
Wild with anger, frustration and a sort of panic from knowing
the wasted value of these slipping minutes and the danger of
overstaying my time as I had already done by a wide enough
margin, I dug out the spanner again, stuck it in behind the joint,
and heaved. Grunting and sweating in the slippery stifling darkness, I struggled until suddenly the spanner slipped, throwing
me off-balance. I gashed my hand badly on some projection,
tried to clutch the falling spanner, missed it and heard it a moment
later as it hit the deck. I thought of trying to bend down to
pick it up, but I knew that even if I managed to get down that
far I certainly wouldn't be able to straighten up again. So I
tried using my knife, forcing its blade into the gap and levering:
the knife snapped in two and I let the useless haft drop down on
its lanyard. I thought: That's about the bloody lot! That finishes
it! I'll have to come down again tomorrow. Or as soon as I'm
fit for it again. But the idea of going up there now, without
the thing I had come for, seemed somehow impossible. I felt
the joint on the cable with my torn fingers and racked my
brains for an answer. And the answer came. *That parallel-rule!*

I groped my way gack to the chart table, opened it and pulled
out the heavy ruler. I took it back to the gadget, and even in
this urgency I couldn't help thinking with a navigator's mind
and regretting this barbarous misuse of a navigational instrument. But pushing away any such technical and professional
qualms I worked it on edge under the bulged and battered con-
duits, took a firm grip with both hands, and, knowing it was
this now or nothing else but an admission of defeat, I put all
that I had and perhaps a bit more into one savage, maniacal heave.
The pipes came free. I clutched for a handhold to stop myself
going over backwards, found one, and found at the same time
that the gadget was now lower down and apparently held by
another stud.

I took the thing firmly under one forearm, shoved the rule
under the flange and pulled. Something parted, and I had the
gadget, free, right in my arms! For the moment, though, I was

too exhausted to cheer, even mentally. I rested the studs of my front glass on a bulkhead I could not see and lowered my face on to the cold metal of the helmet. All I needed now was the strength to get this box of tricks, and myself too, up into the sunlight. We had a little way still to go.

I straightened up, made sure of my grip on the gadget, groped aft to the control panel and there turned right to the ladder. I was glad to find it in the same place—there had already been so many snags that it would not have surprised me overmuch to find that the thing had moved off. I leant against it, chinned the bellpush and called the surface. My words came back at me off the walls of the helmet, and to me they sounded like the pantings of a dog that should have been put down years ago.

'On deck—on deck! Take up the slack—easy. I am on my way up. Send down a weighted bag on the shot.' A distant voice crackled back an anwer.

'Send bag on shot—aye, Sir. Taking up your slack. You—longway—over—time—Sir. Sending—down—diver—to—help.'

That really got me on the raw. I tried to shout though probably it was only a jagged whisper.

'Keep your blasted diver! Keep him where he is!'

'Aye aye, Sir,' the voice said regretfully. Probably Devonshire had been agitating for an hour to be sent down after me. I thumbed the valve with my free hand and waited for buoyancy to build up—the suit distended and the load lifted off my shoulders as my feet left the plates. I guided and checked myself with my hands on the sides of the ladder, but passing the place where the ladder had been blocked I tried not to touch it more than I needed to. Then my helmet scraped against the edge of the top hatch and I heaved and wriggled my way through into the submarine's bridge. With the toe of one boot locked under the hatchway's rim, I opened my exhaust valve by a turn and a half, to keep myself heavy. Then with my fingers on the spindle I called the surface.

'Up top! I've got the bag. Stand by.' I grabbed the canvas, brass-eyeletted bag which swam just over my head in the gently

moving current, and as soon as I had it fast I tipped the weights
—old nuts and bolts—out of it. I settled the precious object-of-
the-operation into the bottom of the bag, and told them up
top: 'It's all yours—take it away!' I watched it rise and vanish
where the streak of the shot-line vanished too, and I told them,
happily, 'I'm coming up'.

Reaching for the shot, I closed the exhaust again. As the corselet rim rose to my chin, the filling dress took me steadily up
the line, while my hands, not feeling much now, slipped loosely
over the oily strands. The black became green and the green
lightened, brightened. I could see tiny shining bubbles clinging
to the line as it passed my front glass; I could see my magnified
hand sweeping those bubbles aside into brilliant fading showers,
like fireworks at a distance. The voice came again out of the
speaker.

'Sir. You're coming up to the stage. Better rest there a bit.'
The suggestion puzzled and irritated me.

'Put the First Lieutenant on the line.'

'Sir?' Number One's voice rattled down.

'Cut out the stage party. Forget the bloody stage—I want to
get out of here. Bring me up and I'll go straight into the chamber.
Got the bag inboard?'

'Yessir. Walters has locked himself in your cabin with it.
We'll bring you up from the stage when you're ready.'

And here *was* the stage. I handed myself over to its rusty
grating and swapped the shot-rope for its wire bails. I was thinking that the nonsensical idea of my waiting down here would
have been Doc's doing. Been reading up too thoroughly on the
bends—but let him worry about me when I get up top. That's
all I want—*to get up top*.

I jerked the breastline four times and the shackles started squeal-
ing as they began to haul me up. I leant back against the bails
and watched the silvery, glittering surface coming down to
meet me. A minute later I was face to face with *Prince Salvor's*
rust-scabbed plates. It was a sailor's dream of home.

Inboard, hands quickly freed me of my weights, helmet, corselet

Lt.-Com. Keeble is brought inboard after his marathon dive to the U-307.

and boots, and for a moment I tasted air, real air. Then I was bundled, still in my suit, through the man-hole into the recompression chamber. I felt awful beyond words, and the Doctor, who had followed me into the chamber, confirmed cheerfully that I looked it. I sagged down on to a mattress and gave up.

When I came round again, the Doc was bending over me with a syringe. 'What's this in aid of?' I asked.

'Anti-tet injection,' the Doctor told me. 'I don't suppose you know it, but you came aboard looking like a pork butcher. It was quite obvious that you'd been doing a bit of dissection down there—and not very scientifically. Thought you might have got a bit of infection through these gashes in your hands. Now don't get up.' He pushed me on my back again. 'You can tell me all about it later, and I'll give you a scalpel for your tool bag. The thing to do now is *rest*.'

I drifted off again, gratefully.

*   *   *

A few hours later, recompressed, decompressed, showered and shaved and in a clean suit of whites, I was abroad again. I begged leave to be admitted to my cabin and Walters opened the door to me. 'All right?' I asked. 'Didn't bring up the wardroom clock by mistake?'

'Perfectly all right,' the boffin beamed back. 'Their Lordships will be very happy with this. I've had it to bits; but what puzzles me is how you managed to short-circuit the demolition charge without touching it off. The contacts were closed, but——'

'The demolition charge!' I said. 'Christ! I forgot all about it!'

IX. MORE TROUBLE

PRINCE SALVOR bustled back to Beirut and there Walters and the machine which had quite unaccountably failed to blow up in my face were disembarked and flown out at once to U.K. I heard no more of them. Captain (S), having expressed his gratification at the outcome of the operation, did not detain us, and we steamed on to Alexandria. I settled once again in the centre of my web in the Fleet Salvage office.

The work of administration was bearing down more and more heavily on me. Well over two thousand men were engaged in salvage work in my area, many of them in remote parties spread all over the zone of operations. Always the work was urgent—an assault on nature, in which, given enough time, nature would win in the end. When equipment wore out or broke down, as a rule no attempt was made to refurbish it on the spot. It would be sent back to Alex, smothered in oil, with some vital part sheered off, often shattered by bomb splinters, for stripping, repairing and reassembly in our workshops. A constant stream of motor pumps, power units, diesel generators, welding units, compressors, mobile cranes and the thousand other devices employed in salvage poured into the base in an endless stream, where fitters and mechanic ratings fell on them and worked far into the night at their benches in our workshop.

Decisions on whether the bigger units would respond to treatment had to be made daily, and responsible priorities assigned to them in a monotonous succession of conferences. An internationally famous firm supplied us with the hundreds of thousands of cubic feet of the vital pressurised gases, oxygen, acetylene and hydrogen, which were in daily use in our underwater work. It fell to me to keep tabs on the gas bottles in which they came and to see that the returned empties went back in sufficient quantities to keep the flow of supplies constant or on the increase. I pursued the heavy bottles all over the Mediterranean area.

Every week American and British ships unloaded tons of new gear on us. Welcome though it was, it contributed to the fat files which were multiplying themselves like rabbits in my office while I cowered behind a towering In-basket. Our staff grew with the paper-work and my first Wren writer was now one of a cheerful and efficient bevy, but we never showed signs of getting ourselves up-to-date. For the most part I enjoyed the administrative work, but I welcomed the diversion of any operation that appeared to require my presence, and they cropped up with comforting regularity.

We had a good team. Our officers were hand-picked for guts, technical proficiency and their powers of improvisation. The ratings were a tough lot and when they were ashore they showed it in bursts of indiscipline, but the threat of a draft back to General Service controlled the most wayward. We were getting results, good results, with just enough set-backs to oblige us to retain our sense of proportion. All the same, we regarded ourselves as an élite corps.

But salvage, at this time, was not my sole preoccupation. Now that the tide of war had rolled away from Egypt and the scarred ports up and down the coast were secure from enemy attack, the civilian contractor of the Middle East made his insidious appearance on our busy scene. Peace was around the corner. The resumption of normal trading was certain in the foreseeable future; and there was no danger from flying splinters.

Civilian supplies of all kinds to the Middle East had virtually stopped at the beginning of the war. There was a flourishing black market in almost every commodity. Taxis in Alexandria bumbled around on the discarded and well-worn tail-wheels of Spitfires, and a good motor tyre would fetch a hundred pounds. Scrap metal was at a premium—and to look at our yards it seemed as if we dealt in it exclusively. On top of that, I had control of harbour clearance at half a dozen ports, and the wrecks with which they were bestrewn represented several enormous fortunes to contracting firms who could get at them. So between my excursions to sea and as I burrowed frantically into the mass of documents that threatened to choke my office, I had regular visits from the emissaries of firms interested in the rusty loot at my disposal.

In these days Alexandria seemed to be peopled entirely by speculators and their agents. In a very short time their visits threatened to occupy me full time, and although I was reluctant to lose the entertainment these suave visitors and their often disingenuous proposals offered me, I was forced to divert the stream from my door. At the same time, we were not above a little trading on the side ourselves. For some reason we seemed always to be short of serviceable jeeps, but we had lying about in sheds numbers of these vehicles which had been damaged by fire or sea water—survivors from the Liberty ship accidentally torpedoed off Tripoli, and the ravaged *Thomas Masaryk*, among others. The difficulty was to get them into commission.

Holloway and our chief motor mechanic hit upon a neat plan. At suitable intervals they would hitch one of these dilapidated machines on to the back of a jeep in running order and tow it off to the R.E.'s mechanical depot—the Royal Engineers were responsible for the supply and maintenance of our vehicles. There they would turn over the scarred and battered jeep to the sergeant in charge of the store with a sorry tale of some silly beggar driving it off the end of the jetty—took us a week to get it up, it did—and please could it be overhauled and put in running order pretty quick. We had a salvage party going out on a big job and were proper stuck. The sergeant would take one look at the hulk, throw up his hands in despair and issue a new jeep. Holloway's timing must have been pretty good and his stories suitably varied for he never failed to come back without a replacement. But to do ourselves justice we often helped the sergeant out with spares from our own caches of loot, and Holloway probably had a few tricks up his sleeve that I never heard about. Either that or the sergeant must have believed that we did most of our driving under water. Anyway it was a great comfort to have this largely unofficial source of supply, and we must have been almost the only unit operating in the Middle East without serious transport problems.

*   *   *

The tempo of salvage operations never slowed. Although by now casualties from enemy action were fewer, marine accidents, particularly to Liberty ships, increased in number. Fully laden vessels went ashore all over the place from the Indian Ocean to the Red Sea and the Mediterranean. Navigation in the Red Sea is difficult at the best of times. The currents of its tideless area set erratically, sometimes with the prevailing wind, sometimes not; and vast areas of water are badly charted or not charted at all. Roughly down the centre of the sea runs a long, hundred-fathom channel, but this slips quickly and imperceptibly into coral shelves, which in turn run into the low sandy coast. Unless a close watch through polaroid glasses is kept for a change in colour of the water, reflecting the change in its depth, it is dismally easy to stray off the channel and over a reef. A haze thick with particles of fine sand limits visibility and provides a still greater trap for unwary navigators in excessive refraction, a deflection of the sun's rays in the shimmering atmosphere which makes sun sights almost useless in the Red Sea. Even star sights can be unreliable and navigational errors of up to thirty miles or more may result.

The *William Hawkins* was a Liberty ship bound through the

Red Sea for the Persian Gulf with a war cargo destined for Russia. Her master, elderly and hurriedly trained, was innocent of all knowledge of these hazards. Accustomed to sailing his Liberty ship in convoy, he was an easy prey to refraction when ploughing his lonely furrow in the Red Sea. Casting about in confident expectation of raising Jeb-el-Tier lighthouse, which was visible with light dimmed in wartime at only ten miles, he was actually lying about sixty miles off it. Inevitably he ran ashore, on to one of the many coral reefs of Dahlak Atoll. His distress signal was picked up by the Naval Base at Massawa and retailed to us at Alex. I seized the opportunity for a vacation from paper work and put out, under the Admiral's orders, in *Prince Salvor*, sailing through the canal and south to the estimated position of the *Hawkins*. If the Liberty ship's master had known where he was, he would not have run his ship ashore in the first place, and Captain Wise and I proceeded in confident anticipation that our quarry would be found almost anywhere except in her radioed position. We were not disappointed. When we arrived on the bearings *William Hawkins* had given, not only was there no sign of her, but the chart gave no indication of a reef in the immediate vicinity. We were forced to carry out a box search, which was not a particularly healthy occupation in these treacherous waters. But luck was with us, and ploughing through the glassy swell on our first leg in the direction of the nearest shallow we saw the bulky, familiar shape of a Liberty ship looming up ahead.

We dropped the hook at a respectful distance, and I ordered the diving boat away to make a preliminary inspection. This revealed that *Hawkins* had got off lightly. Barring a few cracks and splits in her wrinkled bottom bilge plating, she was parked undamaged on a gently sloping coral shelf. We laid out ground anchors to seaward to brace her against any drift farther ashore and got down to welding up the damage to her bottom. Meanwhile the *Hawkins*'s Chief Engineer pumped out her flooded double bottom and found that his pumps could hold the sea off.

Prince Salvor had left Alex with her fuel tanks as low as we dared allow, and now we were able to pump three hundred tons of fuel oil from the *Hawkins* into our own tanks. The fuel was a little something for Admiralty, and the resultant lightening of the Liberty ship made a first contribution to the problem of refloating her.

From her 'tons per inch immersion scale' I was able to calculate that the removal of a further 850 tons of the *William Hawkins*'s cargo should decrease the draft for'ard enough to give us a real chance of moving the ship. I signalled to Massawa for a tug and lighters and had confirmation of their departure with a rapidity that drew my admiration for H.M.S. *Bull*'s degree of readiness.

Standing by for the arrival of *Henrietta Moller*, I watched the first smudge of smoke on the horizon build into the stocky outlines of the powerful little tug. Then I realised with a shock that she had only three lighters in tow. We needed a minimum of four to unload enough of the *Hawkins*'s cargo to ease her off the reef. Nor was I utterly confident that I had not underestimated what would be required to refloat her. With the lighters quickly secured alongside the *Hawkins*, the derricks creaking and clattering, ton after ton of cargo went over the side and the lighters settled ever more deeply in the water. When they had taken about 650 tons between them I decided they had already passed their maximum safe loads, and the *Moller*, like a duck with her family in train, waddled off back to Massawa with the three lighters strung out behind her. But the Liberty ship was still rock-firm on the reef and there was nothing we could do except settle down to wait in prayer in this tideless sea for a north wind that would raise a swell great enough to lift the stranded ship's bows. Another foot of draft would do it, I reckoned.

The first day passed without a breath of relief and the second day after the *Moller*'s departure maintained the flat calm. But early on the third morning the hoped-for northerly began to pile up. We hastily hove down on the Liberty ship's stern anchors, passed *Prince Salvor*'s tow line aboard her and after manoeuvring the salvage ship into position to take the strain, worked up gradually to full revs. The tow line lunged out of the water, straightened bar-taut for a moment, humming and vibrating, then tightened and eased alternately in the rising swell. *Prince Salvor* threw her whole weight into the struggle in a long and patient pull. For several hours her screws lashed the water round her stern to a bubbling, frothing mass of creamy white as she strained at the dead weight of the Liberty ship; but the *William Hawkins* sat fast.

Then I signalled the grounded ship to start her main engines and work them up slowly. I hoped this would get her stern down and start a movement in her inert hull. And it did. With the sea boiling under her stubby stern the Liberty ship yielded unwillingly to the tremendous pull on her and came dragging off her resting place, slowly at first, and then gathering speed as she answered to her engines and charged astern. One moment the combined thrust of two powerful ships could barely stir the ponderous merchantman; the next I was signalling frantically to her to stop engines before she fouled her own ground-gear wires and our sagging tow line. *Prince Salvor*'s skipper, reacting quickly to the danger, sheered his ship away and kept the tow line taut and clear; but for a few alarming seconds in the turmoil following the first free movement of *Hawkins*, it was not clear which ship had taken the initiative in the operation and the salvage ship had to scramble for safety.

With *Hawkins* now clear of the reef, a cursory inspection showed that the little water she was making could be handled with ease by her own bilge pumps and further underwater repairs were not immediately necessary. The chief danger to her was from her master's considerable inexperience. I took over, and with *Prince Salvor* in train, rescued and rescuer nosed off through the East Channel minefields towards Massawa and dry-docking facilities. After an uneasy night in the swept channel, I was glad, as the sun lifted its brassy face, to raise the port right ahead. We stopped engines off the main harbour, now considerably tidier than when I had last seen it, and as a visitor I politely hoisted the pilot signal. From the signal station the bright eye of an Aldis winked out to us:

WELCOME STOP YOU KNOW THE WAY BERTH NORTH
HARBOUR

So we pushed through the boom, past the floating docks, both with craft inboard and working at full clatter, and while I on *William Hawkins* picked up the buoys alloted to us, *Prince Salvor* slid quietly past and tied up alongside.

That night at dinner I saw the familiar Regia Marina silver laid out again and the old faces ranged down the long table. They had a new Number One, Ellsberg had gone, leaving as his memorial the two docks moored in the main harbour and still working under the glare of floodlights, and there were a few unfamiliar faces. But Captain Colin Lucas still presided, and even the steam-heated atmosphere of Massawa could not spoil my pleasure in the congenial company still to be found there.

It was a good party, but I broke off the engagement early. *Prince Salvor* was already under sailing orders for her next task, and next morning I was flying out at first light to investigate a new problem, news of which was contained in a signal waiting for me at Massawa. It promised to be a big job. An Admiralty floating dock, one of the larger ones, had gone ashore on a desolate stretch of coast.

Under tow by two ocean-going tugs, the *Hesperia* and another of the *Empire* class, Admiralty Floating Dock No. 24 was on her way to the Far East. She had been built in three parts, the centre part great enough to house the extreme sections when the dock was on passage. Her design was ingenious. Once she was delivered, it was only necessary to flood the centre section and float the two ends out to provide a dock; but delivery was the very devil. It was like towing a block of flats. The two tugs had picked up the dock at Malta and had been routed up the North African coast, close in, on their way to the Canal area. In the flat calm in which the voyage started, the tugs ploughed doggedly on, holding to their course without difficulty in the absence of wind. But as they raised the North African coast, the wind whipped up and the weather steadily deteriorated until dock and tugs were fighting it out with a steady fifty-mile-an-hour gale.

As the seas mounted the tugs battled to keep the dock on its course, but the mammoth bulk of the monstrous box acted as a sail and for every few yards the cortège gained, the dock skidded an equal number of yards sideways, like a dinghy with centre-board up, and dragged the tugs with her. They edged steadily inshore in spite of the tugmasters' violent efforts to bring the dock head-on to the wind. The trouble was that the dock really had no head. Whichever way she turned she presented an enormous expanse of wall to the wind which pushed with a force and persistence the tugs could not match.

The running battle continued, the tugs losing steadily, until after a particularly violent, plunging sheer, the *Empire* class tug became girt. That is to say, she surged round almost broadside on to the dock she was supposed to have in tow and her wire, running at right-angles over her side, threatened with every movement of the dock to pull the little ship bodily under. Faced with the certainty of foundering, the master of the tug cast off his tow and the whole load fell on the *Hesperia*, plunging and straining in the heavy seas a cable's length away and by now a few hundred yards off the rock-lined shore. It was much too much even for the 4,500 shaft horse-power of the *Hesperia*, and she and her tow were swept remorselessly on to the desolate shoreline between Ras Ameer and Appolonyia.

The boiling surf made short work of *Hesperia*: her bottom was ripped out the moment she struck, and although two of her crew were washed overboard at the moment of impact, the rest of the ship's company managed to cling to the upperworks of the wreck until the storm abated enough to let them struggle to the shore. *Hesperia*'s obstinate charge had been carried after her, broadside on through the seething waters and was lodged, apparently inextricably, on the jagged rocks of the bleak coastline, one wall of the great dock virtually on dry land, the other planted like a giant's boot in the maelstrom of the inshore water. Her passage crew took cover in the compartments of her hollow

An aerial photograph, taken at 750 feet, shows H.M. Tug *Hesperia* and Admiralty Floating Dock No. 24 after they parted company and ran aground. The two ends of the dock can be clearly seen stowed in the main section.

walls, and with their companions in the stranded tug waited for the weather to break. Meanwhile the other tug steamed into Benghazi and reported details of the catastrophe.

My plane touched down at Alex. I transferred to the Admiral's aircraft and flew on to Benghazi. There I decided to have a look at the wreck from the air, take some photographs for further reference, and consider the possibilities of a parachute drop to this remote stretch to organise the salving of the dock if such seemed to be a possibility.

The R.A.F. laid on a bomber without hesitation, but they showed no enthusiasm for my projected descent by parachute. Four days after the dock had drifted ashore the wind had dropped and risen several times, but the weather had not settled down and there was a discouragingly brisk breeze still blowing as we made ready to take off. The country we were flying to was rocky and broken, studded with a wiry, stunted scrub that would tear a man to pieces if he were dragged through it, and the R.A.F. showed no tendency to be party to a display of heroics which might well end tragically without advancing the operation in hand. When I thought about it cold-bloodedly myself the appeal drained quickly out of the idea.

We took off and soon were circling low over the two wrecks. The tug was in a bad way: heeled over at an angle of fifty degrees, her bows were lifted almost high and dry on these unfriendly-looking rocks, and broken water was swirling over her steeply canted after deck and whipping up in spume round her mast. Underneath she must have been wide open to the sea. But the dock was holding together. It squatted massive and grotesque among the slimy rocks, and I sensed rather than saw the shudders that ran through her as the rollers pounded the seaward wall, climbed more than halfway up the sixty-foot high black side and slid back leaving fingers of foam to mark their progress. With the hammering the sea was giving her, she *must* be moving, straining her great frame, yielding under the assault of hundreds of tons of solid water, until the first plate had to buckle, until her own enormous weight, all of twenty thousand tons, started the sag that would finish her. If anything was to be done it had to be done quickly.

On the shore survivors had got a fire going. I could see a tarpaulin stretched over some branches to form a lean-to, and a break in the scrub was dotted with flotsam that had been rescued. Just beyond the margin of the sea a ship's lifeboat lay, capsized, and small figures ranged along the waterline looking for anything worth salving that the sea had thrown up. Others attacked the tough undergrowth for fuel for the smoky embers of their fire. I reckoned there were forty men there. It seemed just possible that with their help I could do something to protect the dock from further damage until a proper salvage force could reach her. I debated with myself for a moment and then asked the pilot to drop me.

The pilot jerked his thumb at the wind-battered coastline, grinned and shook his head. When I persisted I was met with blank refusal. There was nothing more I could do about it, and I couldn't deny that the pilot was behaving a damned sight more sensibly than I. The obvious thing *not* to do in the circumstances was to jump out of a reasonably comfortable aeroplane and be dragged over these bone-breaking boulders, through that cruel, lacerating scrub, at the end of an over-lively parachute. I resumed my seat and the plane banked steeply and headed back to Benina aerodrome. From there I drove back into Benghazi to try a different approach.

By dawn I was doing everything but stand on my head on the minute bridge of a motor launch as, with the horizon seesawing sickeningly, we battled our way through steep, marbled seas to the scene of the wreck. Once there the ML lowered a tiny dinghy and a P.O., who could ill be spared by his skipper, handling the cockleshell with consummate skill, coaxed her into the choppy lee of the dock. I made a hair-raising leap for the lower deck of the dock, poised for a moment with my arms flailing, and then flung myself forward on the cold, sea-washed plates, my fingers scrabbling for a grip among the rivets. I found an eye bolt, fastened on to it, and in a moment was able to lurch to a secure foothold on a ladder. When I got inboard through a hatch giving access to the hollow wall, I found a few of the passage crew who had made their way back on board during a lull in the weather sheltering from the lashing spray and clearing food from the storerooms while they waited for a chance to make the shore again.

Together we made an inspection of every tank in the bottom section of the dock, and we had only to open the pet-cocks tank by tank to hear the quick slapping of water that indicated how extensive the flooding was. Twelve tanks out of eighteen were open to the sea, and I had little hope of saving the dock. But I clambered up the steep steel ladders that ran up the side walls and signalled the ML to call Alex and arrange for a salvage ship to proceed to Ras Ameer. One way or another she would certainly be needed.

When the wind dropped we slithered back ashore across the rough suspension bridge the survivors had rigged between wreck and beach and set about building a more solid gangway of rocks above the surf. It was a miserable twenty feet from the inshore dock gate to dry land. Then with the help of the *Hesperia*'s telegraphist, the tug's wireless set, miraculously undamaged, was dismantled and reassembled aboard the dock. We connected it up to one of the auxiliary generating units in a side tank and before long we were in direct touch with Alex.

But AFD-24 was giving in fast. Great rumples two or three feet deep spread along her sides, corrugating them, then cracking and splitting. It seemed that structurally the dock was a total loss, and when *Prince Salvor* appeared on the scene in response to my signal, a minute inspection of the interior of the tanks and the outside of the submerged portion of the dock made by her divers gave final confirmation of my first diagnosis. Nevertheless, the dock contained tens of thousands of pounds' worth of valuable gear: electric pumps, control gear, switch gear, switch panels, emergency generators. There was a machine shop magnificently equipped with costly precision machine tools. The great valves and vents for flooding the dock were too valuable to lose if they could be saved; and there was mile upon mile of expensive and scarce piping. All these things, whatever could be used in a dock of similar pattern—and there was much— had to be dragged ashore and transported to base before AFD-24 broke up under the stress of her own weight and the incessant pummelling of the sea. We needed a powerful and well-equipped salvage party with crawler tractors and skids or sleds of some kind to drag the heavy plant across the rocks and wadis of this barren terrain to the desert road. I sent off a long, detailed signal to the Admiral in Alexandria and C-in-C at Caserta.

About this time a Cyrenaican police patrol, mounted on sturdy, dainty-stepping horses, turned up to inspect us. They patrolled this dreary coastline monotonously on the look-out for smuggling and trouble-making Bedouin, of which there were plenty. I took advantage of their appearance to borrow a horse and set off briskly across the twenty-odd miles to Appolonyia. After five miles of this mode of transport I had lost all my enthusiasm for it, and I arrived ultimately at my destination in a condition that hardly allowed me to roll out of the saddle. There are few things as pathetic as a sailor doing duty on horseback. Before I was finished with AFD-24 I was to make that gruesome, rock-strewn journey several times, but I never began to get used to it.

A week or so after I had signalled for them, the salvage party under Lieutenant Johansen of the S.A.N.F. landed their gear on the wreck and began systematically to strip it. Handling the heavy parts on the sloping steel decks, hampered by the massive end-sections of the dock which were still stowed in her waist, called for physical endurance of a high order. The toil was back-breaking and unremitting, and it was a race against time, for the dock was slowly breaking up under foot. By night the company was enlivened by visits from marauding bands of Bedouin. They would swoop down on the wreck in search of loot and find a squad of weary men, ready for anything but nonsense, rising out of the debris that littered the shore. This was invariably more than they bargained for, and the Arabs would let off a few rounds from their ancient Italian carbines as a gesture and make off again, riding with reckless dash through the scrub, pursued by an occasional admonitory shot from the salvage party.

I kept an eye on proceedings by flying back and forth from Alex to Appolonyia, and then making that dreadful journey to the dry dock by horse or donkey. On my second visit I found the White Ensign whipping smartly in the breeze and the shore camp tidied up and augmented by neat, portable buildings erected in orderly rows. Complete naval routine, including requestmen and defaulters musters, was in force; and Johansen had inaugurated a perimeter defence against Bedouin forays by posting ratings armed with sub-machine guns and equipped with field telephones in wadis a thousand yards from the camp. If I had not made such a singular spectacle on a horse myself, they would probably have picked me off before I got close enough for identification. It was quickly clear to me that the salvage party was more than capable of looking after itself, and I left them to it, thankful for the shape of my office chair after those memorable hours in a locally-made saddle.

But as usual I was not given much chance to stagnate. Right under our noses in Alex harbour the old *Brambleleaf* began to play tricks. She was a Fleet Oiler that had been hit by two torpedoes in 1942. One had struck in her after-tanks, the other in her engine-room and the damage was extensive. We had managed to get her into port under tow, and although she was too severely crippled to be worth repairing, she had served a useful purpose in Alexandria as a static refuelling plant. For two years she had lain there, refuelling ship after ship, with her wrecked engine-room open to the sea. Now the sketchy repairs to her stern had given way. What was left of her after deck had dipped and slid down to the bottom, leaving her bows above surface pointing stupidly at the sky. She had fifteen hundred tons of oil in her for'ard tanks and before I arrived on the scene somebody had decided that the first move should be to get the oil out. I came just in time to stop this nonsense: it would have been a clear invitation to the remnants of the oiler to try a backward somersault. We needed all the weight there was up for'ard to bring her bows down when we pumped some buoyancy into the after-compartments.

I had a discussion with *Brambleleaf*'s officers, mainly to ascertain which tanks had been flooded, and then I togged up and went below with a squad of divers to inspect the submerged decks aft. While some of my divers set to work sealing and patching around the stern I picked my way across the cluttered, sloping after-decks, checking the oiler's dozens of tanks to determine which might have their buoyancy restored. It was rough work. Each tank was sealed with a heavy top secured by a massive clip called a dog. I had to free the dogs by chipping at them with a heavy hammer, have a look inside the tank, and if it was not badly holed, mark the tank top suitably and send it up to the surface where a suction joint and spill-pipe would be welded on to it. Later, the tank top would be replaced by a diver, a suction coupled on, and the tank pumped free of water.

I was sweating heavily as I worked, constantly stumbling over one piece or another of the mass of gear which litters a tanker's deck, and more than once I had cursed the attendant up top for not giving me enough slack. Nothing is more irritating than to have one's head jerked back by lines held too firmly, to be reined in like a horse feeling its oats.

I was working on one of the last of the tanks when it happened. The tank, I had been told, was flooded, and I was swinging vigorously at the dog securing its top when the cover quivered and a jet of silvery bubbles shot past my front glass momentarily blinding me. I should have been warned, but my temper was on edge and instead of pausing to think I continued to wrench at the clamp holding the tank-top down.

It came loose in my hand and before the fact had transmitted itself to my brain the hatch cover flew open as if it had been blasted. A gigantic air bubble belched forth from the open hatch, picked me up inside its tensile walls and threw me sideways along the deck. I cannoned painfully off a number of projections as I was catapulted along and finally bumped to rest,

lat on my back under a nest of pipes. Blackness hovered ready
o come down on me.

I tried to relax for a moment to gather my thoughts. The
ressure in my helmet seemed to have risen sharply, and as I
urned my mind blearily to this I suddenly felt the deathly cold
ouch of water on my chin. My helmet was flooding!

Violently I clawed at the nest of pipes and dragged myself
nto a sitting position. With my helmet upright the water dropped
n inch and then slowly, menacingly, started to mount again.
shook my head to clear it and reached with my right hand for
he valve at the side of the helmet. A few quick flicks closed it.
This held the water, now quivering almost at my lips, at bay
ong enough for me to ask the surface for more air. As the
humping of the pump quickened its tempo in response, the
xquisite fresh air flooded into my helmet. The pressure built
p. The water level in my suit was forced down inch by inch,
lown to my chest. And there for the moment it was held.

Now I could give some attention to the cause. So far I had
peen solely and unhappily concerned with effect. There was a
strange sensation in my right leg and groping downwards with
my hand I was horrified to feel the wet wool of my pants' leg
through a gash in the twill of my suit. I traced the rip up to my
thigh and then, wriggling my foot, which answered with unusual freedom, guessed that I had lost a boot. Often before I
had torn my suit and felt the damp spreading through my heavy
underwear as water seeped in. But with a gash of these dimen-
sions I was lucky that the pump was holding the water in check,
and it was questionable if I could move.

By this time my attendant was pretty sure that something
was wrong and was stuttering into the telephone. It would have
been more sensible to have sent one of the other divers to have
a look at me, but that had not occurred to him. I told him sharply
to start taking in slack—and to go easy. I fumbled with numbed
fingers for a grip on the nest of pipes that had stopped my head-
long sprawl and fought my way upright. Moving very slowly,
ponderously, I stumbled across the slippery steel deck, picking

my way through the snags, until I could feel my lines go straight up overhead. Four pulls on my breast line and the surface began to haul me in. I was carrying so much water that it took four men to get me inboard from the ladder.

Damage, apart from my suit, was confined to a few bruises and to my morale. With my helmet and weights off I inspected the rip in my suit with interest. The right leg was torn completely open and hung uselessly by a reinforced section at the back. My boot was still somewhere down below. At twenty feet it had been all right, but at twenty fathoms it would have been a different story. It would have been a different story, too, if the tank-top had caught me squarely as it flipped back. Far from being flooded, the tank had been full of air at pressure which had blasted out when I opened the hatch. There were a few words to be said to the officer who had misinformed me.

That was the only snag we struck in recovering *Brambleleaf*. The rest of the operation went smoothly, and in a short time we had the battered oiler back on the surface again. But that was the last time I ever took another man's word for a fact which I could check for myself.

*　　　*　　　*

Often the greatest danger lurked in these simple, apparently routine jobs. In a really complicated operation we allowed for almost every eventuality, planned everything down to the most minute detail, and where possible exercised every step. But a straightforward job presented its own hazards, not the least of them being the tendency to take things for granted, and the slipping of concentration on what seemed an automatic task. Always in underwater work a single lapse could be fatal.

Shortly after we finished on *Brambleleaf* I had orders to send a party to a cruiser lying just outside the Great Pass. She had reported a leak and was calling for a diver's examination of the bottom plating next to the Asdic dome before she resumed her passage. I took a party out to the cruiser and stood by while he preliminary survey was made. It was pure routine. The weather was fine, the sea calm and clear, and the men of my party worked cheerfully with the ship's company in passing bottom lines. These lines, which were run from the ship's rail under the keel hard by the Asdic dome and up the other side, served as a guide and a handhold to the divers making the inspection.

The diver, a shipwright, experienced and one of my best men, stood quietly by until it was time for him to go over the side. He went down the ladder quickly, leaving a little flurry of bubbles behind him as the dome of his helmet dropped down below the shining surface. I could picture him underneath, making his way along the bottom lines hand over hand, his helmet occasionally striking the ship's side as his buoyancy pushed him gently upwards. On the telephones we could hear him grunting when he twisted to get his front glass close up against the plates swimming hazily in front of him. As he got farther under the cruiser he called for more slack. I estimated that he must have been almost under the keel plate when his voice rattled in the telephones again. It was only just audible, calling for still more slack. The attendant eased on his lines and moved over to increase volume on the communication set. The diver must have chosen that precise moment to release his grip of the bottom line. Unattended, his air hose, with his life-line lashed to it, flicked over the side and eluded for a few seconds the frantically grasping hands of the horror-stricken attendant. The whole party pounced on the lines, got them, made them fast. But in these few moments forty feet had gone over the side.

In silence, hand over hand, the dripping lines were hauled slowly back inboard. No sound came in answer to my urgent appeals over the telephones. The swish of air washing round a helmet was clearly audible in the speaker on deck, but it seemed only to intensify the silence. Foot after foot the lines came in. The diver on the end of them was without buoyancy, a dead weight.

His helmet broke the surface. Another heave and the suit came

into sight, dangling emptily on the air hose. The arms hung life
less, the rubber cuffs empty but for a trickle of water dripping
from them. The water was deeply tinged with crimson.

We pulled the limp suit over the bulwarks into the diving
boat and dropped the horrifying bundle on the bottom boards
Somebody, with a shaking hand, reached to unscrew the front
glass of the helmet—and released a warm, sickening flood. Hur
riedly we threw a canvas engine cover over the pitiful, terrifying
remains. One slip, and the accident we had lectured on, threatened
about, painted ghastly pictures of and done our level best t
guard against, had happened. Casually, the unfortunate ship
wright had been allowed to drop forty feet and the instant
change of depth and pressure had produced the giant squeeze
Most of the diver had been forced into the copper dome of his
helmet.

We summoned the cruiser's launch to ferry the body ashore
while another diver got dressed to complete the survey. The
inquest would have to wait.

X. 'OPERATION MANNA'

SINCE the beginning of 1944 the islands of the Grecian Archipelago had been visited—in fact, haunted—by our Special Service parties. They were of all sorts—young British Naval officers, Greek Navy men, British and Norwegian and French Army types—all of them having the time of their lives in an uncomfortable sort of way. In caiques, they flitted among the islands maintaining contact with resistance groups and 'bandits', bringing back prisoners, escaped Allied P.O.Ws., and, now all-important, the vital Intelligence reports which we needed as a background to our plans for the invasion. Now, with Italy surrendered, our forces well into Normandy and the German campaign in Russia pretty thoroughly bogged down, Metropolitan Greece was humming with rumours of an imminent withdrawal of enemy forces. There was at any rate no doubt that the Germans were shifting uneasily from foot to foot. I was delighted at the prospect of going back. Three years ago we had taken our last glasses of whisky from Nikolai, the barman of the Grande Bretagne Hotel in Athens, and almost before he had had time to rinse the glasses he was taking similar orders from German parachutists. They had come in hard on our heels, red-eyed and merciless with benzedrine and the fumes of destructive power. For three years Germans had been the masters of that ancient land; their submarines had used the Greek ports, and from the airfields of Crete had come the Stuka dive-bombers to scream down on our almost defenceless convoys. Now the sands were running out for the master race and we, the ordinary people, were ready to move in again.

The Intelligence reports that most deeply engaged me were, of course, those concerning enemy plans and moves to sabotage and block the Greek harbours. The more we could know of the Germans' intentions, the readier we would be to go straight into the job when we could get to grips with it. From Piraeus, for instance, we had heard that S.S. demolition squads had been flown in to prepare for wholesale destruction in the port. As further details came in from the same quarter we were able to prepare the stores and equipment most likely to be needed. All routine salvage work ceased, and *Prince Salvor* and *Captive* were put in hand for repairs, re-equipping and storing. Fleet Salvage went into top gear. I detailed off the various parties and sections, appointed their Officers, Petty Officers and Leading Hands—and at once found that nine out of every ten men who had been allocated to base duties were furiously endeavouring to wangle themselves into the operation. It was a heartening sign of their spirit, if any such sign had been needed. But not everyone could go. The base had to keep working and I had to turn down dozens of requests from able men. I heard that Holloway, still my Cox'n, and the Leading Writer never had to buy their own drinks at the Fleet Club these days. They were followed around by a body of sailors anxious to buy the beers for these important men who had their hands on the operational lists! It made no difference to the composition of the lists, but it made Holloway and the Scribe, as they called him, into V.I.Ps. overnight. They began to be careful whom they spoke to.

Meanwhile, as we straightened our plans and marshalled our resources, Fleet Sweepers were already nibbling at the fringes of the Greek minefields. There were R.A.F. mines as well as

German ones to contend with. All of them spoke the same lethal language, whatever the intention had been when they were laid, and as the reports came in from the sweepers I realised that we would be more than lucky if our invasion fleet got through without a bang or two on the way. For all the sweeping, there were far too many mines about in those waters. Sweeping is never a hundred per cent effective, and this job was being done in a hurry.

I took advantage of a temporary lull, for everything was set and we only needed the word to go. With Admiral Rawlings's permission I flew up to Naples to report to Captain Rippon and get whatever advice he could give me on the forthcoming operations. In Naples I found terrific port-clearance activity, conducted jointly by British and American forces. Commodore Sullivan, U.S.N., was most kind to me, and I had only to admire certain items of his salvage equipment for him to promise to transfer similar gear to us. I accepted the offer as a sign of good will and co-operation, but I could not for the life of me see how he would be able to spare the stuff or get it to us in time. I should have known the Commodore better. When I got back to Alexandria, it had already arrived—by air!

Then out of other talks in Naples, yet another R.N. salvage ship was allotted to us. This was the *Salvestor*, and it was decided to man her with South Africans. With so much accomplished, and with a mass of valuable advice from Rippon, I flew back to Alex—and found unexpected trouble.

The Greek fleet, never too stable politically, had gone so far as to mutiny. When I heard this I remembered how in that bloody period in Crete when the local populace was helping and harbouring our battered garrison, they still found time, off-duty as it were, to tear each other limb from limb on matters of internal politics. It was said then that at any gathering of five Greeks there would be five bitterly opposed political parties represented. But now they could not have picked a worse time to fly off the handle. The issue, Communist-inspired, was anti-Royalist versus Royalist. The first stirrings of discontent had developed rapidly into open insurrection in the ranks of the Greek Army, and our own forces had promptly corralled the lot in the desert; now it had spread to the Fleet. Royalist officers and men in the ships which were waiting in Alexandria for the start of 'Operation Manna', the invasion of Greece, had been overpowered, and the mutineers had taken the liberty of issuing an ultimatum to our Commander-in-Chief. The answer they got was a rigid deadline for their unconditional surrender.

The Royal Navy had acquired some experience in dealing with threats of this nature. We had French units in Alex harbour, and once or twice it had been expedient to moor a few submarines so that their bow torpedo tubes pointed at possible sources of trouble. No open threat, of course: just a few submarines in berths not usually allotted to them. I arrived in Alex to find some of our fleet units similarly disposed. At the same time, while he was naturally committed to enforcing a surrender, the Commander-in-Chief was unwilling to cause any unnecessary bloodshed or damage, and I was immediately briefed on the part Fleet Salvage was to play if the worst came to the worst. We were to stand by with rescue tugs and with *Prince Salvor*, ready to fight fires, haul damaged ships clear of the navigational area, and so far as possible save life.

Such was the unhappy state of affairs on the eve of the liberation of Greece.

Just before the expiry of the ultimatum, a party of specially trained Marine frogmen, armed with Sten guns which were packed with water-resisting grease, and wearing rubber Sladen suits, were embarked in a patrol launch. The launch slipped quietly out into the dark harbour, towards the Greek ships, and we in *Prince Salvor* slipped equally quietly from our buoy and edged, blacked-out, into a pre-arranged position.

The minutes ticked away as we strained our eyes into the darkness, but from the direction of the Greeks came no sound or light. Behind me, Holloway muttered, 'Now, Sir——' and at that very moment we heard a sudden rattle of automatic weapons, while searchlights broke out blindingly from several points on the perimeter. In *Prince Salvor* we increased speed and closed up to our limit berth. The ships were floodlit now, but there was no more shooting and presently we picked up Aldis signals cancelling the rest of the operation and instructing us to retire and remain at immediate notice for further action.

In the morning we heard how the Marine boarding party had taken the rebel committee ship completely by surprise and captured the whole bag of tricks with few casualties. For the time being, at any rate, the situation was under control. But it was an unfortunate preliminary to 'Manna', and it made a great deal of difference to the strength of Greek participation in the liberation of their homeland. In a new disposition of units, only the cruiser *Averof* and the hastily repaired Hunt-class destroyer *Adrias*, together with a few Greek-manned MLs, represented the Royal Hellenic Navy.

Day by day the P.R.U. aircraft supplied us with air photographs of the Greek harbours, and we scanned them closely for evidence of blockships. But here was a snag. The deep waters, characteristic of most Greek ports, effectively hid any wrecks. Knowing how thorough the Germans were in their blocking technique, we could be sure that they would sink ships on top of each other to combat the same snag from their own side of it and to gain some accurate and first-hand knowledge of the situation, it was decided that I should pay a 'cloak-and-dagger' visit to Poros. Accompanied by Lieutenant Noel Rees, R.N.V.R., who was with us because of his knowledge of Greek and the Greeks, and of course by the indispensable Holloway, I set out in the hydrographic ML commanded by Lieutenant Paisley of the Royal Navy.

Our small craft put to sea in a fresh wind and a lumpy sea and behaved in a fashion much too lively for the comfort of poor Noel Rees. He was used to what has been described as a 'full' life, and now he was having to pay for it. I could see that he was suffering acutely from the ship's motion, but sheer courage or obstinacy kept him down with us in the small and smelly cabin—until the arrival of a surprisingly well-cooked meal sent him in one swift wordless rush to fresh air and darkness on the upper deck. I reckoned that he had done pretty well, at that.

When the meal was finished and the wreckage cleared away, Paisley brought out his charts and we went over the details of our trip. We planned to push on at maximum speed so as to arrive off the minefields outside Poros on the second night. Thanks to the R.A.F. having gained mastery of the air, it was unlikely that we would be spotted by enemy aircraft during daylight hours. The chief danger—and a considerable one—would be mines. The waters we would be passing through were alive with them, and while with accurate navigation and a draft of only about four feet we could hope to sneak through or over the moored ones, we had to bear in mind that after recent sweeping operations there were bound to be hundreds of 'floaters'—mines that had been cut adrift and not sunk. All we could do was to keep our eyes skinned and hope for the best. I remembered Saint Paul's decision in danger in these same waters—to 'cast four anchors out of the stern and pray for the day'. We didn't have that many anchors on this little hooker, and moreover such an operation was not in the *Manual of Seamanship*.

The plan was that when we arrived off Poros Bay, as close in as we could get, our own people ashore would meet us. All being well, Rees and I would go ashore while Paisley would stand off with his ML and come in for us at the same time on the following night. Failing a rendezvous then, he would retire and try again the next night, and if this drew a blank as well he would give up and head for home. This last possibility we touched on only lightly as if it could not possibly happen—it was just that we had to have a plan to cover all eventualities. Well—those were the plans, and pretty simple they were. But it is odd, how when men with any war experience worth remembering discuss these things, they are all of them in their own minds quite sure that nothing at all will turn out as expected. In his own mind each man is working out alternatives and emergency procedures: the plan itself is rarely much more than a peg on which to hang the start of the operation. All the same, we nodded at each other, said Yes, that was how it was all going to be, never voiced a doubt that it would go as simply as it did and always does in discussion.

Paisley stuck a woollen cap on his head, pulled on a scruffy battledress jacket and climbed the small, steep ladder, pausing to have a word with the telegraphist who was wedged in his cramped compartment off the wardroom entrance. I wrapped my watch coat around me and settled down on the spare settee, blew up my Mae West, and slept.

In that close and fuggy atmosphere I woke feeling like a slug under a stone. Holloway was shaking me by the shoulder; he had a cup of strong tea in his other hand and daylight was filtering in through the narrow ports. As I gulped the bitter tea, hoping that it would burn my mouth clean, I saw that Holloway was offering another cup of it to Noel Rees, who was shrouded under a blanket on the other settee. Rees opened one yellowish eye and requested my Cox'n to remove both himself and the tea in double-quick time. Rees did not look very well. Holloway shook his head, sad to see his tea wasted, then he saw that I had just about finished mine, and he changed the cups round. He gave Noel one more glance, then told me loudly that breakfast would be ready in half an hour.

This quite finished my stable mate, who sprang from his blanket and just reached the heads in time. Holloway left, chuckling, managing the ladder easily with two cups and saucers in his left hand and with still a considerable motion on the ship. I stirred myself, shaved, and cleaned my teeth in the small compactum on the for'ard bulkhead. Feeling much better, I climbed up to the bridge and joined Paisley and his Leading Seaman. Paisley could not have had much sleep, but he was in high spirits and puffing strongly at an unusually large pipe. The day was fine and the visibility excellent. Although we were still moving quite a bit, the sea had gone down considerably. We decided to have our breakfast up here on deck—then I would take over, and Paisley could get his head down.

The day passed without incident. I sighted several floating

mines, but none of them close enough to necessitate an altera-
tion of course: I noted them in the log with their positions and
the times. Later Paisley came up from his bunk in the chartroom,
under the bridge, and joined me in tea and toast. I did not know
it, but he had already checked our run and now he told me
that under present conditions we would be up to our position
by midnight. Noel came on deck—he looked a lot better and
managed to drink some tea. We went over the plans again, as
he had not been in a state to hear them the evening before. The
day closed slowly with as fine a sunset as I have ever seen in
the Mediterranean, and as the light failed our lookouts spotted
more mines on all sides—none of them too close, but soon it
would be dark and none of us rejoiced at the thought of pursuing
our course blindly. Silence fell on us as we all concentrated on
a binocular search of the dark sea ahead; the ML thrust her
sharp bow into the small waves and her twin diesels growled
smoothly into the dark. Looking astern, the wake was almost
invisible five yards clear of the ship. The stars came out and the
hours slipped by, then we raised the dark loom of land high
over our port bow. Paisley set our position on the chart, then
altered course for the run-in.

Noel and I went down to the cabin and changed into battledress and dark woollen diving caps. We put on rubber-soled
shoes and, feeling rather self-conscious at this, buckled on web
belts and pistols. In my pockets I stuffed biscuits, some chocolate and a pocket compass; then we checked our watches by the
deck-watch in the charthouse and went back up to the bridge.
I had seen films of this sort of thing, and had an idea that we
ought to have blackened our faces and hands, but although we
discussed the idea we never got around to doing it. For one
thing, we did not know what to use for blackening—I had no
shoe polish with me. The headland loomed tall above us; Paisley
slowed his engines and we crept in with the echo-sounder tick-
ing rhythmically as it recorded the soundings. The Cox'n was
steering from the upper bridge position, and both Lewis guns
were manned. We heard the breakers on each side of the gap,

stopped engines and drifted. The only sound now was that of the sea.

Nor was there a glimmer of any light on that big length and height of shoreline. All dark, just us here with the waves lapping at the ML's hull and farther off the rumble of surf. Everybody jumped when, way off to the north in the direction of Piraeus, the beam of a searchlight shot skyward, hesitated and died abruptly as though someone had made a mistake and pressed the wrong switch. Now, again, nothing at all . . . I could hear Noel's breath, and he was standing several feet away. I couldn't help wondering if something hadn't gone wrong, if our reception committee hadn't fallen foul of the enemy. And then? I refused to consider the question, told myself to relax, that we'd only just arrived and that after three days' steaming there was nothing in a half-hour's delay. All the same, the minutes dragged heavily by. Then, and it came as a surprise, we all heard the sound of the boat's oars. On the port side the Lewis gunner brought his gun to the bearing of the sound and watched keenly over the top of the sights. A moment later a small boat slid out of the dark and slewed round neatly to settle quietly alongside. Noel jumped down to the deck, spoke quiet, excited Greek— treble voices answered him. I peered hard, and saw that the occupants of the boat were children. Three of them. Noel straightened, and told me that this was the planned reception: two of the kids were sons of the Mayor and in their parents' house, the 'cloak-and-dagger' boys were waiting for us. Not one of the children was more than twelve years of age, and the big pistol heavy against my thigh made me feel just plain silly. I was suddenly awfully glad that we had not blackened our faces. Noel went on to explain that the Germans were making one of their routine check-ups, so it had not been possible for any of the men to come. The children, who were in any case quite used to this sort of thing, would not be missed.

Bidding a quick farewell to Paisley and to Holloway—the latter was vigorously making 'V'-signs at me from the after part of the bridge, I supposed as an encouragement—I climbed down into the boat and perched myself on the after thwart, careful to balance the boat as Noel dropped down after me. Without a word the young oarsmen shoved off and rowed us rapidly away into the dark: the ML vanished and we were left entirely in the children's hands.

Skirting the shore close to the entrance we slipped along past fishing boats up on the shingle and bigger caiques at their moorings, until something loomed up ahead. It was a wooden jetty, and Noel interpreted a muttered warning to 'mind our heads'. Abruptly our small craft swung round between the piles under the jetty. Here it was all pitch black, and there was a stink of seaweed and fish. The kids tied their boat up, and just as I was wondering where we went from here a small hand grabbed one of mine and guided me to a ladder. I hauled myself up it and emerged on the back end of the jetty under the shade of an irregular white wall. Noel joined me and we set off behind the youngsters, shuffling along close to the wall and round a corner. Here there were coils of rope and a mass of nets: our guides crawled under the nets and we followed to squat there in the dark like so many boy scouts playing cops-and-robbers. There was a lot of rapid Greek, all in whispers, and Noel told me that we were to stay here until the German patrol passed. Then we would know that the check-up was over, and it would be safe to carry on into the village.

We didn't have to wait long. Soon I heard the sound of tyres on gravel, and the squeak of pedals. Peering out, I saw the bicycle patrol passing, eight of them riding in pairs behind a leader, with automatic rifles slung across their backs. As they vanished round the corner we crept out from under our nets and followed the children along the edge of the gravel path. Without meeting a soul we filed quietly into the village, keeping on the shadowed side of the narrow streets. On each side were low, whitewashed dwellings, a small vineyard to each of them. Presently we came to a more pretentious homestead which Noel whispered to me was the Mayor's. Here we turned in, and in the large, stone-floored kitchen we were greeted courteously

by the principal citizen and his wife. Sitting round the table were
a number of scruffy-looking ruffians wearing beards and British
battledress—one of them sported R.N.V.R. stripes on his shoulders. This was a good-looking Jewish lad who would have
passed for a Greek anywhere—he was an accomplished linguist
and had been doing valuable undercover work in the islands for
some months past. While Noel lost himself in a torrent of
Greek conversation with the others of the party, I got down to
business with the R.N.V.R. Lieutenant. He had been questioning various fishermen and sponge-divers who had been hanging
around the docks in Piraeus and Leontas, and he had plenty to
tell me.

The gist of it was that S.S. demolition teams had scuttled
several ships alongside the quays, then blown in the quay walls
and covered the wrecks with rock and rubble. Most of the cranes
and other installations had been destroyed, but the big 100-ton
floating pontoon crane had been sunk by her own Greek crew,
and they had arranged things so that salvage would not be difficult. But there was one particularly worrying bit of news—
the German experts had manœuvred the big floating dock into
the gap between Leontas and the outer harbour, skilfully capsized it and sunk it upside down! That would indeed present us
with some headaches, and I was glad to be forewarned.

The steep-sided Corinth Canal had been blocked with trucks
and locomotives, and some parts of its sides had been blown in.
In the entrance they had scuttled a small motor-ship, but here
again the sinking had been done in such a way that my informant
thought her refloating would be pretty simple. He added that
the power station was to be destroyed just before the evacua-
tion, but the Greek underground boys had a counter-plan to
attack the S.S. when they started operations. With any luck
the power station might be saved.

Delighted to have all this first-hand and up-to-date intelligence,
I did full justice to the simple meal which was now set out on
the table together with several bottles of home-produced wine
which was most drinkable. Noel told me that while there would

be no more routine visits by the Germans until next morning, a surprise raid was always on the cards, particularly now that the garrison were on edge and showing signs of nerves. For this reason, we were to remain hidden until the following night. The two of us were led out to our sleeping quarters: as we crossed the farmyard I realised that we were heading for a large pig-sty, and sure enough we were ushered in among the grunting, honking swine. Our guide crawled into the covered section, which was occupied by a huge sow, removed a section of the boards at the back and indicated to us that we were expected to climb through. I squeezed myself into the dark aperture and found a small cubby-hole lined with empty but odorous sacks. Here we were to spend the next twenty-four hours. At any rate, it was warm. We took off our belts and pistols, made pillows of our jackets and disposed ourselves as comfortably as possible for sleep. Our companions on the other side of the wooden partition made the most awful racket, wheezing and snoring. The atmosphere was one of pigs and garlic, but I suppose we were very tired, and both of us slept soundly throughout the night. When I awoke, sunlight was filtering in between the split boards, my watch showed the time as eight-thirty, and I was feeling hungry. I woke Noel and we shared some chocolate and had a drink from our water bottles. Then we relaxed in silence and I turned my mind to the problem of raising an upside-down dock: it might well be the trickiest job I had yet faced.

Presently someone came into the sty to attend to the pigs, and started muttering to himself—actually the man was talking to Noel, but it sounded as if he was only grousing at the animals. Then the boards were lifted and in came our breakfast—slabs of dark bread, looking rather like pancakes, pungent garlic polony and a can of warm goat's milk. Not very appetising, but we dealt with it out of sheer hunger. Noel told me that there had been one inspection, at dawn, while we were asleep, and that there would be no other visits until sunset or later. To pass the time we talked in whispers, discussing the dinner we would have at the Bretagne once the landings were over—

knowing Noel and his connections in Greece, I was prepared to
bet that it would be a party to remember. Next to us, all the
time, the sow was carrying out her matronly duties to the litter,
and until it was over the noise was terrific. The hours passed,
and I watched the changing angle of the sun's rays as they slanted
in through the cracks over our heads. Soon after noon we were
given more food—a delicious grilled fish, garlic-infused salad and
a bottle of that pleasant wine. Probably as a result of that wine
and the warm, stuffy atmosphere I fell fast asleep again, and
when I awoke with Noel shaking my shoulder the luminous
hands of my wristwatch pointed to eleven o'clock. Noel had
been warned that the patrol had arrived, and the children were
in the sty keeping the pigs quiet. I did not quite understand why
this should have been necessary, or for that matter how they
did it—perhaps scratching the animals' backs, or something of
that sort. We lay there in the dark, listening with our pistols in
our hands. Voices and laughter indicated that the Germans were
in a cheerful mood. We heard heavy boots on the flagstones
outside the sty, then a muttered order and the rattle of bicycles
as the patrol mounted and rode away out of the yard. At about
eleven-fifteen we were let out into astonishingly fresh air, and
what a luxury it was to stand upright! We were taken into the
kitchen to bid farewell to our hosts. The 'cloak-and-dagger' boys
had gone about their business, but the R.N.V.R. Lieutenant had
left a message to the effect that he would 'see us in Athens'.
We hoped he was right.

The children led us back to the net sheds; we were anxious
to get clear before the patrol came back, and we lost no time in
getting aboard the little rowing boat and pulling out seawards.
We rowed out very quietly through the entrance; the land's
bulk towered across the stars behind us, and trailing my hand
in the water I found that it was almost milk warm.

Just before midnight, well out to the pick-up position, Noel
stopped our young rowers. We waited, listening, and almost
immediately heard the rumble of engines closing from seaward
—it had been as simple as that! Paisley was right on time, to

the minute. I handed the rest of my chocolate and biscuits to the youngsters, and Noel told them in Greek how well they had done and what fine chaps they were. The ML showed up out of the gloom and lost way, drifting to a stop as we pulled alongside and climbed aboard. They all seemed very pleased to see us, and Paisley passed a canvas-wrapped bundle down to the children; it held tobacco, cigarettes and bully beef, a present for the Mayor. Turning, we headed out to sea at our best speed.

Over hot drinks and cigarettes we told Paisley about our experiences ashore. He had filled in the time by taking his small ship down to Milos, but he had not closed the island when he had spotted one of our sweepers under '88' fire from the shore. He told us that he had never seen so many floating mines as he had that day: to use his own words, 'The bloody ocean was lousy with them!'

Three days later we secured alongside the jetty at Ras-el-Tin; the Duty Officer 'phoned for my jeep and with Holloway driving like a madman Noel and I hurried to Navy House to make our report to Sir Bernard Rawlings. It was all taken down by a Wren officer, to be included in the planning files for 'Operation Manna'. And then off again in the jeep—for a hot bath to chase away the haunting smell of pigs.

*　　　*　　　*

A couple of days later I was sitting in my office in the dockyard when the signal arrived for all ships to come to immediate notice for sea. I ordered our parties to embark at once, and made a round of our Salvage Units to ensure that there had been no slips in the drill. All was well. The main advance party was in *Barclose*, a boom defence vessel which we used as a lifting craft, and secondary groups were crowding out the accommodation in *Captive*, *Prince Salvor* and *Salvestor*. With my Senior Engineer Officer, and of course, Holloway, I embarked in the cruiser *Black Prince*. That afternoon we put to sea with the Fleet Sweepers and Destroyers leading *Ajax* and the 15th Cruiser

Squadron, followed by the whole invasion fleet, down the Great Pass and heading north. 'Operation Manna' was at last under way.

Right in the middle of the fleet, the old Greek armoured cruiser *Averof* lumbered along, belching clouds of heavy greasy smoke from her funnels. Irate signals from the Admiral only seemed to make the smoke thicker, and as darkness fell that ancient Greek was still befouling an otherwise clear sky.

Black Prince's wardroom and all the adjacent alleyways were crowded with stretcher beds and heaps of Army kit. The wardroom itself was packed with naval and military passengers as well as many more war correspondents than I should have thought necessary. They were being entertained by those of the ship's company who had no watches to keep. The roar of conversation and the pall of tobacco smoke decided me against seeking refreshment. I went forward, and climbed a ladder into the bridge superstructure, located the Navigator and introduced myself. He took me up on to the cruiser's bridge, and pointed out the position of my small flotilla in the convoy disposition.

He told me, too, that he had had my gear put in his cabin in the lower flat. It was kind of him, and delightful to know that I would have a peaceful night instead of having to doss down on one of those wretched little stretchers. After a turn on deck I went down to the wardroom for dinner, then sent a messenger to find Holloway—I found he had already discovered my billet, turned back the Navigator's bed and spread out my pyjamas! When he turned up a few minutes later I asked him if he had been looked after and he assured me that he was comfortably settled in the Leading Hand's Mess. Some hours later I was reading in bed when I heard a knock on the bulkhead, and here he was again, bringing me a large enamel mug of cocoa laced, so my nose told me, with rum. Holloway had obviously made himself well at home, as a proper sailor should.

In the morning, after a shower and a good breakfast, I was up on the signal bridge in time to see the first floating mine explode after it had been hit by a well-directed burst of Oerlikon shells from the mounting below me manned by Marines. The mines now appeared thick and fast and most of them went up in columns of water and clouds of brown smoke that drifted back down the lines of ships. As the sweepers out ahead cut mines loose from their moorings the rattle of Oerlikons and Point Fives was almost continuous, punctuated by the crashes of explosions as one after another those floating horrors were disposed of.

By afternoon we were just south of Poros. We were coming up to a turn in the swept channel when the leading sweeper, *Clinton*, caught a mine under her bow and stopped, down by the head, with vented steam feathering from her funnel steam pipes. There had been so many bangs all day that it was a minute or two before we realised what had happened. We were not given much time to get over the shock, either, because almost immediately *Clinton*'s next astern, the *Larne*, reeled to an immense explosion next to her boiler room, and in the same moment a Greek ML literally vanished in a cloud of splinters. As I hurried up the ladder into the bridge space I heard another crash astern of us, and turning I was just in time to see *Petronella*, a water carrier, sink like a stone leaving nothing but oily debris and some light wreckage to mark the spot where she had gone down. I reported to the Captain, who told me that they were detaching two of my ships to take care of the mined sweepers and that a launch was coming to transfer me to *Barclose*.

Orders from the Admiral turned the rest of the fleet back on its tracks to wait until a more effective sweep had been carried out ahead. This was completed without further casualties, and I was soon on my way in the launch to join *Barclose*, which was waiting in the channel. I boarded her, went straight up to the bridge and told the C.O. to pick his way through the floaters and close the *Clinton*. I signalled *Salvestor* to get the crippled *Larne* in tow and then to beach her in Poros Bay. Meanwhile we threaded an erratic course between the mines and got ourselves lashed alongside the *Clinton*. Thanks to the fact that her crew had been on deck closed up to sweeping stations, she had

Photograph by S. A. Public Relations Film and Photographic Unit

H.M.S. *Larne* beached and listing in Poros Bay after being mined. H.M. Salvage Ship
Salvestor is seen in the background.

no casualties other than superficial injuries to a few men who
had been in the way of the blast, but she was well down for'ard,
floating on her battened-down upper mess deck and there was
an enormous hole under her starboard bow. Her Damage Control
party were already busy shoring decks and bulkheads. It was
amazing to see how this light ship had survived the force of
that violent explosion. With *Barclose* tight up alongside, we
kept ourselves in position and clear of the floating mines until
the fleet turned again. Then we followed in the broad pattern
of their wakes, and once in the anchorage I secured both ships
for the night. By morning we had got *Clinton* into a reasonably
safe condition so that at least she would stay afloat, and working
our way into the outer harbour we moored her to await repairs.
Meanwhile, *Salvestor* had managed to get her lame duck into
Poros Bay and had secured her there with her bows up on
the beach.

Now I borrowed Paisley's hydrographic ML, and made a
quick survey of the outer and inner harbours. What that young
man had told me in the farm kitchen was dead right—the
upside-down dock effectively blocked the passage into Leontas
harbour, and the channel was closed to ships of any size. First
priority was to clear this entrance, and for all the advance warning, I still had little idea as to how we ought to go about it.

Moving on around the port, I visited the small dry dock.
They had sunk its caisson inside it together with a couple of
lorries and a crane. These would not present much difficulty,
but it was a waste of time.

Next to this dock was the power station. It was hardly damaged at all, and around it and on the quay lay the bodies of the
SS. demolition squads. The underground resisters had carried
out their intentions with great efficiency. I was filled with respect for these courageous fisherfolk and tradesmen, all small
people who stood to win no medals as they fought their silent,
dangerous war. I wondered what casualties they had suffered in
this quick, fierce battle.

Now we had to face the problem of mines inside the harbour

areas. We would have to work down there, clearing the wrecks that had been scuttled alongside the quays, but until the bottom had been cleared of mines, every dive would be intensely dangerous. Yet with the many different types of mine which we knew to have been laid inside the port, normal sweeping methods would take more time than we could afford to waste. I determined to put into action a method we had worked out in theory just before the start of the operation, and for permission to adopt a very unorthodox procedure I requested an interview with the Senior Naval Officer, Captain Campbell, and the Commander, Mine Sweeping.

At Naval Headquarters I outlined to these two officers the plan I had in mind. Briefly, it was to mark or disarm the mines by direct diver approach. We would have every diver I could muster carry out an organised search of the harbour bottom, and when we met a type of mine we could not disarm under water we would mark it with a pellet buoy to simplify the work of the sweepers. Then we would be able to get on with our own work at speed and in reasonable safety.

While I spoke, I realised that my proposals were causing alarm to the Commander M.S. By the time I had finished he was purple in the face and his mouth was opening and closing as if he had a lot to say and was unable to find his voice. He turned to Captain Campbell with a gesture indicating plainly that in his opinion I was either drunk or mad. But Campbell, who had more than once taken a gunboat inside Benghazi harbour to shell the startled Italian forces there, was not opposed to the idea at all. In fact, I could see, much to my relief, that it definitely appealed to him. It was not a new idea, although it had been decried by many people, that the closer one could get to a source of danger the more effectively and safely it could be dealt with. In any case it would speed up the search for mines that were virtually unsweepable by normal methods and it would permit us to get on with our wreck clearance with the minimum of delay.

After a certain amount of discussion it was decided with one abstention that we should proceed forthwith to tackle the mines

Photograph by S. A. Public Relations Film and Photographic Unit

Salvestor stern-on to the damaged *Larne.* On the right of the picture a mammoth steel patch is being prefabricated to be welded on to the hole in the *Larne's* boiler room.

where they lay. I went back to the harbour to give the necessary orders. My fellows were delighted. Now they had a chance to show the rest of the Navy what they were made of!

Soon we had all the craft in position and the divers went down to start looking for trouble. One by one they signalled their finds. Primers and detonators were removed and any unknown or complicated types of mine were buoyed off. Many of them were the German 'O' type, which were fired by the change in pressure as a ship passes over, and we had been well briefed by the experts on the method of rendering them safe. It took us three days altogether before the job was done and the surface of the harbour was dotted with coloured pellets. Then one day's sweeping cleared the entire area and the worst task of all was my own—compiling long and detailed reports of what had been done. But now mine disposal by diver was established as not only possible but also highly effective, as it was to prove itself over and over again in the mine-infested waters from Cherbourg to the German ports. Volunteers were trained and back-room boys devised special equipment; but our early success using ordinary diving gear, guided by faith and protected by nothing but sheer good luck, remained for long a source of pride to us. Not one man was lost, and there were no incidents apart from occasional heart attacks when something peculiar happened.

But mines kept turning up in the most unlikely places, and we had to move warily under water. It was still something of a surprise, though, when I had an urgent signal from the unlucky *Clinton* to the effect that she had a moored mine tangled up in her anchor cable. We rushed over and went down close to her bow. We did not have to look far. The mine's wire mooring had several turns around the anchor cable, and the mine itself, swinging like a balloon on the short free end of wire, was almost scraping its deadly horns on the ship's hull plating. The only possible explanation was that when we dropped anchor outside in the channel, we had picked up the mine and mooring and hove it in when *Clinton* weighed anchor and towed the whole lot into harbour with us.

It was a miracle that when we dropped anchor the second time we hadn't tweaked a horn and sent the mine and *Clinton*'s bows sky high. As it was, sorting out the tangle would be a tricky job. I quickly grew to loathe the sight of that weed-covered, barnacled sphere. There was quite a bit of movement on the sea, here in the outer harbour, and at any minute the brute might swing the wrong way and then they could send for a new salvage officer. But eventually, after some gruelling hours during which we nearly died of fright several times, we managed to get a line from the mine out to a launch. The launch took the strain while we cut through the mooring wire close to the sweeper's anchor chain. As the last strand of wire parted the mine suddenly bobbed away and up to the surface, clear of the ship. The launch towed it out into the channel where it could be exploded in safety, and I felt ten years older. But now work on the *Clinton* could go ahead. Down in Poros Bay, *Salvestor* was busy prefabricating a massive steel patch for her wound.

To assist in the clearance of the port I recruited a number of Greek sponge-divers, who took their pay part in cash and part in rations. Food ships were arriving daily now, and an earlier danger of famine was fading rapidly as these cargoes of victuals streamed ashore for distribution. Yet the political situation was far from settled. Trouble was brewing, and all of us knew it. But that was not my concern, and as fast as we could we forged ahead with port clearance and salvage. The first obstruction to be tackled was that capsized dock, and here, while we were making the first surveys, Petty Officer Devonshire came near to losing his life. Only a caution born of long experience saved him.

He was crawling along the uppermost plating when he almost blundered up against a thin wire that seemed to be stretched right across the dock. He stopped dead, almost losing his balance and falling across the wire. Then, wary of booby traps, he slipped carefully over the side and traced the wire downwards. It led him to a large canister and was itself attached to a pull-type detonator. He called me on the telephone and told me about it.

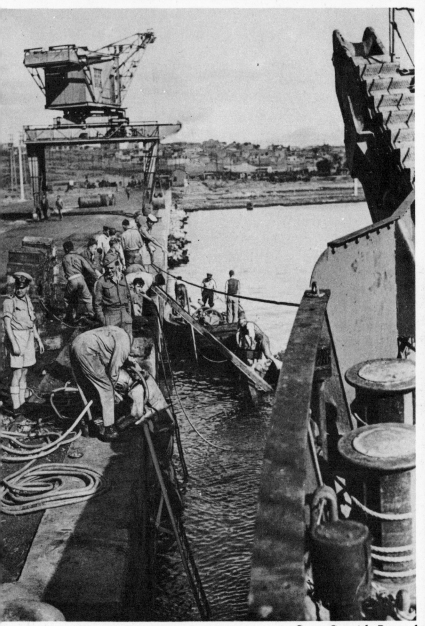

Piraeus. The author embarks on a descent to the bottom of the
harbour on an expedition to disarm mines infesting the port.

I thought his voice sounded a bit shaky, but I told him to climb up again and trace the wire across to the other side. Over the 'phone I could hear him grunting and cursing as he dragged himself across the slimy plates, keeping the wire in view but not getting any closer to it than he had to. I watched over the side and saw his bubbles rising from the far side of the dock: then he told me that he was going over that side, and a few moments later he called again.

'Yes, Sir—here's the other bastard!' There was a huge demolition charge on each side of the dock, and one pull at that wire anywhere along its length would have blown the lot, including Devonshire, to Kingdom Come.

We made up two wire ropes with eyes at their ends and sent them down. Devonshire looped them over the two canisters, and I called him to come up. As soon as he was inboard we carefully took up the slack on the wires, passed the ends to our ML and got them turned-up on the after towing bollard. Then we started towing, towards the harbour entrance, but we had hardly made a hundred yards' progress before both charges went off on the bottom raising tall pillars of water astern of us. It was as well that Devonshire had seen that wire when he did.

But the dock itself turned out to be much less of a problem than I had anticipated. Devonshire and I were down on the bottom seventy feet below the surface, and the simplicity of it struck both of us so that when we came up and our helmets were whipped off by the attendants we started to talk immediately. After seeing that most of the dock's sides was built of open lattice-work steel and not the usual closed-tank construction, we both had had the same idea. If we blasted the lattice-work the whole dock would collapse on to itself and there would be at least forty-five feet of water clear over the top of the wreckage—quite enough water for any ship that needed to use the inner harbour. And so it worked out. We made up long charges of explosive-packed hose, and divers threaded them in and out of the girders on both sides. Detonators were fitted, and from them a cable was led up to the surface. From a launch, at a safe distance, I pressed down on the plunger handles. The whole surface of the entrance heaved, erupted as though from a submarine volcano, and the stink of explosive fumes swept past us. When all the fuss had died down we worked our way over the wreck, sounding with a lead line, and we found that the least depth was forty feet. That was enough, and I was happy to go ashore and report to Captain Campbell that the passage was clear.

*　　*　　*

Meanwhile, our rugged lifting craft, the *Barclose*, was doing valiant work all over the Piraeus. With her powerful gear she could tackle just about anything and she certainly performed in many ways that her builders had never intended. Her captain had been a trawler skipper on the English east coast, and in spite of his present rank of Lieutenant R.N.R. he had shed none of his independent attitude to life and more especially to Naval customs and regulations. He was a law unto himself, but he was such a cheerful, engaging sort of chap that the many Powers which ruled us acquired the habit of turning blind eyes to his frequent lapses from normal Service behaviour. Really, they could not have done much else because everyone appreciated his magnificent seamanship and they realised that it would be a waste of time to try making him behave like a naval officer. He handled his massive and clumsy ship as if it were a small launch.

As tenders to the 15th Cruiser Squadron we drew some of our stores from the flagship, and one morning I signalled *Barclose* to arrange for their collection. I meant, of course, that she was to send a boat for them. For some reason which he never afterwards explained, the skipper took it into his head to fetch the stores in person: *Barclose* swept out of port, and ran down the Fleet at full speed. Turning in a wide sweep and still moving fast, she headed for the flagship's gangway. Our skipper ignored frenzied hails from the cruiser's Officer-of-the-Watch, put his engines hard astern at just the right moment and stopped dead alongside the Admiral's own gangway without removing one splinter from it. Yelling for the lines to be made fast, he hopped nimbly on to the gangway and shambled up to the quarterdeck, where he spotted the Captain in conversation with the Commander and made a bee-line for them. He was in his shirt-sleeves and braces. The two officers were goggling at this apparition, when Admiral Mansfield, who had chosen this moment to come up on deck for a look at the weather, came face to face with our boom ship hero. The Admiral smiled.

'Good morning, Captain!' The skipper grinned broadly and touched his greasy cap with one finger.

'Morning, Guv'nor.' The Admiral kept a straight face, and asked, easily, 'Can we be of any assistance to you?' My old friend nodded violently.

'I 'ope so, Mate! I been sent for the bloody stores, baccy an' fags like.' He pulled a crumpled sheet of paper out of a pocket in his trousers, smoothed it out in his big hands. 'I got a list 'ere, Mate.' He held it out to the Admiral, who took it without hesitation and passed it to the horrified Commander. 'My Supply Officer'll take care of that for you,' he told the Skipper. 'While you're waiting, perhaps you'll take a little wine with me?' Admiral Mansfield grasped one hairy arm and led its owner to the companion-way leading down to his quarters.

Later, *Barclose* returned at her usual speed—flat out—and her captain came over to tell me how nice the Admiral had been to him. 'Decent geezer, that!—Gave me a couple o' gins. . . .' That afternoon I had a signal inviting me to join a dinner party in the flagship and when the port was going round for a second time the Admiral spoke to me down the length of the table, across a sudden silence.

'Oh, Keeble. D'you get the—er—bloody stores all right?' A roar of laughter greeted his question. The story had already gone round the Fleet and was widely appreciated. Both Admiral and Skipper came out of it well, and *Barclose* had become legendary in a day.

*　　*　　*

First thing next morning, I was summoned to report to Admiral Rawlings. He informed me that I was required urgently in Alexandria and would be taking passage with him and his staff in *Ajax*, sailing that afternoon. I whipped round quickly, seeing that things were organised and would carry on according to plan while I was away. Then I collected the reports which I had compiled and which would be wanted in Alexandria, rounded up my gear and joined the cruiser in the anchorage. An hour later she shortened-in, and soon after tea we weighed anchor and headed off at twenty-two knots.

Now that we were at sea, Admiral Rawlings was prepared to be more explicit. He called me to him on the quarterdeck where I matched his pacing (up and down and a neat turn at each end without changing step) while he told me that the battleship *Valiant* was in serious trouble in Trincomalee, Ceylon. The floating dock in which she had been berthed had collapsed under her and caused considerable damage to her screws and rudders. The *Valiant* was urgently required for our new offensive against the Japanese, and to get her operational again was a matter of the highest priority.

XI. SURGEONS TO 'VALIANT'

H.M.S. *VALIANT* was one of a class of five battleships which were laid down before the First World War and re-designed and modernised just before the Second. She was the same *Valiant*, of course, that suffered at the hands of those Italian human torpedoes in Alexandria at the time when I first entered this salvage story. From that savage attack she had emerged with comparatively light damage and in fact she had right through the war borne something of a charmed life, often damaged and even more frequently near-missed but never for very long out of the fighting line. Now, through no effort of any enemy, she had taken the hardest knock of her career—and in dock, of all places!

The dock in Trincomalee was one of the Admiralty's latest and heaviest floating units. It was there to handle the capital ships which were now being deployed for offensive action against the Japanese in the Eastern sectors of the Indian Ocean. Regular docking was a necessity, partly for routine inspection and main-tenance of rudders, propellers and other underwater fittings, and also because of the rapid marine growth in tropical waters. Weed and barnacles on the underwater hulls of ships built up

at such a rate that, unless they were docked and scraped, every
month in the water meant a loss of about one knot in speed.
Some idea of the profusion of this marine growth may be
gathered from the fact that a man could stand on the edge of
a crust of barnacles and coral sported by two of the depot ships
in Alex Harbour. So, taking her turn with the rest of the Eastern
Fleet, the 36,000-ton battleship had been raised in the dock for
a timely trim and shampoo.

The dock that was to take *Valiant* was similar to AFD-24 in
general construction. So that it could be towed easily from one
place to another it was built in three separate sections, the larger
having two-thirds of the buoyancy capacity and the two detach-
able end-sections making up, between them, the other third.
Under tow, the ends were docked inside the main, central part,
thus making a handy package for the tugs to handle. When a
ship is to be docked the dock is flooded down by its ballast tanks
for the ship to enter, then the tanks are pumped to raise dock
and ship out of water. The flooding and pumping controls are
in three separate groups, one for each section, on the manifold
control board which is under the eye of the dock master in his
control room.

Work on *Valiant* was finished late one evening and that night
it was intended to flood the dock down so that the battleship
could vacate it at first light. The vents were opened, and the
dock began to sink. But not all of it—the vents in the two end-
sections stayed shut, and with the massive weight of the centre
part flooding down, those two ends were being dragged down
under terrific strain against their full buoyancy. Something had
to give way. Before anyone realised what was happening the
fore and after ends ripped off with a noise like the coming of
Judgement. They crashed up powerfully under the battleship's
bow and stern, and the centre section of the dock, badly holed,
sank like a stone into nearly a hundred and eighty feet of water.
Eyewitnesses later told me that the scene resembled some inferno
as the huge ship rolled and bounced with the wreckage of the
dock fittings all around her. Considering the weights and forces

which had been so suddenly released, it is amazing that *Valiant* suffered as little damage as she did. She was making water for'ard, and the steering flat had taken it hard, but these troubles were quickly and easily controlled. The real damage was to her rudders and screws. One of the twin rudders was set up by several feet and the other damaged, and the inner propeller shafts jammed solid so that they could not be turned. At daybreak divers went down and found that both inner shafts were out of alignment, the screws were damaged and the huge cast steel 'A'-brackets which gripped and supported the propeller-shaft housing were fractured and distorted. Both inner screws would be out of action until the ship could be docked again, and the nearest dock big enough to take *Valiant* was now at Alexandria.

It was a sad blow to her captain, officers and men, all of them keyed up as they had been for the forthcoming operations against the Japanese. After the Naval Constructors had conferred, it looked as if *Valiant* would be out of the war for good.

Her sea trials off Trincomalee had shown that when the outer screws were worked up to even moderate revolutions the drag of the useless inner propellers caused heavy vibration in the turbine space. The best speed she could make without actually shaking herself to pieces was about eight knots, and at that, with one of her twin rudders altogether out of action and the other only temporarily repaired, she responded so reluctantly to steering that she was a danger to herself. Everyone began to believe the Constructors. But she was of such importance as a bombard-ment unit that it was decided to get her over to Suez and attempt the passage of the Canal, on a short-cut to docking in England. Escorted by destroyers, *Valiant* made a snaky course at an average speed of less than eight knots, and it was early in October when she limped into Suez Bay and dropped an anchor into the grey, stinking mud. And here, only three hundred miles from Alex-andria's dry dock, further manœuvring trials demonstrated that she could not possibly manage the narrow waterway.

High-level discussions took place in Cairo and in Alex between the C-in-C, Sir John Cunningham, who had come over from

Malta, Sir Bernard Rawlings and Vice-Admiral Tennant, who
was about to relieve him. They, with Sir Bruce Fraser, on his
way to the Far Eastern Command, consulted long and anxiously
with the Naval Constructors. It was Sir Bernard Rawlings who
suggested that I might produce the answer with underwater engineering, and thus it was that I arrived in Alexandria and was
summoned to meet the new Flag Officer Levant and Eastern
Mediterranean, and the Fleet Engineer Officer, Captain Murray.
We talked the thing over and when I was asked for my views
I told them that my own plan would be to cut away the dead-
wood—to remove all the damaged inner part, shafts and the
'A'-brackets that held them, so that the ship could run on her
outer shafts alone.

'Certainly,' Captain Murray nodded, 'but—er—*how*?' I drew
a deep breath, expecting opposition. After all, it had never been
done before, and I had no absolute certainty that it was going
to be done now.

'By cutting the shafts close up to the glands, and then cutting
through the "A"-brackets and dropping the whole lot on to the
bottom. If we try to sling them off we'd run a grave risk of
damaging the outer shafts.'

I told them that only two divers would be needed, myself
and one other, and that if the job could be done at all—we
could not be sure of that until we got down to it—a week ought
to see it through.

The upshot of this discussion was that the Admiral passed me
on to Cairo, with his official approval of my suggestions. Before
I left, I went down to my dockyard office and sent for Petty
Officer Nichols. With an underwater cutting torch in his hands,
Nichols was something not far short of a genius. For some time
he and I had been assembling our own sets of cutting equipment,
and by combining the British and Italian types we had succeeded
in eliminating most of the usual faults, and had already pulled
off some very useful and difficult jobs below the surface. Often
we had discussed the possibilities of boosting the torch's capacity
enough for it to cope with heavy sections—now we would have

a chance to put our theories to the test. I explained the problems ahead of us, and the Petty Officer's usually poker face broke into a wide grin. I told him to get busy perfecting the modified torch and to have a three-ton lorry ready loaded with all the gear we might need. Beside himself with enthusiasm and delight, he dashed off to commence his preparations. Nichols's enthusiasm matched his confidence.

*   *   *

I was delighted to hear that for my trip to Cairo I was to have the use of the Admiral's own aircraft. Holloway drove me over to the Fleet Air Arm base, H.M.S. *Grebe*, as it was called, and I found the neat little Cessna and its Air Arm pilot waiting for me. I was engrossed in my own thoughts and in worries, too, as to how my ideas would be received at this Cairo meeting, and I hardly realised we were airborne before we were losing height over the green patchwork fields of the delta with the pyramids on the horizon and the sandy runway of Heliopolis sweeping up to meet us. Still preoccupied, and definitely nervous, I humped my bag into the waiting staff car and was driven off into the closely-guarded HQ area. Somebody gave me a cup of tea, and then all too soon, for I was still revolving my arguments in my mind, I was pushed into a large office containing the Commander-in-Chief, Admiral Sir John Cunningham, Admiral Sir Bruce Fraser, and two Naval Constructors who had flown in from Ceylon. These gentlemen wasted no time, but opened up at once with a detailed description of the damage to the battleship and its effect on her range and performance. They made it sound very depressing. My confidence dwindled and in front of the two famous admirals I began to feel very small and uncertain indeed. But I realised that if I did not make my attack now I would be at the mercy of the Constructors, so I swallowed hard and began to talk. It was my own voice but to me it sounded weak and far away. I outlined my proposals and when I had finished the Senior Constructor fixed me with a coldly merciless eye and said that my solution would be highly satisfactory—if only it could be regarded as feasible! They had considered it, he went on, in Trincomalee, but they were then and now of the opinion that to cut such heavy sections of metal under water was beyond the capabilities of tools and men. It had never been done before. In fact, the old argument! The Commander-in-Chief went on smoking and Sir Bruce Fraser finished a doodle on his blotting pad and gave me an encouraging smile. It made me feel rather better, and I hurriedly explained how we ourselves had developed the technique of submarine cutting, and how with several years' constant practice and our own modified torches we had, in my opinion, a very good chance of doing this job.

The C-in-C looked up to ask me how long I would need just to ascertain whether or not we could do it. I told him that a couple of hours on the job would prove it one way or another, and added that with adequate supplies of oxygen and hydrogen bottles we could expect to complete the whole thing inside seven days.

Calmly Admiral Cunningham asked me: 'When can you start?'

'Within a day, Sir. I have a truck ready loaded in Alexandria, and my Petty Officer Diver is standing by.' At this Admiral Fraser smiled again, and a minute later I was dismissed with orders to go ahead. To give the Constructors their due, I must admit that they were trying hard to look hopeful.

*   *   *

A telephone call to Navy House in Alexandria resulted in my being given permission to retain the Admiral's aeroplane so that it could take me on to Suez, and next morning we took off after an early breakfast. I had given orders for Nichols to come down with the truck, and with twelve hours' start he could be expected to arrive within a few hours of me. There was a car waiting at the Suez R.A.F. station. It decanted me on the pavement by the wooden jetty opposite the French Club in Port Tewfik, and there, alongside the jetty, waited a picket boat from the *Valiant*. Ten minutes later I climbed the gangway to the battleship's quarterdeck. Not only had Nichols arrived ahead of me—he had driven hard all night after leaving within ten minutes of my message reaching him—but he was already at work, with the ship's divers, rigging the pumps and diving gear in the launch alongside under the *Valiant*'s stern. I was welcomed by the Commander and by Captain O'Donnell, D.S.O., R.N., and in the Captain's cabin I outlined for the third time what we planned to do. I was getting just about word-perfect, and I was beginning to convince myself that it would be as easy as I had been trying to make it sound. The Captain told his Engineer Commander to give me all the assistance I might need in the way of Engine Room Artificers and stores, and we made a signal to the local barrage balloon depot asking for all the hydrogen bottles they could spare. From the sappers we called for supplies of oxygen. In a very short time we had all we needed, and I was finding such a high degree of co-operation almost embarrassing. It reached the limit when I asked Captain O'Donnell, who was about to leave for discussions in Cairo, if Petty Officer Nichols could be berthed somewhere on his own where he would get the maximum advantage from such short rest periods as we would be able to allow ourselves between spells under water. It would be murderously hard work, and a berth in a communal mess plus the inevitable hospitality of the lower deck was something to be avoided. Captain O'Donnell immediately offered his own sea cabin on the bridge. When I told Nichols of this, he stared at me in amazement and his only comment was the single word, 'Blimey!'

As the boat-loads of gas bottles arrived from the shore, the E.R.A.s positioned them on the quarterdeck and we ganged them in series, controlled by manifolds. I showed the artificers how to control and vary the pressure in response to the diver's instructions over the telephone. To the 'phone set in the diving launch we connected a relay loudspeaker which was set up on the battleship's quarterdeck, close to what had already become known as the Gas Works. Meanwhile, sailors were rigging heavy wires over the stern and around the inner shafts to keep them from striking the outers when, as we hoped, they plunged away to the sea bed a hundred feet below. I walked over to the guard rail and looked down. Nichols, ready dressed for the first dive, was sitting in the launch. I went down the gangway and joined him, squatting on the thwart while I gave him his instructions. He was to get himself comfortable as close as he could get to the shaft gland, where the shaft entered the ship's hull, and let us know when he was ready for the torch to be lowered to him. When he had made a deep cut and was sure that he could burn right through into the inner bore he was to report to me so that I could signal Cairo that we were going ahead. They would be waiting anxiously for that news.

The underwater cutting torch we were going to use was similar to that used for cutting steel on the surface, but it was a bulkier tool and it used oxygen gas with hydrogen instead of acetylene. Acetylene has a tendency to detonate under great pressure and our mixture would serve us better. Apart from this, our torch had embodied in it an extra sleeve orifice on the outside through which air at a low pressure could be fed to form a sort of air shield round the flame. Without this jet of air protecting it the flame would have been nipped out as soon as lit by the pressure of water. But with fluctuating pressures calling for constant adjustment of gas pressures up top a diver had to be constantly alert when he was using the tool. Sometimes, as we had learnt often to our cost, the thing would blow back, transforming the torch instantaneously into a red-hot menace which the diver could only drop or lose his hands in cinders. Then it would pop out, and we would have all the tedious business of pulling it up and relighting it. Then again, wartime gas bottles varied both as to fittings and pressures. One way and another, this undoubtedly valuable tool could be as temperamental as an opera star and a good deal more dangerous. We had the more advanced oxy-electric cutter, of course, but in its early form this too had been known to put up some quite peculiar performances, extremely disturbing to a diver. In any case, it was limited in its depth of cut.

Yet, in Nichols's adept hands, these temperamental weapons behaved like lambs. His skill would be a major contribution to the success we hoped for.

*   *   *

The attendants dropped the helmet over Nichols's head, and I climbed the ladder to the quarterdeck to get the torch adjusted, ready to be lowered as soon as he was ready for it. Meanwhile, he was going down under the battleship's stern, and while I fiddled with the torch I could hear his heavy breathing and an occasional muttered epithet coming out of the loudspeaker. I had the torch ready for him and from his broadcast comments I knew that he was easing himself along the slimy barnacle-spotted shaft, thirty feet under the surface. I heard the clang as his helmet rapped the ship's side.

'This is as far as I can get, Sir. 'Bout five feet off the gland. Torch, Sir.'

I took up the torch and opened its controls. An E.R.A. applied a light and it ignited with a solid bang. I adjusted the gas feeds and checked the gauges, then we lowered it, roaring, to the surface of the water. It went under with a deep rumble and a burst of steam and bubbles. Holding it, we adjusted again for water pressure and set the balancing diaphragm, a clever device perfected by the Italians, which automatically adjusted the high pressure of gas in the bottle to the pressure required in the torch for maximum efficiency of operation at different depths. Down below, Nichols would hear the noise of the flame loudly in his helmet. He pulled in the down-line and presently reported that he had the torch in his hands. When we had slacked away on the lowering purchase, I hurried down into the launch and sat myself beside the telephone set. Nichols's air bubbles were streaming away aft, deflected by the curve of the stern plating.

Over the speaker I could hear the torch roaring. Nichols kept up a running patter of instructions to the Gas Works. 'Step up oxygen! . . . whoa! that's enough. . . .' The speaker crackled and behind the voice all the time was the noise of the torch. In the disturbed water that lapped the boat's sides, carbon particles danced black against the white foam and a tiny jet of vapour rose from each bubble as it burst. Suddenly I realised, looking at my wrist watch, that Nichols had been at work for more than half an hour. I flicked the switch over and called him.

'Nichols!' The roaring faded as he thumbed his exhaust spindle. 'How's it going? Any progress?' I turned the switch back and his voice came through as clearly as if he was sitting next to me.

'It's all right, Sir. I think I'm into the bore—can't see properly, but there's a ruddy great jet o' steam hitting me front glass.' I thought that one out—and realised that he must, indeed, have cut right into the bore: the steam would be from sea-water inside it boiling and jetting out. I called again, very happily: 'Carry on as long as you can. I'll be on deck.'

Nichols grunted an acknowledgement, and I headed for the quarterdeck. A delighted commander immediately wrote out a signal to Cairo to the effect that we were making progress and intended to proceed.

Three hours later, a union blew out in one of the hydrogen manifold sets, so I cut the supply and used the opportunity to get Nichols up for a rest. He had been cutting for nearly four hours and he would be in need of a break. The ship's artificers fitted a new joint while I went down to the boat again and found Nichols, damp with sweat, lying back in his sodden diving suit and puffing rapturously at a waterlogged cigarette while a sick-bay attendant was putting a dressing on a badly burnt thumb. It was hardly surprising that he had burnt himself. That steam jet, loaded with carbon, had etched a sort of frosting on to his front glass, and he had, in fact, been working blind, entirely by feel. I suggested that I should relieve him now, but he insisted that he was all right for a few more hours, and since I realised that with the damaged thumb we would have to cut the wrist-cuffs to get him out of the dress, I agreed. Soon he was dropping down the shot-rope, back to the job. But two and a half hours later, after listening to the weakened muttering from our 'phone set, I brought him up, protesting but definitely exhausted. We cut his cuffs, eased him out of the dress and sent him away to eat and sleep. It was getting dark by then, so I got myself rigged and had floodlights slung over the battleship's stern.

I went down into pitch-black water and felt my way cautiously along the shaft until my helmet clanged against the ship's stern. It was not difficult to find the gaping cut which Nichols had made. He had carved in through more than two-thirds of the diameter, and I could almost get my hand into the inner bore. But I found it a tricky business to balance astride the smooth round of the shaft, and I made myself a set of rope stirrups before I called for the torch to be sent down. Then when they told me they had it ready I pulled in on the light line that was secured at this end to the shaft. As the torch came down, the enveloping dark gave way to a golden glow, a fantastic flickering brilliance as the cutter came down into my hands. I wriggled myself into a more or less comfortable position astride the shaft and started the heating oxygen. I watched the glow of melting steel as the burner did its work, then put on the cutting mixture and the brilliant sparks of oxidised steel flaring out from the cut made a picture like some fairyland on a technicolor screen. After a few slips and re-starts, I got into the swing of it and cut steadily until the sweat pouring down my face just about blinded me. I stuck at it, gritting my teeth against the discomfort that increased steadily until it became an all-enveloping, agonising ache. My thigh muscles seemed to swell with every passing minute from the strain of gripping the shaft. My hands, wrapped round the heavy cutter, seized up at regular intervals, and I had to exercise them one at a time as best I could without releasing the torch. I thought my back would never straighten again. Time lost all meaning as I fought off dizziness and exhaustion. My whole existence narrowed down into the roaring, white-hot flame eating its way with maddening slowness into the eighteen-inch shafting. I could see nothing beyond the flame, only guess at the progress I was making against the stubborn toughness of the steel. Then suddenly, astonishingly, as I pushed the nozzle of the cutter into the gap, I found that there was nothing solid to meet it. I could hardly allow myself to believe that the shaft was cut right through and I pushed the torch round to the other side of the shaft to see if its glow would show through: I strained my eyes and thought that I could make out a serrated cleavage all round, broken by bits of molten steel that still clung to the cut edges. I called the surface and Nichols answered.

'I think we're through. How long've I been down?' There was a pause, then Nichols told me.

''Bout six hours, they say, Sir.' As far as I could tell, it might have been six weeks. My body felt broken, my hands hurt abominably and I was nearly blind as well.

'Take up the torch. And my slack. I'm coming up.' The line began to run over my arm and the torch rose in its halo of golden light leaving me in the dark. I looked up, saw the shimmer of the surface like silver with the arc-lamps lighting it from the ship's stern. I fingered the spindle and sank into my suit as the buoyancy grew and lifted it around me. Presently I was hauling myself painfully into the boat, and the attendants twisted off my helmet, relieved me of the lead front and back-weights. The relief was tremendous.

Nichols, his face grey and lined in the hard glare of the lights, was already dressed and booted. I noticed that his thumbs were encased in bulky fingerstalls, and I had a look at my own—they were swollen grotesquely and dripping blood, scorched from contact with the hot metal close to the cut. The attendant began to slit the rubber cuffs of my diving dress, and I spoke to Nichols.

'See if she's really through, and let me know. Then start on the vertical leg of the "A" bracket, as high as you can get.' Nichols nodded. He was down again before I was out of my gear, and while the sickbay man was wrapping my hands in burn dressings the telephone came to life with the welcome news that the cut was definitely through, and that the strained and warped shaft had actually dropped about an inch at the break. That was fine, excellent—but I thought to myself, wearily, more than twelve hours' continuous work for one cut, and we have five more to make!

On the quarterdeck I met the Commander. He led me down to the wardroom and shoved me into an easy chair—Lord, what comfort!—and fetched me a large, strong whisky. The Surgeon Commander joined us and inspected my tortured thumbs. He didn't like them, but he said brightly, 'They're no worse than your P.O.'s. We'll fix you up with waterproof dressings and you'll be all right so long as you don't want to play the piano. . . . Here's a pill to put you to sleep.' I had no need for a sedative except that the smart of the burns might have kept me awake. The last of the whisky helped the little capsule on its way, and within a minute or two I began to feel it doing its work. Hours later I woke from a dreamless sleep to find that someone had covered me with a rug, and the sun was shining in through the wardroom ports.

Anxious to know how Nichols was, I started up, but a steward came over with a cup of tea and a message to the effect that Nichols had been to report and had departed to get himself some sleep. I drank the tea, and limped stiffly off to find the Commander in his cabin. He gave me a cigarette and told me that Nichols had completed the cut through the vertical bracket in less than four hours. This was wonderful news.

But now we had the ticklish part of the business. The whole weight of shaft, propeller and bracket was held by the one remaining horizontal limb. When that parted, the whole issue would leave instantaneously for the sea bed seventy odd feet down—we would have to be very careful not to go with it. I knew what a diver looked like who had been squashed by a sudden increase in pressure, and I was anxious to avoid a similar fate either for myself or Nichols.

However, I had a scheme designed to minimise any risk. The

plan I had in mind was to have two gelignite charges made up in canvas stockings with tail lanyards so that we could lash them round the inboard end of the lower brackets. I reckoned that 15 lb. of explosive would do the job without damaging the ship or the outer screws. If we stopped cutting about two-thirds of the way through the last bracket, when it was nearly giving under the weight, we could fix the charge, surface, and set it off from an exploder on deck.

I asked the Commander to send for his explosives expert and a smart-looking Gunner (T) arrived promptly. I explained to him how I wanted the charges fitted, and he went off straight away to get them ready. Then Nichols arrived, told me that he had slept enough and was ready to start again. I told him of the explosives move, and I had an impression that he was considerably relieved to know that he wouldn't be jockeying the shaft until it dropped. He hadn't raised the subject, although it had plainly been worrying him, and my estimation of the Petty Officer rose a great deal in the knowledge that he had, in fact, been prepared to take that chance without so much as mentioning it.

Back in the diving boat, preparing for another descent, Nichols told me how he'd managed to cut through the vertical limb of the 'A' bracket so quickly; there had been a partial fracture already and he had had only half the thickness to sever. They clamped the helmet on him, and watching over the boat's side, I lost sight of him as he went down into the dark water. I hung around, keeping a check on the Gas Works and an ear cocked for reports. After two hours' work, Nichols called up that the cut was half made. I dressed, and slipped down to join him where he was working astride the horizontal leg of the 'A' bracket hard under the stern of the ship. Tying a line to his wrist, I took the slack with me and crawled out to the enormous collar through which the propeller shaft passed at the junction of the two legs of the bracket. Then, pulling myself up to be level with the scorched gap Nichols had previously made in the vertical leg, I peered through the front glass of my helmet. I could see the sloping cut, more than two inches open on the outside. At a signal from me Nichols started cutting. The glare of his torch flickered in my helmet and I kept my eyes fixed rigidly on the gaping cut. Time passed, and I had to blink to clear the sweat that was half blinding me, but I dared not rest my eyes for more than a second. I had to see the first slight widening of that gap which would warn us to stop cutting while we got clear. Suddenly, as I stared, it moved and I jerked hard on the line fastened to Nichols's wrist. The torch snapped out immediately in reply, and I saw it dangling on its lanyard as Nichols's brass toe-caps flashed upwards past my helmet as he surfaced. Hardly daring to breathe and with my heart thumping like a trip-hammer, I crawled along the weakened bracket over the almost completed cut and straddled it with my back to the ship's hull. Here I was safe, even if the shaft and brackets fell away. I called the surface.

'Send me down the charges!'

Nichols's voice asked: 'What's it look like, Sir?'

'Almost too good. This thing's ready to go.'

It was, too. I pulled in on the down line, and presently the long canvas sausage was lying on the bracket in front of me. I passed the lanyards and secured them, checked the detonator. Then I looked it over and couldn't see anything else that needed doing. I rose quickly up the shot-line and was soon on my stool, freed of helmet and weights.

Without boots, but still in the dripping diving dress, I flapped up the gangway to the quarterdeck and invited the Commander to fire the charge. He glanced at the wires leading down over the stern, then looked at me again; I nodded, and he pressed the handle of the exploder. A muffled thump—the deck vibrated —and that was all. But from the stern guard rail a Petty Officer turned and called excitedly.

'There she is, Sir!—hundred feet astern!'

He was referring to the buoy we had shackled to the propeller with a coil of wire rope—the sight of it floating out astern there was all we needed to tell us that the shaft, propeller and brackets, all twenty-six tons of them, were now safely settling into the ooze on the bottom. The Commander slapped me on the shoulder—'Nice work, Keeble! Let's get ourselves a drink and draft a signal to shake up their ideas in Cairo!'

The battleship's leading diver knelt down and slid a knife under my cuffs. I sent a message down to Nichols to dive and check up under the stern. Then in the Flag Lieutenant's cabin I shed my grimy woollen underwear, had a hot bath and put on a uniform. I found the Commander in the wardroom, and he handed me a signal with one hand and a glass of Scotch with the other. The signal read, STARBOARD SHAFT PROPELLER AND BRACKETS REMOVED STOP NO DAMAGE TO HULL OR FITTINGS STOP COMMENCING PORT SIDE IMMEDIATELY ENDS

It looked good to me, that message, and as I handed it back to the Commander I couldn't help grinning to myself as I imagined the reception this news would get in Cairo. It should do something to improve the long faces of the Constructors!

Valiant's Senior Lieutenant (E) came in at this point, clad in a soiled boiler suit, gloved, and with a greasy torch, the badge of office of the Senior Engineroom Watchkeeper. He reported that an inspection of the gland-space had revealed no damage at all: as far as they could tell, total losses were two electric light bulbs in the steering flat. And from the quarterdeck came a message from Nichols: a clean job, he reported, only stumps left to show where the shaft and brackets had been.

*   *   *

Within an hour, Nichols was back at work—on the port shaft. The ship's divers were passing wires under it, and no doubt sneaking over now and then for a peek at Nichols in his blaze of light. There was already a noticeable change in the morale of the ship's company. After months of pessimistic reports, their ship was undergoing a highly successful operation. At this rate, touch wood, she would be something like her old self again within the week. You could see the new cheer in faces, hear it in sailors' voices. The last month or two hadn't been happy ones for *Valiant*.

Darkness fell, and the glare of our floodlights attracted swarms of fish which leaped around the stern and at the feet of the ladder, where sailors with buckets scooped them out for tomorrow's breakfast. After dinner, Captain O'Donnell returned from Cairo. He came up the gangway with a copy of our signal in his hand, and I have rarely seen a more delighted man. He told me that the C-in-C was extremely happy about it and the Constructors blankly incredulous. I told the Captain that now we had the hang of it we would likely finish the port side even faster than we had dealt with the starboard—and so it turned out. To save ourselves from overdoing things, Nichols and I took shorter shifts, turn and turn about. He, in one amazing effort, cut right through the port shaft in less than four hours. In the early afternoon of the fourth day the gap in the vertical limb opened, and soon afterwards the two of us, utterly exhausted, lay on the deck in our wet diving dresses and watched the Captain explode the last charge. The same thump, slight lift of the deck, the tinkle of a glass breaking somewhere down below; but from the men at the stern rail, no shout. The buoy had not appeared.

Disheartened, I asked a ship's diver to go down and see what had happened. It seemed a long time while we waited in silence for his report. Then he called up that all was well, just the stumps and no sign of other damage. What had taken place was that the shaft had dived to the bottom, screw first and of course revolving, and the buoy's wire had been wound round the propeller. Later a diver from the ship's cutter found the buoy astern and well under the surface.

That night, with the help of the doctor's special knockout drops, we slept like logs, and the next day I was able to appear like a civilised naval officer on the ship's bridge while Captain O'Donnell took *Valiant* to sea for trials. Meanwhile, Nichols was the honoured guest of the Chiefs' and Petty Officers' Mess.

Valiant reacted splendidly to our underwater surgery. As the engineers worked up the revolutions she kicked up her heels and without any trouble below touched something close to seventeen knots. She steered well on her one working rudder, and of course manœuvred perfectly on the outer screws. Trials completed, she boomed up the Gulf of Suez, once again an active ship of war. At sunset we anchored in the Bay, off Tewfik, and before I left the bridge a messenger handed me an invitation to visit the Warrant Officers' Mess. I mentioned it to the Commander and he laughed. 'Well, take it easy. We'll want to see you in the wardroom afterwards, and I've an idea that the Captain'll be dining you!' I quaked inwardly, but the thing had to be seen through to its grisly limits and presently in the W.O.'s Mess the 'Backbone of the Royal Navy' entertained me in their own fashion for a full hour. The Mess President suggested that I might like Nichols to be asked in for a drink: I was delighted at their gesture and soon my Petty Officer was manfully standing up to the same violent entertainment. I took myself away to the wardroom and more whiskies, then, careful of my movements and speech, to dine with the Captain. To do justice to our joint Irish ancestry, Captain O'Donnell called for a special bottle of Irish whiskey which he had been saving for the Armistice. Hours later, full of good food and at any rate half a bottle of whiskey, I was just able to find my way back to my cabin and fall into bed. The past few hours had been the most gruelling of all. Next morning, much the worse for it, I flew back to Alexandria in a Beaufighter and was met at the airfield by Holloway in the jeep.

Congratulations were overwhelming—from Admiral Tennant and the Fleet Engineer Officer, a message from the Admiralty Salvage Division, and, to cap it all, a Highest Commendation from the Commander-in-Chief. There followed a couple of days spent in compiling long and detailed technical reports, and as soon as they were signed and dispatched it was time to start thinking about the Greek ports again. There was still a mass of work to be done over there, and from what I heard in Alexandria I gathered that we would be facing trouble above as well as below water—a civil war had started. I wondered what they would think up next for us.

XII. INGLORIOUS EPISODES

So it was back to Greece. As the dusty airstrip of Megara outside Athens rushed up to meet my Blenheim, I knew I should find many changes in this turbulent country. I stepped out of the 'plane and was greeted by a young, tough-looking officer of the 2nd Independent Parachute Brigade, whose men were guarding the aerodrome from the insurgents. It was an order in the Middle East that all officers should carry side-arms, and the young paratrooper took the liberty of pointing this out to me. He seemed to be unaware that G.O.C.'s order was qualified by an unwritten law that naval officers did not in normal circumstances observe it, and I brushed the well-meant advice aside. As it happened, it would not have helped me later, even if I had had a revolver.

In the aerodrome office a few minutes afterwards I was asked for my identity card for the first time in months. It was becoming obvious that this civil war was being taken seriously and was going to be a considerable nuisance. Then, instead of the usual staff transport, an armoured car pulled up outside the shack where I had been interviewed and I was ushered into its cramped and stuffy confines and jolted in great discomfort to Athens. Lugging my bag into the Grande Bretagne Hotel, I looked for a drink. From the outside the place was almost unrecognisable under the weight of sandbags and barbed wire, while inside the Army had done much to reduce the general plushiness carefully preserved by the Navy into the gleaming orderliness and cheerless hardness of a barracks. Then I was outraged to discover that strict Army drinking hours had been enforced. Nikolai's dispensary was deserted—here indeed was proof of the seriousness of the emergency.

I wandered unhappily back to the foyer and there ran into Captain Campbell. It was good to find a friendly face in this desolation and I gladly accepted his invitation to lunch. Over a meal clearly devised from Army rations he told me something of the new troubles. Apparently sniping and ambush were daily occurrences. Everything was on a war footing and my salvage parties, isolated in the dock area, were providing a natural target for the insurgents and were continuing their work under fire. Captain Campbell himself had been ambushed a few nights earlier and was hobbling about with a foot in plaster as a result. He promised to take me into the port in his car after lunch— the road between Athens and Leontas, the inner harbour of Piraeus, was reasonably safe during the hours of daylight.

The drive to the harbour was in fact quite uneventful, but when we had parked the car and were walking down the quayside to where the crippled *Clinton* was moored, the quick bark of a mortar was followed by graceful fountains of water rising close to the minesweeper's hull. The working party below could not have cared much for this sort of performance. True, the hammer of a ten-pound mortar bomb would not travel far through water, and the danger to our divers was no more than that of having their teeth rattled unless the Greeks got a superbly accurate shot in. But even the remote chance of a mortar shell going off at one's feet is a singularly disquieting background to underwater work.

Luckily the Greeks were short of mortar ammunition and they fired only an occasional round. But they had plenty of rifle ammo and they amused themselves by sniping irregularly at our chaps throughout the day and night from a vantage point several hundred yards across the harbour. There was little point in sending a patrol round the sweeping perimeter of the harbour, for long before it could reach the rebels they would have melted into the hills behind them, or lost themselves in the swarming warren of Piraeus's slums. But my salvage party bore it all very well. For all the interruptions the repair work was well under way and the ragged fire from across the harbour had produced no casualties. Morale was high and heightened by the fury which the men felt at being fired on with their own ammunition —either provided by the Allies to the Greek Resistance, or stolen from our own occupation forces. The murderous inclinations were strictly mutual.

I was soon rigged in a diving dress, and down on the bottom under *Clinton* to see for myself how the patch was doing. It was in an advanced state and a magnificent job. At the end of the patch I saw a busy diver. When I moved up behind him and rapped on his helmet, he turned his face-glass to me and I could see the white tip of his nose pressed against it. It was Devonshire, and when he realised who I was he grabbed my hand and shook it in a grip which made me grunt with pain. I raised my hands to let him see the sodden bandages so that he would never do that again. Then I pointed to the surface. We came up together, and as soon as the attendants had our helmets off we were exchanging news. Devonshire was delighted to hear of our success with *Valiant*, and he told me that he reckoned another week would see the *Clinton* ready for her trip to dry dock in Malta.

Everything was hearteningly in order here despite the mortar fire, but there had been no reports on what was happening with *Larne* down in Poros Bay, and that would have to be my next visit. I had no doubt that Commander O'Brien and his *Salvestor* were making all possible progress, but the repair to *Larne* was particularly tricky because of the position of the damage. The thought of another visit to Poros Bay appealed to me, and I was looking forward incidentally to renewing my acquaintance with the Mayor and his family—including the dear little pigs I had bunked with on my first visit. I counted with confidence on the unchanged attitude of the swine, but I was much less sure of the Mayor's position. Nobody in Athens could tell me whose side he had come out on. Even Salonika, I heard, had gone fighting mad, and that was another place I would have to visit, to survey it before *Prince Salvor* finished her work on the blockship off the Corinth Canal and was ready to move north.

I decided that after breakfast next day Holloway should drive me up to Captain Campbell's HQ so that I could discuss these plans with him and get his approval, and that settled, sporadic rifle fire in the neighbourhood of the port and the occasional rattle of automatic weapons as dark wore on neither spoilt my sleep nor gave me any premonition that my plans were to be rudely interrupted.

*　　*　　*

Early next morning I went ashore and climbed into the jeep beside Holloway. He let in his clutch and we were off at the usual breakneck speed favoured by my cox'n, twisting and turning through the narrow streets and alleys of the dock area. The sky was overcast, and there were driving rain squalls. Holloway drove snuggled down in his oilskins and with water dripping off the rim of his cap on to his nose. He seemed to know the maze of wet, grey streets, and he flung the jeep round corner after corner with absolute nonchalance while the tyres screamed and an occasional passer-by hurled himself in sudden terror flat against the nearest wall. But I was used to his reckless driving, and we had never yet come to grief, so I turned up the collar of my watchcoat, tilted my cap forward to keep the rain out of my eyes and thought about the notes and reports which I had stuffed in my pockets. It was much too early for conversation.

I was thinking about the repairs to *Larne* as yet another blind corner rushed up ahead of us, and out of the corner of my eye I saw Holloway's hands shift their position on the wheel ready to drag it over without slackening speed. The jeep skidded round, shaving the kerbstone and straightened out. Then suddenly out of the morning drizzle a solid barricade of donkey-carts, barrels and sacks loomed up a few yards ahead of us. The street was completely blocked as we tore in at the obstruction. Instinctively I flung up my arms to cover my face while Holloway stiffened with all his weight on the foot brake. The wheels almost locked, and we slid at terrifying speed across the wet street and charged full tilt into the road block. The air filled with flying earth and wood and the world spun violently round me as I was catapulted out of my seat into the debris. Holloway had shot over the windscreen somewhere to the right.

When I dragged myself to my feet, dazed and very badly shaken, it was a moment or two before my head cleared and I realised that I was staring down into the barrel of a Sten gun. Then I felt a hard prod in my back and that was another Sten. A handful of extremely hostile-looking Greeks who had converged on me threateningly quickly became a crowd. They were dressed in filthy overalls, odd remnants of battledress and German scuttle helmets, and all of them were bristling with small arms. I looked round for Holloway and saw that he was being taken care of too. I was still shaking from the shock of our collision and I was not thinking very clearly, but I did not care for the Sten that was pointed at my chest. I thrust it away and it came back to bear on me with a vicious flourish that indicated its owner was not joking. I started to protest, but a burst of torrid language from one of the unshaven company was accompanied by a violent thrust in the back from the second Sten, and I began to stumble forward. Holloway was pushed up beside me, muttering and growling and looking far from happy, and the two of us were propelled roughly along the street. After fifty yards or so our escorts came to a ragged halt and Holloway and I were bundled into a decrepit-looking baker's shop. Half of our captors went back to what was left of their road-block and the others continued to push and prod us through a low brick archway and down a flight of steps into the bake-house, a lofty and very dirty place, the greater part of it occupied by an ancient double oven. Seated on a heap of sacks were more Greeks of similar unprepossessing appearance, and I noticed that for all the business-like weapons and ferocious expressions several of them could not be more than fourteen or fifteen years old. It occurred to me that many of these men/had helped to push back the flower of the Italian Army in 1941 and side by side with our own troops had fought the tough losing battle against the Wehrmacht hordes. More recently, as likely as not, they had formed part of the band of gallant patriots who had killed so many of the S.S., in the battle of the power station. Whatever they were fighting for they were a people who fought magnificently; and they had little respect for human life, their own, or others—which in the circumstances was not a particularly comforting thought. I told Holloway, who was still fuming and fidgeting, to take it easy; there was no point in aggravating the situation with a show of belligerence. But even so I had no real feeling of great danger. The whole performance had about it an air of melodrama, an absurd theatricalism that robbed it, at least to my reeling mind, of perilous undertones. I was about to shout for somebody who could speak English so that we could get the nonsense stopped, when Holloway nudged me and jabbed with his thumb at a corner of the room.

There, flat on its back with one arm outflung was the body of a short, stocky man in British paratroop overalls. The face was putty-coloured and still shadowed with a dusting of youthful acne—the boy could not have been more than twenty. His beret, mud-soaked, had been dropped casually on his chest. I looked sideways and saw the twin tracks of his heel-marks where his boots had trailed over the dirty floor as he had been dragged in. They must have shot him outside and hauled him into their hide-out to conceal him from a chance patrol. I stared in horror at this plain evidence of murder, and then it came home to me what it meant to us. It was like seeing the judge don his black cap.

I was frightened and angry. Since the days of Crete I had always admired these people, even respected their ruthlessness. Now it was clear that we were to be slaughtered like cattle by the men we had fought with as Allies. We were already in the *abbatoir*.

I cursed the fact that I had no knowledge of Greek. At least there would have been some small satisfaction in telling these thugs what I thought of them and their gallant form of warfare. I seized Holloway's arm and began to tell *him*, to relieve my feelings, gesturing with my other hand at the toughs now leaning slackly against the wall. At once the suddenness of my movement brought them to the alert, a Sten jabbed me agonisingly in the side, and several other Greeks tensed and raised their weapons, eyeing me malevolently. I did not try to talk after that, only kept my eyes away from the body in the corner while our captors conversed rapidly in Greek. Presumably they were discussing how we should be dealt with, and it was a small relief to think that the subject was not entirely closed, although I had the feeling that only the means were under debate. The end, I felt sure, was already settled. Their decision, whatever it was, was soon reached, and we were forced over to some stone steps next to the huge oven. With guns jabbing in our spines we followed a Greek youth who led us up the steps and along the side of the oven-top to a battered steel door which, standing open, revealed a dark space stinking of soot. The guide stood to one side and we were thrust roughly through the small opening. The door clanged shut and a bolt went raspingly home on the outside. At least we had not been shot—yet, but the darkness of our prison was impenetrable and we were both chilled and shivering. Holloway clicked his cigarette lighter into action while I made a quick but careful inspection of our accommodation.

We were in a kind of outer casing to the oven which had been built to draw smoke and fumes from the furnaces and convey them through a long and completely unscalable chimney above our heads. The rear of the oven jutting into this flue narrowed our circulating space to a small girder-obstructed corridor running round the back of the oven. Soot lay in thick banks on the walls, topped with dust and flakes of fallen rust, and the fire-brick lagging was worn and broken. Clearly the oven had not been used for many years, at least not for its original purpose, although it might have served before now as a condemned cell —its walls were solid enough.

I poked and prodded over the filthy surface of the flue's interior without finding anything to raise our hopes of escape, and then, as a last resort, clambered on to the rounded top of the oven itself. There was little more than two feet of clearance between this and the ceiling of the oven's outer casing, and I squirmed about uncomfortably, grubbing without much hope for a grating or vent of some kind. I was thinking of giving up when I discovered by touch, below an inch of soot, a change in texture from the rough brick. Scraping away the soot and cursing softly as it spurted up in my face, I got through to the smooth steel of what was probably a manhole cover. It seemed not unlikely that there had to be access from the oven to the flue for cleaning purposes, and this no doubt was it.

I put my mouth close to Holloway's ear, on the off-chance that somebody outside understood English, and whispered to him to douse his cigarette lighter and start talking while I investigated further. Silence from us might arouse the curiosity of the Greeks, and I did not want them poking their noses in if I was on to something.

Holloway embarked on a monologue as confidently as if he were rehearsing for a ship's concert party, interjecting a few remarks from time to time in deeper tones which I took to be his version of my voice. While he gabbled on I scrabbled around in the soot, trying to find a break in the brickwork I had located a few minutes earlier. In the pitch darkness and clouds of soot it was not easy to rediscover the opening, but I was used to working blind underwater and before long I got it. I groped round the manhole cover, suppressing the desire to sneeze, feeling for the boltholes. Only one of them had a bolt in it! This was too good to be true. There had to be a snag, and I expected the bolt to be rusted solid, which would have been enough to put a stop to any further progress. Fumbling painfully with my damaged hand, I got my fingers round the head of the bolt and tugged speculatively at it. Luck was with us all the way: the bolt came soundlessly out of its socket and slipped out of my fingers into the darkness. It had no nut.

I crawled back to Holloway and told him about it.

For an hour or so we kept watch on the revolutionaries, squinting down through the cracks around the door. After a while they started moving about in a dilatory sort of way, apparently getting ready for a sortie, checking their arms and ammunition. Then they had a meal out of tins—it looked to me like N.A.A.F.I. bully beef—and washed it down with wine. I watched enviously; with my mouth lined with soot I had a haymaker's thirst and my liking for these brigands was not increased by their omission to think of their prisoners at mealtime. Probably the fact that they had not bothered to feed us indicated that they did not expect to have us with them for long —and I could not imagine that they were going to turn us loose to bring a patrol down on their lair. Obviously, the sooner we found a use for that manhole the better. I reckoned that we were no worse off making a break for it, however slim the chances, than waiting for events to take their inevitable course. But the odds at present were hopeless, and we settled down to wait and pray for the departure of the men who had been getting ready for a raid.

Hours went by and our thirst mounted. Holloway dozed off, and I did not wake him because his snores would be audible and reassuring to the guards. At intervals I peered through the narrow cracks of the ill-fitting door and ultimately I was able to discern that it was getting dark outside—the circle of light I had once been able to see penetrating a knot-hole in the boards covering a window near the entrance had disappeared. Some of our captors had also been sleeping, but now they began to stir again. My field of vision was strictly limited, but the shuffling and coughing, the strike and flare of a match told their story, and occasionally an uncouth figure crossed my line of sight. It was obvious that something was afoot, and I woke Holloway. Then the outside door creaked open and shut, open and shut again, as the raiders crept out one by one, presumably to avoid disclosing their strength to any casual passer-by. As the movements continued I cursed myself for not having counted the departures from the start; that would have given us some idea of how many men we would have to tackle if we did succeed in breaking out of this dark and filthy prison.

In any case, it would be better to take a chance as soon as the party was clear than to wait until they returned in force, and I crouched tensely, waiting for the noise of the departing men to stop. I allowed about fifteen minutes after the last of the party seemed to have gone, then whispered to Holloway that we could try to get down into the oven below. We crawled over the soot to the manhole, found it and very cautiously set ourselves down with our fingers gripping its rim, our hands evenly spaced around it so that the lift would be clean and silent.

'Ready?' I asked. He grunted. 'All right—*lift!*' The cover came up easily enough and quietly. We put it down on a bank of soot and I eased myself through the aperture, my legs swinging in space until a foot found the lower floor of brickwork. Then I reached up through the manhole and tugged at Holloway's ankle. I helped him down, guiding his legs, fearful that he would miss his footing and make some noise to warn the guard—or guards.

We looked around this annexe to our prison, assessing its possibilities. Ahead of me an edge of light showed between the double doors of the oven, and when I got close to them I found a half-inch gap: I explored it gingerly with my finger-tips, and as far as I could tell there were no fastenings, on the inside anyway. The strip of light had been unbroken suggesting that there were none on the outside either. Better still, I found that by peering through the gap from this lower position I had a far clearer view of the darkened room; I watched carefully, sorting out shapes and distances, and I reckoned that the man squatting just below the oven doors, so close that only part of him was visible, was the only enemy we had to contend with. Certainly we had a chance. I spoke very quietly into Holloway's ear, told him to take the left-hand door while I took the right, that when I said 'Now!' we would heave the doors open and jump the sentry. If there were no others, out of sight, it ought to work.

We crouched behind the doors with our hands flat against them, and I kept my eyes on the man down below. He hadn't moved. I whispered hoarsely, '*Now!*' The doors swung back violently and noisily and the man below started to his feet as I launched myself into space and landed on his shoulders. He was off-balance and he went sprawling under me. Holloway crashed down on top of me like a ton of bricks and my mouth caught the edge of the Greek's tin helmet. Some teeth went and I tasted blood, but I had the man by his shoulders and I was banging his face against the stone floor of the cellar. Then my hands were jarred by a sudden thud, and the man's struggles ceased abruptly. Holloway had scrambled up and got in a full-blooded kick at the Greek's head. The body under me was limp, unconscious, possibly even dead. We didn't stop to investigate, but rushed up the steps and out into the empty street, into the wonder of fresh air and space. I grabbed Holloway's arm.

'This way. Run!' We fled across the cobbled street to its darker side, headed for the corner at a rush and as we reached it and turned right a jeep full of men nearly ran us down. We dodged frantically as it braked, ran on down the street close to the wall. Just before we reached a crossroad there was a burst of automatic fire from behind, and I saw sparks as bullets ricochetted off the stones and sang away, whining past us. Then a sudden blow on my right foot nearly tripped me, but stumbling I ran on, the breath sobbing in my lungs as we turned the corner. Our course was downhill now, in the direction of Piraeus, and there was no more shooting. We stopped to get our breath back and to listen, and there was no sound of pursuit either. It seemed too good to be true.

Holloway was panting as though he had not run so fast in the last twenty years. I was just about on my last gasp. My mouth was full of blood and I had already swallowed so much of it that I felt sick. A moment's rest and then we loped on as fast as we could, dodging from doorway to doorway, pausing often to listen for sounds of our murderously-inclined allies. But there were no further alarms, and when we were about halfway to the harbour area we met one of our own patrols in an armoured car and threw ourselves thankfully into the safety of its head-lights. Our delight at finding ourselves among friends was rather damped by the obvious distrust with which they greeted us. The interrogation seemed to me to be unduly prolonged—I could hardly speak anyway—and I had an impression that they thought we were Greeks in disguise. It seemed silly to me. But they drove us to the Sixth Airborne Division's control post, and here, in the light and confronted with a mirror, I understood their doubts. We were both of us covered in soot, most of my brass buttons were missing, and my hands with bandages hanging loose were dripping blood. Some of it was mine, and some of it was the Greek guard's. My lips were swollen up so that I could not speak clearly, I had lost four front teeth, and my second-best Gieves's half-Wellingtons were scarred by the ricochetting bullet that had nearly bowled me over as I ran.

Once they were satisfied about our identity, the airborne men decided to flush out the nest of revolutionaries at once, and Holloway did his best to provide directions. The patrol were filing out to their transport when my cox'n suddenly thought of something else. He grabbed the arm of the last man and with a look of intense supplication asked him: 'Try an' get our flippin' jeep back, Mate!' The soldier nodded dubiously and hurried away into the dark. We were left with the C.O. of the post and a handful of men, and I told them about the murdered paratrooper we had seen in the bakery. Their eyes darkened with anger, and I did not give much for the chances of those Greeks if the patrol caught them with the corpse of the airborne man on their hands. The C.O. told me grimly that he had had several men missing in the last few weeks.

Just before dawn the patrol came back. They had with them the body of the paratrooper, and they confirmed that the Greek we had jumped on was dead. Holloway's kick had been a good one. None of us had any tears to shed for that. Holloway was upset, certainly, but only because they had not found the jeep.

*   *   *

Greece held no further surprises for us, and in due course the insurrection dwindled to a form of uneasy truce. But at least we were permitted to carry on our salvage work in peace. I paid a quick visit to Poros Bay to satisfy myself that work on the *Larne* was going ahead on the right lines, then took myself back to Alexandria. The war in Europe was on its last legs now. Ship recovery on a peacetime basis seemed a little tame to me, and I was ready for fresh fields. There was still plenty of work to do—the procession of ships bound for the Far East left in their wake a trail of strandings, collisions and vessels damaged by explosions of stray mines, but the desperate urgency and the battle against odds of earlier days seemed to be gone. I made a tour of Middle East ports which included an Alpine excursion across the bottom of Tobruk harbour, labouring up the slope of one bomb crater and sliding down the side of the next—hardly a square yard of the harbour bed had been left where nature had put it. But post mortems followed by endless reports were stale stuff, and I looked with eagerness to my draft to the Far East. It was preceded by a dreary tour of the war-shattered ports of Europe, slightly enlivened by a brush with an unexploded V-2 on the bottom of the River Scheldt and by the advent of my brass hat. But, as it turned out, the brass hat only foreshadowed a bowler. Before I got to Hong Kong the two atomic explosions, whose pall still stretches over the world, had taken place and the war was at an end. All that was left for me was to dot the i's and cross the t's of port clearance plans and get myself back to the bits of my peacetime job.

I heard—and still hear—regularly from some of the lads: the unquenchable Holloway, now driving an electric train in London; Wilber Rippon, returned to a more exotic Genoese background; Nichols pursuing the quiet life in Streatham. When I get the

Christmas cards with the scrawled post-scripts, I feel rather like an old-time actress thumbing the faded pages of her album of Press clippings. For a time after the war Devonshire and I linked forces in South Africa and pulled off one or two mildly sensational salvage coups; but now, at the backward-looking age of fifty, I find myself too often contemplating my thickening waistline and muttering into my evening drink about the good old days. And sometimes, when I read the daily headlines, it has occurred to me that I may yet, before hardening arteries quite rule me out, have one last fling.